BROOKLYN
BOUND

MARIA N. GRECHENKO

Print ISBN: 978-1-950685-67-7
Ebook ISBN: 978-1-950685-68-4

Printed in the United States.

To my children and grandchildren, lest they forget they are

Grechenkovskoy porody

NOTE FROM THE AUTHOR

The names in this book have been changed to protect the innocent and the not-so-innocent. Even though the latter don't deserve it. In fact, if I didn't have such an aversion to legal action, I'd use their first names, patronymics, last names and last known addresses to shame them publicly.

However, I have chosen to take the high—and less litigated—road to show that I really *am* a better person than many of them turned out to be. Bless their hearts.

So, if you think you're one of the characters in this book who is described in unflattering terms, you're probably right. Bless *your* heart.

Read on if you really want to be sure.

INTRODUCTION

The first man I ever loved was tall, dark, and handsome.
A natty dresser, with coordinating hat and gloves in winter.
Broad shouldered, athletic, a great dancer and a lover of music.
Worldly, charming, a great conversationalist.
Demanding, yes; generous to a fault—yes, a flaw inherited from his mother.
A man who taught me how to laugh, how to dance and how to have fun.[1]
A man who showed me unconditional love every day of my life that I was
with him until, suddenly, he was gone.

If you're looking for one of those bustier-busting books, this isn't it.
Move on to the romance section of the bookstore.

This is a book about a little girl's first love—one she never, ever
forgot.

It's a tale told by a *dame d'un certain âge* as she closes the memory
loops of her life, recollection and remembrance fused together. He appears, life sized, on the projector screen of her life review.

Be careful: you just might find yourself falling in love with him,
too.

---

[1] There is *no word* in Russian for *fun*. I am **not** making this up.

1

There is nothing in the world like the smell of a freshly opened pack of unfiltered Camels. The aroma is sweet and spicy—it tickles your nose, it hits all your happy places and makes you want more. The problem, of course, is that the second sniff never measures up to the first one. And if *that* isn't a solid hint about certain Life Experiences, I don't know a better one.

Still.

One of my earliest and fondest childhood memories takes me back to the dim landing outside our shotgun apartment on Berry Street in Brooklyn. Papa and I have come out here so that he can have a cigarette after supper, since cigarette smoke always makes Mama cough. There's a polished dark wooden railing along the hall that runs the length of the Mironovs' apartment and leads to the staircase to the third floor. Papa makes a space for me to sit by brushing away some dirt and spreading out his hanky on the floor. A thoughtful builder had spaced the balusters so that my chubby legs fit through the gaps when I sit down. I always come out to smoke with Papa because I can talk to him one-on-one without Mama listening to what I have to say—and possibly adding her own opinions—and because it's such a peaceful, quiet few minutes. Sometimes we don't say anything and I watch Papa as he exhales the smoke and it swirls and curls, rising to the upper floors. I've never been all the way to the top of the building and often wonder if the smoke continues to live up there, always swirling and twirling in an endless ethereal dance.

My favorite smoking time happens when Papa has to open a new pack of unfiltered Camels. The ritual is always the same: the thwack-thwack-thwack of the new pack on the back of his left hand, the search for the tab and removal of the cellophane around the top. Finally, the coup de grâce: the careful tearing off of the foil on one corner of the pack and the proffer of that lovely, crumbly, different-shades-of-brown-enrobed-in-white little Rockettes lined up in rows.

"Wanna sniff?"

"Uh huh."

And I'd inhale that captivating scent as hard as I could, diving head-first into olfactory bliss. It always made me want to come back for more.

"Mozhno yeshchyo raz?"

"Mozhno."

And he'd hold the pack up to my nose one more time. True, it still smelled nice but had somehow lost the spellbinding power of that first virgin sniff.

The ritual continued with Papa forming his left hand into a fist and hitting the sealed part of the pack on the back of his index finger. As if in response to an unspoken command, one cigarette would raise its head above the rest of its brethren, and Papa would ease it out. Pack secured in his shirt pocket, Papa would twirl the fresh cigarette into his *mundshtuk*, flick his Ronson once, and inhale deeply. I inhaled right along with him, pretending that I had a cigarette, too. It was these times, these quiet, neither-one-of-us-talking times, the times when we simply sat together—Papa on his haunches, me on the floor next to him, my right shoulder to his left side—that made my world feel safe and good and true. I knew in my heart of hearts that as long as Papa was here—and he'd be here forever, of course—I would always be loved and protected. Always and always.

On weekday evenings we could smoke in the apartment because

Mama was at work. I guess the smoke would disperse by the time she got home, because I never heard her say anything about it and I never heard her cough. Or perhaps she learned to live with the Camel treillage. That said, the smoking-in-the-apartment ritual differed slightly from the smoking-on-the-landing ritual. While the opening of the new pack was always the same, where we sat was quite different. Papa's chair was in the left corner of the living room, angled toward the TV, clear glass square ashtray always on the right arm. My official seat was on the sofa, where I was supposed to sit to the right of Mama to watch TV. Since Mama was not home to enforce the rule during the week, I usually opted to sit on the left arm of Papa's chair. After he finished his cigarette, I'd move to Papa's lap and lean against his chest, where I could feel the thump-thump of his heart with the back of my head. I tried to match his inhalations breath for breath until it felt as though we were breathing as one.

Once upon a time, when Mama was again obsessing about her weight, Papa offered up that, when he stopped smoking (every year for Lent) he gained weight. But, as soon as he started smoking on Easter, the weight quickly came off. Pause. Pause. Pause.

Mama: "Do you think, if I started smoking, I could lose some weight?"

Papa: "*Ne znayu*, I'm not a doctor, but it probably wouldn't hurt to try. Want to try?"

Mama: "What? Right now?"

Papa: "Why not? I'll show you how."

Me: "I wanna watch!!!"

What followed was a rather interesting (for me) scene. Papa did his usual careful-removing-of-the-cigarette from the pack and twisting it into his *mundshtuk*. A flick of the Ronson, a strong inhale, and the tip glowed red.

"OK, I started it. Now, come on."

"What come on? How do I do this? What am I supposed to do?"

(Geez, I thought. She's acting like she's never seen someone smoke before. I could practically see feathers flying off her like they did off the chickens at the live poultry market we frequented. What is *that* all about? Faker.)

With a gentle, "I'll hold the *mundshtuk* to your lips, you slowly suck in the smoke," Papa attempted to induct Mama into the World of Smokers.

About two feet shorter than Mama, I stood to her right and looked up to see whether it would work. A quick puff, a short inhale gasp, and a very loud "aaaaahhhh khah khah khah khah!!!" Mama bent nearly double expelling the smoke, coughing and gasping for (non-smoke-filled) air. A clear *fail* of the smoking fraternity initiation ritual.

After Mama stopped retching and we'd all had a good laugh about her disastrous maiden voyage into the magic world of smoking, she decided that she'd give this thing another try. (Ah, what price slender beauty?) For the results of this second attempt, re-read the above paragraph, except for the laughing part. After Mama had finished her second bout of hacking and wheezing, for some reason she was far less pleasantly disposed than after the first bout. In fact, she sort of yelled at Papa for engaging in this filthy, disgusting habit that was making her sick. My little brain couldn't quite reconcile this fit of pique with Mama's recent willingness to acquire said habit, but there was much about the grownup world that I didn't understand back then. All I know is that Papa laughed a bit and said something about how they probably couldn't afford to have two smokers in the family anyway.

Many years later, while finishing up a cup of coffee and a cigarette—my version of a breakfast of champions in college—I was hurled headfirst into a remembrance of that particular episode. And, because I still had a little time before class, I walked across the street to the local deli and bought myself a can of Tab and a pack of Camels (filtered). I had been a devotee of the Virginia Slims brand myself (because I'd "come a long way, baby") for a number of years, and I'd heard that Camels were not for the newly minted smoker. However, since I had a few years of nicotine addiction under my belt, I thought I was prepared to venture into Papa's tobacco territory. Maybe make him miraculously appear or something, even if only to scold me for smoking in the grand "do as I say, not as I do" parenting tradition, which we all contemptuously condemn until we become parents ourselves and use it practically on a daily basis.

When I reached my usual pre-class hangout space on the fourth floor of the Walsh building, I dropped my brown bookbag onto one of the ancient wooden "iron maiden" style seats and myself into another. I pulled the fresh pack of Camels out of the top of my bookbag (with the very French GARBÀGE stamped on the front) and studied the picture on it. It wasn't the same as Papa's—I'd wimped out and bought the filtered version because I didn't have a *mundshtuk*—but I figured it was a logical progression of the camel's evolution, since he looked more contemporary and a tad snazzier. Everyone has to change with the times, I guessed, even dromedaries . . . unless this was a Bactrian. Whatever. Still, hoping to recapture some of the magic of our old smoking days on the landing, I mentally invited Papa to join me and, holding the fresh pack in my right hand, smacked the filtered end on my left hand three times to pack the tobacco down.

I found the tab to the cellophane wrapper and pulled it around the top to remove the transparent cap.

I opened the corner to reveal little filtered soldiers all lined up for action.

I gave the pack another tap—this time on the left index finger of my fist—and propelled one of them out of the pack.

I popped the filtered end between my lips, flicked my disposable blue Bic, and inhaled. Eyes closed, I flashed through a time tunnel back to Berry Street.

And got punched in the throat.

The throat punch immediately was followed by "aaaaahhhh khah khah khah khah khah!!!" and the head spins.

I threw the still-smoking remnant of my childhood memories into my freshly opened pink can of Tab and lurched to the ladies' room, where I did *not* retch. But I did spend a little time engaging in measured breathing and splashing cold water on my face and wrists to keep from passing out on the tile floor.

As a result of this experience, I gained a newfound respect for Papa and his demonstrated ability to smoke Camels (unfiltered, no less!) not only as though there was nothing to it, but even to enjoy the process. Wow. I guessed that I was probably behind the smoker's power curve since I only started to smoke seriously in college. Papa, on the other hand, had started when he was seven.[2]

---

[2] I loved Papa's stories about smoking. He had a number of them, but this one appealed to me on several levels, most likely because of my grandfather Fedor's instruction to Papa at the end of the episode. Here goes:

Back in the day in pre-Revolutionary Russia, the Grechenkovs lived about as well as any other peasant family, even better than some. Not only did they have a house, but they had a barn for their milk cow and horses. One evening, Papa strolled into the barn and took a *samokrutka* one of the older boys had given him out of his pocket, struck a match he'd stolen from the kitchen stash and, putting the cigarette between his lips, inhaled as he lit the end. This wasn't his first cigarette, but it was the first one he'd smoked anywhere near his house where his mother might catch him. She was beautiful, he said, dark haired, blue-eyed, and very strong . . . in other words, one of her whippings was a memorable occasion. After his third-or-so drag, Papa suddenly heard footsteps approaching the barn. With no time to extinguish the remaining half of his cigarette, he quickly slipped it under the hay drying in the loft.

The door opened with its habitual creak.

My grandfather appeared in the doorway. According to Papa, his father was tall and strong as an ox. He'd once single-handedly lifted a horse-drawn wagon off a man trapped under its front wheel. After stopping the horse that had been spooked by something. Fedor was of legendary strength, at least in their village.

Surprised to find his son in the barn, Fedor—naturally—asked what he was doing there. Papa made up some lie about looking in on the horses. At that very moment, Fedor noticed a wisp of smoke coming from the hay loft directly over Papa's head. As my grandfather grabbed at the hay to find and extinguish the cause, he found Papa's hand-rolled, half-smoked cigarette. The dialogue, as Papa remembered and retold it, went like this:

I suddenly realized why Mama would have been a tad miffed after her second smoking attempt: she'd been punched in the throat twice. And we'd laughed at her.

In moments of stress, my brain would produce—for some inexplicable reason—advertising jingles or pithy sayings related to the cause of the stress. In this instance, my mind reproduced a couple of phrases from a magazine ad for Camel Filters: "They're not for everybody. (But then again, they don't try to be.)" Yeah, buddy, I thought. Older, wiser, and more experienced in the smoking discipline, I left my fresh pack of Camels on the blue counter facing Key Bridge. Maybe some poor schnook who was short of cash and cigarettes would pick it up. And maybe quit smoking.

Fedor: Is this yours?

Nick: Uhhhmm . . . uhhhh . . .

F: I said, Is this yours? Just don't lie.

N: It's mine.

F: Oh, so you're smoking now?

N: Uhhhm. Uhhh . . .

F: *Tol'ko ne vri!* (another exhortation to be truthful)

N: *Nu, da.*

F: If you're going to smoke, go ahead and do it. Just don't burn my barn down. Understand?

N: (Beginning to realize he was not about to be killed) *Ponyal.*

F: And make sure your mother doesn't find out.

N: She won't.

And that simply, between two men, a conspiracy was formed. Fedor lightly slapped Papa on the back of the head, then put his arm around his son and walked out of the barn . . . having first thrown a bucket of water on the offending area.

And Papa kept his promise for years, until he was ratted out by one of the older village boys. But that's a story for another day.

2

One cold winter Saturday, Mama and I had walked out to the subway station near the park to meet Papa after he'd worked some welcome overtime at the Jaguar Match Factory—an opportunity he never passed up. My favorite game back then was to run in front of my parents, turn around, throw my arms into the air in front of Papa and say "Na menya!³" He'd pick me up with an Op-plya!, carry me for about half a block, and set me down only to have me repeat the drill. We both loved it; I, especially, loved the feel of his cold cheek against mine and how safe I felt when he carried me. (I've spent a lifetime looking for that selfsame feeling and thought I'd found it. It was close, but not quite the same. And then it was suddenly gone, too.) On this particular Saturday, I had come up with a brilliant—to a three-year old—idea and launched it immediately upon being returned to the sidewalk. The fact that my parents were in the middle of a conversation on some ridiculous grown-up topic only spurred me to let it out:

"Guess what?"

Pause. Silence. I'd done the unthinkable: I had interrupted two adults in the middle of a conversation. Had I been alone with Mama, the punishment would have been swift, not necessarily accompanied

---

³ "Pick me up" or "Here I am"

by yelling. Simply the Hand of Justice meting out what it deemed appropriate for such an offense. Fortunately, Papa was there, so I hedged my bets and figured he'd probably provide pretty good cover . . . . . or at least interference. Undaunted, I sallied forth.

"Guess what?"

To my immense relief, the baritone responded: "*Nu*, what?"

"Do you know what I'm going to do when I grow up?"

"*Nu*, I suppose you'd like to be a teacher like Mama, no?"

"Well, not exactly. Do you want to know?"

"Yes, tell me."

"When I grow up, I'm going to marry Papa."

There it was. My secret was out. For better or for worse.

And then, of course, Mama had to add her two cents' worth, doubtless because she could sense that the jig was up for her:

"And what am I going to do? Are you going to throw me out of the house?"

To show her that there were no hard feelings after my most recent experience on the receiving end of creative child discipline—involving my old potty chair and some colorful handkerchiefs—and that I could be far more merciful than any example she'd shown me, in all seriousness I turned to her and said,

"No, I won't throw you out of the house. You'll be able to stay. But you will have to cook for us."

And she never let me forget it.

3

Being a widow and empty nester has its advantages. Not many, but some. For instance, you can eat your dinner seated on the sofa, plate in your lap, whenever you want. No one is around to shame you for your sloth or slovenliness, no one to insist that the table be set properly. It's OK to use paper towels instead of a napkin and to cut all your food into bits and season it before you sit down. While some might accuse such a person of lapsing into DILLIGAS[4] mode, I see it, rather, as a loosening of one's belt and restraints once the inflictors of norms are no longer present . . . even though some of the restraints and behaviors might have been self-inflicted. But anyway.

Picture this: I'm seated on my sofa, watching yet another episode of *Law and Order* because I cannot get enough of Sam Waterston as the Passionate Prosecutor, feeding myself by alternating bites of chicken and green beans. Baked together for convenience, they actually make a nice pairing. No potatoes, pasta, rice, or other grains, because I'm on yet another one of my diets in pursuit of an elusive much smaller size. I have a long way to go, but that's another story. As the TV drama goes to commercial break, I contemplate my sad chicken breast (no skin—my

---

[4] I learned this acronym from my (late) former Marine officer spouse. It deciphers as: Do I Look Like I Give a S%$#.

favorite part, dammit!) and the ribs curving up and one word pops into my brain: *Рёбрышки. Ryobryshki.* Little ribs. Riblets. Defenseless, I'm Wizard-of-Oz-tornado spun into a sunny day some fifty years ago and an after-dinner walk with Papa.

There's nothing unusual about our being out for a postprandial promenade; in fact, it was an everyday occurrence. As soon as the dishes were washed, dried, and back in the cabinet, Papa and I would don our outside shoes, coats, hats, and gloves (when necessary) and head out to explore the neighborhood. Not that there was anything particularly new out there, but Papa always had some sort of project underway, so we'd go in search of parts he needed. Most often, this search took us not to the hardware store (I didn't learn what one was until after we'd moved into our house on Sixty-eighth Street), but to the junkyard, where I was allowed to range free in search of who-knows-what while Papa searched through another man's trash for his own treasures. All kinds of things were to be found there—pipes, toilets, sinks, nuts and bolts, wires, even toys.

I remember one particularly spectacular find of mine: a gorgeous china-faced doll with long golden curls and a (somewhat *schmutzig*) long, light blue gown. I couldn't believe my luck! What a find! I quickly scrambled over the pile of metal pipes and ran as fast as I could to where Papa was still looking for a special kind of pipe joint, brandishing my newfound treasure.

"Look! Papa! Look what I found! She's BEAUTIFUL!! Can I keep her? Please? *Mozhno?*"

"Ah? *Chto ehto u tebya?* What is that? *A nu-ka, day syuda.* Give it here."

I surrendered my lovely china doll to Papa for examination and waited breathlessly for his verdict.

"She's pretty, but a little dirty . . ." Papa said and made the *tsk* noise that always preceded some form of negative response. I waited, then decided to risk another pitch:

"Yes, but I can bathe her after I take her home. And Mama can wash her dress the next time she washes our clothes . . ." my voice dropped off in a final sigh of near-desperation. I tried to pout, to add a bit of oomph to my plea.

"Well, whether Mama washes her dress or not is another question, but did you look closely at the doll?"

"What do you mean?"

"I mean, look closely at her face. Here, look at her face and tell me what you think."

I took the blonde beauty from Papa's outstretched hand and studied her face. She was beautiful beyond description, if you discounted one minor flaw. She was missing her left eye. The right one was bright blue.

Still, not to be outmaneuvered, I negotiated a deal with Papa whereby, if I found the matching eye, he'd try to fix the doll. I searched the entire junkyard for a bright blue eye, alas, in vain. I found quite a few brown ones and a couple of green ones that might have fit the bill, but I figured it might take away from the doll's beauty if she had different-colored eyes. Not that it would bother me, but my urchin friends might talk . . . or worse, laugh. Evidently, Mama's perpetual "what will people say" had already been drummed into my brain and cellular memory.

But, it was starting to get dark and Papa was rounding me up to walk home with the fweeeeeeeeeeeee-weet whistle I could neither ignore nor disobey. In a flash of clarity, I realized that—despite my best efforts to find a prosthesis—I'd have to abandon the search and leave my one-eyed beauty behind. For some reason, this infuriated me. I blamed the nameless doll for having had the stupidity to lose an eye and deprive me of such a prize. In fact, so enraged was I by this turn of events that, for the first time in my life, my vision blurred and I could hear nothing but a whooooooshing sound in my ears. With nothing else left to do, I grabbed La Belle by the legs and whirled around like a discus thrower, gaining speed and strength with each spin. Finally, I let her fly as far as my five-year-old arm muscles would allow and followed the trajectory until she landed with a satisfactory thump in a pile of broken toilet ceramics. I'm not really clear on this last part, but I think I might have spit at her. I'm Russian, after all.

But I've digressed.

So, getting back to the walk, here's what I remember about that particular undated early evening.

Somehow, Papa and I had gotten onto the subject of what his life was like as a child back in the Motherland—the *Rodina*. I don't remember how we got on the subject, but I suspect it was because I hadn't eaten much of my dinner, even though it was one of my favorites: chicken soup with Mama's homemade hand cut noodles (some of which I swiped while they were drying on the table before being added to the soup). After the soup, I'd always get the little piece of chicken with riblets still attached because I loved to strip the chicken off them—it tasted better than anything else. Except chicken feet which, for some reason, I really, really liked. Go figure. But I couldn't help the fact that I was born a painfully slow and picky eater whose table habits occasionally prompted Papa to let loose with a *"ZHUY!"* ("CHEW!") at me. Whereupon I would move my teeth really, really fast but not really chew anything. It was my best attempt at compliance.

I distinctly remember that day as being sunny and not too cold because I wasn't wearing (some cursed) hat. Papa was on my left, holding my hand as we walked along, trying to explain in words and intonation that I would understand what it was like to have nothing to eat. Nothing. Not a thing. Clearly, my pea-sized brain was having trouble imagining what it was like asking your mother for something to eat and having her start to cry and tell you that she had nothing to give you. So I asked Papa a series of questions, such as:

"Not even a potato?"

"No, not even a potato."

"Not even an onion?"

"No, not even an onion."

"Hmmm . . . not even some *рёбрышки?*"

"*Especially* no riblets."

"It must have been terrible to be hungry all the time."

"Yes, it was very terrible. And many, many people died, and the last thing they asked for was bread. When you grow up to be a big girl, I will tell you all about the Revolution and how the *proklyatyye kommunisty* tricked simple people into supporting their cause by promising everyone they could have land. And the poor stupid people didn't realize that you can't eat dirt."

And he made one of those "yah" croaking noises when he was trying not to say anything else.

"But why can't you tell me now?"

"Because right now you're too little to understand. But when you get older, I will tell you everything so that you do understand, because the *Russkiy narod* has always suffered. Under the tsars. Under the Bolsheviks. Under the *proklyatyye kommunisty* who destroyed the country. Right now, it's too much for you to know."

"OK, but you promise to tell me? You won't forget?"

"Promise. And I won't forget."

As we walked past the subway station entrance, I got a whiff of that distinctive subway smell—something I miss to this very day. Then again, maybe it's not the smell so much as where it takes me: a place of security, love, and knowing I'd always be taken care of and have enough to eat because Papa was there to hold my hand.

Over the next few years, I heard all kinds of horror stories from family friends and my parents at their frequent gatherings over plentiful food and vodka. There's an expression in Russian (OK, there's an expression in Russian for *everything*) that describes what a table should look like: *stol dolzhen lomit'sya ot yedy.* The table should start breaking from all the food on it. And it was like that at everyone's house—the table would be so covered with dishes of food that it would be hard to tell what color the tablecloth was, even though usually it was white and starched.

The endless *zakuski,* followed by a soup with *pirozhki* on the side, the main entrée with all the different composed salads—*vinegret, stolichnyy, kapusta*—amid rounds and rounds of toasts. And, finally, dessert with tea. Then there'd be a respite from the food while people got up and stretched their legs, smoked their cigarettes . . . and then, out of the blue, someone would say, "I wouldn't mind having something salty . . ." And the hors d'oeuvres would be brought back out and Round Two would begin. Maybe that's why no one had leftovers—we kept eating until the food or booze ran out or it got too late at night to eat one more bit. And neither the food nor the booze ever ran out. If it looked like the booze supply was getting low, one of the men folk would run out to the liquor store to resupply. It was New York—something was always open.

I loved the occasions when we entertained at home, because not only did I get to drink soda (cream being my favorite), but because all my toys and books were there and I found it easy to occupy myself outside the grownups' field of vision. It made listening to their stories easier. Unless, of course, there were other children present. On those days, we'd be left to our own devices to do as we would while the adults ate, drank, told jokes and stories and, after dessert, sang songs they remembered from their youth. Not once, not *ever*, did anyone break into the Soviet National Anthem—any version of it. Stalin had changed it a few times.

The downside to being at other people's homes was not only that I had to be on my best behavior, but I had to eat what they set in front of me without making a peep, which could be incredibly hard to do at times. I'll give you a for instance . . .

We had been invited to an elderly couple's home for one of these get-togethers. I *hated* going to their apartment because the entry hall always smelled like cats peed there and the old man had false teeth that clacked when he ate. It was very distracting. And, since they lived alone, they had nothing to occupy my attention. Instead, Anna Stepanovna would let me go play with stuff in their bedroom, like her silver hair brushes and her beautiful perfume bottles. A poor substitute, but better than sitting next to Stepan Andreyevich, listening to his teeth clack while he ate.

On this particular occasion, I'd been ROR'd—released on my own recognizance—to the bedroom while the grownups did their grownup eating, drinking, and reminiscing thing at the table. I remember that I was in the middle of staring at myself in the old-fashioned mirror on the dresser, wondering what I'd look like with long blonde hair, when my reverie was interrupted by Anna Stepanovna's gentle voice calling me to the table for dessert. Ah! Dessert! Yum! She was a great cook and always had something special only for me. In fact, she said as much when I came out of the bedroom:

"Oh, Mashen'ka, come sit down. I have something very special for you! Here, come sit next to your mama and I'll bring it straightaway."

For the few seconds that Anna Stepanovna was gone, visions of rice babka with strawberry or cherry *kisel'*—my favorite comfort food in the world at that time—danced in my head. The gentle lady with her gray hair twisted in the back of her head in what I assumed was the style of her young days, came toward me carrying a dessert bowl.

"Aha!" I thought, "it's the rice babka! Yay!!"

As Anna Stepanovna reached my chair, she set the bowl down in front of me on the starched white tablecloth. Her right hand on my shoulder, she smiled at me and said, "Look, Mashen'ka, I saw on the television that all children love this dessert! So I went and bought a whole jar of it for you! Here, eat some."

Oh. My. God.

Only I didn't think in those words back then.

The bowl contained an emerald-green, jiggling mass. It smelled sickly sweet. I detested all things green (including Mama's choice of iceberg lettuce green for the kitchen cupboards)—life savers, green peppers, the stupid geranium plants in our kitchen that never bloomed and only stood there, waiting for you to touch them so they could emit their stink.

So, there I was, with everyone's eyes focused on me and that damn bowl of jiggly slime.

I looked up at Anna Stepanovna and—the perpetual truthteller fled, replaced by a creature called the Polite White Liar (PWL)—said,

"Thank you very much, Anna Stepanovna, but I'm not hungry."

I could feel Mama's *don't embarrass me in front of others* energy lashing out at me like porcupine needles from every single pore of her body. Knowing full well that I was beaten (and likely really would be when we got home should I refuse this treat), I tried another ploy:

"Well, I'll eat a little bit because you got it especially for me. Would it be OK if I ate a bit more later?" Simpering, questioning smile.

"Of course, *detka,* of course. Eat as much as you like now and finish the rest later. What a very polite girl you are!"

I felt Mama's porcupine needles retreating to their home pores and caught Papa's right eye winking at me. I picked up the dessert spoon, skimmed a bit off the top of the gelatinous mountain, and maneuvered it carefully into my mouth. It melted into a saccharine sweet glob, then puddle. I swallowed. Carefully. In case it tried to come back up. I tried to turn my grimace into a smile.

"Nu, Mashen'ka, what do you think? Is it good? Do you like it?" Stepan Andreyevich clacked at me.

The PWL came out with flying colors.

"Oh, yes, thank you, Stepan Andreyevich. It's very tasty, but it's just that I ate so much before that I don't have room in my tummy. But I like it very much."

"Anya, make sure Mashen'ka takes home the rest! She says she likes it, so let the child have it to take home. Right, Mashen'ka?" And Stepan Andreyevich winked at me. His left jaw clacked.

"Thank you so very much, Stepan Andreyevich! This way, I can eat a tiny little bit every day." Smile, simper.

And damned if they didn't pack the entire remains of that jar of green apple jelly for me to take home.

The above is an example of why you should always tell the truth.

But, why green apple jelly, you might ask?

That's a legitimate question from a native speaker of American

English. However, I'd like to remind you that these were people who immigrated to the US of A in their golden years. They understood English poorly and spoke it even worse. So, when Anna Stepanovna saw a commercial for JELL-O on television (black and white), she naturally decided to thrill little Mashen'ka with this special dessert that all American children apparently loved.

The linguist in me can't resist pointing out the obvious (in case you haven't yet guessed): there's only a one-sound difference between JELLY and JELL-O and, if you don't hear so well or understand even worse, you'd naturally assume that these things were one and the same.

Yeah.

That's right: she served me a heaping bowlful of green apple jelly, straight outta the jar. Bless her well-intentioned heart.

I still pray for the repose of her soul every night. And Stepan Andreyevich's, too. Because I'm sure he got his real teeth back in Heaven.

4

My first ice skates were beyond beautiful; they were gloriously splendiferous and extravagant. Bright shiny white with real fur trim and soft plaid lining, their silvery blades reflecting the light, they arrived in a huge box on Russian Christmas borne aloft by my *Krestnaya*[5] and her family. But that wasn't all . . . I tore through the wrapping paper and the tissue paper and discovered—Holy Toledo!—a hooded white fur jacket, thick red socks, and mittens to match. I thought I'd died and gone to Heaven: not only were all these unbelievable gifts FOR ME, but two of them were RED—a color forbidden in our house. When I came out of my stupor, I bounced over to my *Krestnaya* and covered her with kisses. After being directed—and slightly shamed into doing so—I meandered over to her husband and boys with my somewhat more restrained thanks.

Vera was the mother of two boys. For years, she had prayed for a girl but none was sent from Heaven. So, when she was asked to be my godmother, she seized the opportunity with both hands and never let go; indeed, Vera turned into a true Fairy Godmother for me. Of course, she didn't have a magic wand nor did she sport poufy dresses like the Good Witch in *The Wizard of Oz*, but she always was beautifully turned

---

[5] Godmother

out in form-fitting dresses and smelled like Heaven (or my concept of it). *Krestnaya* spared no expense in buying me extravagant and frilly dresses (incredibly precious gifts for a child dressed in Mama's home-made clothing), dolls so fine I was not allowed to play with them (outside her presence, of course), and a host of gifts my little eyes never would have seen had it not been for her love and largesse. On top of this, my godbrothers—*Tolya* and *Vitya*, who were much older than I—adored me and indulged me in all my little play fantasies. Indeed, their participation in my tea parties was almost as good as Papa's. Once I had mastered English, I discovered that my *Krestnaya* had a minor flaw: her pronunciation of "that's right," an expression she used with great abandon, came out as "dat's ooorahyt." A half-century later, I can still hear her and it makes me smile.

As I think back on those years, it seems to me that her love, perhaps, was the closest I came to receiving what most people would call "a mother's love." In her eyes, I could do no wrong. In Mama's eyes, I could do no right. So, I suppose that on average—looking at it from a baseball-stats perspective—I was doing pretty well, batting .500 as far as being loved by a mother goes.

Vera had been married once before to someone named Misha—the Russian equivalent of Mike—her first love. In fact, Tolya was Misha's son. But The Great War for the Motherland wolfed Misha down like so many other young men She used as cannon fodder: untrained, unequipped, unarmed. Like so many millions of others, he never returned. But she carried a torch for him her entire life despite having married another man—*Kolya Koom*—whom she truly loved and with whom she had a son, Vitya.

I guess it's like that with your first love: you keep that little tiny flame in your heart burning with hope. Even after he's dead and buried. Maybe it wasn't him after all? Maybe somebody got the ID wrong? What if he's really out there, somewhere, unable to get back? Shouldn't you keep waiting, staying faithful and true like Odysseus' Penelope, weaving the hope tapestry every day, unravelling it every night? The morning I woke up and discovered my husband not breathing, the morning an ambulance took him away and the police locked up our house, the morning I don't remember getting to the hospital, the morning my children and I walked into a sterile ER and saw his pale still body—half of it covered with a hospital sheet—the morning my daughter threw herself on him, screaming "Wake up, Daddy, wake up," the morning I knew beyond a shadow of a doubt that he was dead, dead, dead, I still went home and thought about icing the cake layers I had made because he would have liked the new recipe. I spent years waiting for him to show up unexpectedly and tell me it was all a misunderstanding. In a tiny chamber of my heart lives the undying hope that, one day, I'll open the front door and there he'll be—older, grayer, but still broad in the shoulders with those mesmerizing changeable hazel eyes. Hope springs infernal.

Vera tried; she waited and waited and waited. But the War was coming to a close, she was alone with a two-year-old little boy, had no means of support, and a very nice *Kolya* came along. He offered her protection, safety, and love—not necessarily in that order—and a father figure for Tolya. The chaos of advances-retreats-advances by both sides made the decision for her: they packed up what meager belongings they still had, hitched a couple of horses to a cart they managed to find, and headed west, as many Cossacks did. The rest, as they say, is history.

Krestnaya and her husband ("*Kolya Koom*" as I dubbed him in my early speaking days) were Kuban Cossacks who managed to evade the Great Betrayal at Lienz by sheer dint of luck and maybe Divine Intervention. My godmother embodied the physical traits that the phrase "Kuban Cossacks" evoked in my little mind: she was tall, slender, dark-haired, and dark-eyed. Her voice had a clear and bell-ringing quality to it; her eyes sparkled when she laughed, which was often, and sometimes gently misted over when she looked at me and called me *ditya*[6] right before hoisting me up in one of her bear hugs and covering

---

[6] child

me with kisses. No matter what I did—or what Mama told her I did—she always delighted in seeing me. It was always a holiday and a party whether they came to visit us or vice versa.

Once they moved out of the city and to the countryside in New Jersey ("The Garden State"), we saw them less frequently. However, we did spend a week or two with them in the summers when, as a cute and bouncy blonde three-year-old I was put to work selling tomatoes from my godmother's father's roadside vegetable stand. My job was to look for oncoming cars and, as they approached the stand, to run into the road waving my arms and yelling "Tomatoes! Tomatoes!" I got paid a precious nothing for this exercise in near-death experiences, but I did it because I was more terrified of the Old Man than I was of oncoming cars.

Ded "sobach'ye myaso"[7]—as I referred to him (I got the expression from him because that's what he called all his grandchildren . . . who were, every single one of them, boys)—was a holy terror and ruled his family roost with a fist of iron. He had been a trained gardener in Imperial Russia and used those skills to grow an abundance of vegetables on their land in Fernwood Acres. He viewed his grandsons as a free unskilled labor force whose only good use was hauling fertilizer (chicken droppings from their poultry enterprise), pulling weeds, and picking vegetables as they came ripe. I was a marketing ploy: blonde, cute, could speak no English, and too scared to contradict him in anything. My job was to lure in the unsuspecting driver. It's the only time in my life that I was chosen for something based only on my looks.

I can see you're probably a tad confused by now, so let me explain: the entire Krestnaya clan lived together on four large parcels of land they had purchased in New Jersey. The first parcel already had a large farmhouse on it, so the entire multigenerational clan moved into that one house. I'm not making this up. The *Ded* and his wife (one of the

---

[7] Old Man "Dog Meat"

unrelated *babushkas*[8] in my life)—a tiny, shriveled woman with a heart of gold who had weathered a lifetime of her husband's belligerence and knew how to both avoid and get around it; my *Krestnaya* with *Kolya Koom* and their two boys *Tolya* and *Vitya*; my godmother's brother *Dyadya Shura* ("*Shurey*" to all the grownups) with his shrieky-voiced but beautiful and benevolent wife *Liza* and three boys, *Sasha, Alik,* and *Mitya.* That's right: eleven. *Eleven* people in one house. I don't remember whether it had one bathroom or two, but it really didn't matter much because all of us youngsters were forbidden by the *Ded* to use the toilet for peeing. If all we had to do was pee, we were forced to run out to the woods behind their extensive property and pee there so we wouldn't raise the water bill for the house by unnecessary flushing. I was small (and female) enough to elude *Ded* most of the time and find the bathroom on my own, tiptoeing gently through the house. I don't remember being caught, so I must have been pretty good at the stealth thing. Stealth peeing at the ages of three, four, five, six, maybe more. It was only after they had built my *Krestnaya's* house that I stopped worrying about stealthily peeing in a toilet.

The menfolk called each other *koom* and the womenfolk *kooma,* uniquely Russian terms for the parents/godparents of one's offspring. For example, both Mama and Krestnaya called each other *kooma,* while the menfolk called each other *koom.* Which is where my name for Krestnaya's husband—Kolya Koom—originated. His real name was Nikolai, like Papa's, which reduced to the diminutive Kolya in Russian. To avoid Kolya confusion, evidently, I dubbed him Kolya Koom and the name stuck for the rest of his life.

Time after time, as I think about those happy summer days, I return to the non-visual senses: sounds of laughter and happiness that, to me, had a sort of golden glow about them. Six people who had no pretenses, didn't try to impress each other with knowledge or possessions, but simply *enjoyed* being themselves together. They formed a cohesive

---

[8] grandmothers

group that was the closest I'd ever come in my life to knowing what a big family must be like. As the only girl in the bunch of offspring, I was coddled and pampered by all my "Big Brothers," but my heart belonged to Alik—born somewhere in the middle of Shurey and Liza's litter—who adored me more than anyone else and would carry me around like a princess, even after my hair started to turn dark, my front teeth fell out, and I could speak quite nicely for myself. In two languages.

Many years later, Alik would show up in my life in a military uniform. He had tracked us down lakeside at ROVA, the Russian resort. True to our past relationship, he got me away from Mama—after asking her permission, of course—rented a rowboat, and rowed me all around the lake. It must have been hot that day because I remember the sweat beading on his forehead and temples, running wet lanes down his clean-shaven face. So self-absorbed was I then and over the following years that it was only now, when I returned to that particular memory, that I realized he was in the Army in the blistering heat of Vietnam. I never looked for his name as the evening news scrolled the names of those killed/wounded and/or missing in action. Many years later, I overheard Auntie Liza telling Mama how he'd come back a drug addict and married a totally unacceptable—in her eyes—woman. As for me, I never saw Alik again.

But back to the family compound and its gardens of Ded-planted delights. To this day, I can remember the smell of a tomato picked warm and fresh from the vine. I remember walking down the rows of beefsteak tomatoes, my hands ever so gently brushing the plants, inhaling the almost citrus-sweet yet earthy aroma of ripe tomatoes.

I remember eating a carrot I pulled from the soil and rinsed with water from a hose. The crunch and sweetness of something that had just left its earthen womb and still carried the fragrance of Mother Earth. It was something to be prized.

I remember all the womenfolk, myself included, going to an orchard to pick fruit as each one came ripe. I'll never forget the look, smell, or taste of the special green plums (who knows what kind they were and does it matter?) as I yanked one off the tree, stem still intact, and bit into its sharp end. The juice and flavor exploded in my mouth and ran down my chin. I'd never tasted anything like it in my life, nor would I, but not for lack of searching and trying.

One of my most vivid memories of those sunshiney days is Alik sticking up for me, like the true prince that he was. He actually stood in front of me like a Viking Shield and asked Mama to beat him instead of me. Chivalry at such a young age! I got the spanking anyway, but Alik stood by while I took my punishment and cried along with me. I wonder now, if we were to meet again, whether he'd remember the incident. Alik, wherever you are, I love you still, my brother.

But, getting back to the idea of Krestnaya's extravagant gifts, I remembered her wedding gift to me: a Sunbeam stand mixer. It was the most up-to-date and high tech mixer I'd ever seen, so her largesse held true for all those decades. Years after it had stopped working, I stubbornly hung onto her gift to me. I simply couldn't bear to throw out a gift from the only person who'd ever called me "*ditya*" and "*zo-lotse*[9]." Every time I opened the cabinet that housed the defunct mixer, I'd hear her calling me. No one ever used those terms of endearment toward me again.

---

[9] Little golden thing

5

For the life of me, I do not know what brought the memory of the awful blue knit hat to the forefront of my brain. Hand knit. With spangles. Ugh. One of my mother's friends had knitted a *real wool hat* for me for Christmas. Mama, of course, made me try it on immediately in Auntie Julia's presence. As soon as it was clamped onto my mouse brown hair, ties fastened snugly under my chin in a stranglehold bow, my entire head began to itch. My head, my ears, my chin . . . everywhere that stupid spangly thing touched me, I itched. My parents' generation of Russians or other Slavs had no idea that such a thing as allergies existed. Any aberrant behavior was deemed to be precisely that: bad behavior that could be "corrected" out of a kid. With the proper (disciplinary) approach.

Taught to respect my elders (on pain of one of Mama's disciplinary methods), I couldn't say, "Get it offa me!! It *itches*!!!" Instead, my new blue *store-bought* winter coat was produced and buttoned onto me up to my chin to show how well the hat matched. Little beads of sweat were starting to break out on my overheated, itchy body, yet no one seemed to notice, engaged as they were in admiring Auntie Julia's creativity and handiwork. The ladies commented on how the spangles caught the light and how surprisingly well the hat fit me. And matched my new coat *perfectly*.

Indeed, to record this momentous occasion for posterity, the family camera was brought out to capture the moment. I don't remember how long I had to sit on the (itchy) metallic green sofa (the slip covers had come off for the holidays and the inevitable "company" we would have), but there's a picture somewhere in an old family album of a five-year-old girl with a very forced smile on her face.

One of the final indignities I had to suffer was that I had to kiss Auntie Julia and thank her for the "beautiful hat." She had, after all, as Mama informed me, "spent so much time creating this especially for you" (i.e., be nice *or else*. I knew too well what *or else* meant coming from Mama). As he always did in similar situations, Papa came to my rescue. While noting, in a very *en passant* way, that "it's unhealthy to have her get overheated. Maybe we can take the coat off now?" he started unbuttoning my coat, putting an end to any possible objections from the women.

Papa gently untied the blue bow under my chin and swept the offending bespangled bonnet ceremoniously off my head. Naturally, every single strand of my flyaway mouse brown hair stood straight out like rays from the sun in a demonstration of static electricity. Papa gave me a brief hug and a kiss on the top of my head while smoothing my errant locks and removing my new coat. I knew I couldn't say anything out loud without offending Auntie Julia or pissing off Mama, so I locked my brown eyes onto his grayish-blue ones and telegraphed my thanks. He knew. I knew. We both knew we had to make nice with the womenfolk. After all, they cooked.

As a result of this trauma, or from a bona fide allergy, I can't say, but to this day, I cannot wear anything made of wool next to my skin. If you want to know whether a garment has any wool in it, pass it to me and let me hold it up to my face for a few seconds. If I produce a sound similar to "ghack!" and throw the item back at you while scratching the place it touched, you can rest assured that it contains wool. I offer this up as a public service, especially if there are children and winter hats involved.

6

An only child has few options in the "confidant" department. True, some only children become "best friends" with one of their parents; some develop a wide circle of "best friends" (see the Myers-Briggs definition of *extrovert*); some never learn to relate properly to their peers and create imaginary friends, while still others develop a trusted relationship with an inanimate object such as a doll or stuffed animal. That Mama and I were never going to be "best buds" was a given; and, while I adored Papa and told him almost everything that happened in my little life, I saved my deepest soul secrets for my *Zaychik*.

Zaychik appeared in my life one Christmas morning, a dapper dresser in a plaid vest with a little gold chain coming out of his pocket. He was pink and white, had soft floppy ears and a fluffy white tail that looked like a cotton ball. He looked particularly festive under the little tree on top of the coffee table, and it was love at first sight when I saw those pink button eyes sparkling up at me. Too young to have a variety of names at my disposal from which to choose and too overcome with love for this little beady-eyed creature, I fired off the only word that came to mind: "*Zaychik!*" Thus christened, he became my constant companion and truest confidant I'd ever know.

At first, he went everywhere with me. But time marched on, and one fine day Mama informed me that I looked silly dragging a stuffed bunny around with me. In true allegiance to the shaming culture in which she—and now I—was raised, the opening salvo started with the usual,

"*Kak tebe ne stydno?*[10]" and continued with the piling on,

"Look at you, such a big girl and walking around with a stuffed animal. *Posmotri!* Look at all the other children: nobody has a stuffed animal. They're all going to look at you, laugh, and call you a baby. Do you want them to call you a baby, point at you, and laugh? And what are all the other mothers going to think? That I don't know how to raise a child? Put that thing away."

And so, shamed into submission yet again, I temporarily parted company with *Zaychik*. However, I always knew he'd be waiting for me at the end of the day when I came home from school, an outing to the park, or from a trip to the local A & P or deli. Always constant, he sat on the pillows of my pink and green bedspread almost blending in, given away only by his urbane vest. He was always as happy to see me as I was him, always ready to hear about my latest exploits or how I'd been mistreated by someone in the outside world. He never really offered me any advice, but he was an exceptionally good listener and secret-keeper and never let me down in the hugging department. In fact, he was the first person I ever told about my yearning for a pair of white go-go boots with black heels.

I knew I was venturing into forbidden territory, since all my shoes were bought at the German Salamander shoe store in Manhattan (the door handles were brass salamanders, which is how I learned what one was) where Mama spoke German with the salesgirls to identify the best sensible shoes for me. Shoes were a serious thing, apparently, and their selection and purchase required an hour-long commute by subway into Manhattan. Go-go boots, on the other hand, were to be found at the "cheap" shoe store down the block and around the corner from us. I

---

[10] How are you not ashamed of yourself?

wished as hard as I could for them. I prayed for them. I conspired with *Zaychik* on ways to convince The Authorities to get me the go-go boots All the Other Girls were wearing to school while I shuffled along in my brown lace-up leather "Marta" shoes.

Mama tried to shut down the first feeler I sent out on the subject by pronouncing that: a) the boots looked ridiculous; b) they clearly were bad for your feet; and c) we weren't rich enough to buy cheap things. I went back to *Zaychik* to redraw the battle plans.

In all fairness to Mama, I have to admit that c), above, made sense, but only decades later when I needed to buy appropriate office attire. Through trial-and-error experience, I learned that clothing (and shoes, of course) should be treated as an investment, and that spending more **now** meant that the good quality stuff would last longer. The cheaper stuff was exactly that: cheaper in all ways and usually started to fall apart after the first trip to the dry cleaner's. So, wherever you are, Mama, you were right on this issue. But I've digressed. Again.

Over the years, *Zaychik* lost the gold chain and misplaced his dashing plaid vest. His whiskers started to look more like a Chinese emperor's than a rabbit's, but *Zaychik* and I grew closer and closer to the point where I couldn't remember my life before him and couldn't imagine life without him. As soon as I came home from school, even before I had my snack, I'd run into my room for a quick hug to reassure him that I was back and still loved him as much as I had that morning when I left for school. My playmates and schoolmates all had older or younger brothers or sisters, but I had my *Zaychik*, who never tattled on me or sprinkled salt on my cereal. This special little Lepus Roseus held a very special warm place in my heart.

Perhaps, what happened one otherwise unremarkable day was inevitable, perhaps not. I find it interesting—as I get closer to the finale than I am to the introduction to my life—that I have trouble remembering most of the transgressions for which I was punished. True, the exile incident left an indelible impression on both my memory and heart, but the other mischief or disobedience for which I was punished evaporated from my mind. The "disciplinary actions" did not.

If you've read this far and, assuming you started from the beginning, you may have formed the opinion that Mama was the parent who administered "justice," and you'd be right. She was the cop who caught me red-handed, the investigating officer, the judge, jury, and executioner all rolled up into one. I became familiar with the implementation of the Sixth Amendment to the US Constitution before I even knew what the Constitution was. It could be that the physical, emotional, mental, and spiritual burdens she carried weighed heavy on her shoulders; maybe, she simply had a short fuse when it came to me and my shenanigans—I don't know. I'm in no position to be an apologist for the disciplinary measures taken to ensure that I grew up properly and became an educated, refined *kul'turnyy chelovek* in the eyes of the world. All I can say is that the methods were harsh, yet creative (cf. the Exile episode).

Hence, I do not recall what it was that I said or did to set Mama off in the half-hour between when I got home from school and Papa appeared on the doorstep. No clue. However, her yelling hurt my ears to the point where my eyes (involuntarily) started to water as she covered the full range from *"Kak tebe ne stydno?!"* to the usual "I don't know WHAT to do with you!!" For the first time ever, I tried to retreat to the sanctity of my pink room and find comfort in hugging my *Zaychik* instead of standing still and being the target of all that heated verbiage. Uh oh. Wrong move.

Before I knew what had happened, Mama had swirled into my room like the tornado in *The Wizard of Oz*, yelling "WHERE do you think you're going?!? How *dare* you walk away from me?!?" And then, before I knew it, she had snatched my *Zaychik* out of my arms and, yelling things about having had enough of me and that stupid rabbit, she stormed out of Apartment 2R and down four flights of stairs to the basement. I knew, because I heard the basement door slam open and shut. I heard her decisive clomping coming back up the stairs and wondered what would happen next. My eyes watered and my hands started to shake. I wondered if, somehow, one of Papa's leather belts would be produced from the closet (again) and how many strokes I'd get this time. I heard the door open, then close, then the locks clicking into place.

"Well, that's it," she said. Her face was all red and beads of sweat were rolling down her temples; she furiously brushed them away. "I've thrown away your *Zaychik*. Tomorrow the trash truck is coming, and he'll be gone for good. Now, go to your room and do your homework." My chest hurt (was I having a *serdechnyy sluchay*? I briefly wondered) and I could almost hear my heart breaking at the thought of my beloved little *Zaychik* stuffed into a metal trash can, suffocating under heaps of potato peels, onion skins, rotting bananas, and coffee grounds.

I commenced my usual begging, pleading, and abasing myself. I tried to grab Mama's hands with my own shaking ones, but she whisked me off like so much dirty dishwater and pointed out that it was too late for any apologies. *Zaychik* was gone for good. "Nooo, pleeeeeze, nooooo!! I'll do anything, but please let me have my *Zaychik* back. Pleeeeeze!!!" I started gasping for air and crying at the same time; I could feel my nose running abundantly as I cried and cried and cried. A tissue was handed to me with a firm "wipe your nose, your snot's running all over your face." I blew my nose and watched Mama disappear into her bedroom to dress for work with the final words, "And I'm going to tell Papa everything when he comes home."

I was stunned by how the world appeared to go on despite this horrible thing that had happened to my *Zaychik* and me. I went back to my room, sat down at my desk, looked out the window up at the sky, and wondered if my Guardian Angel could be convinced to watch out for my *Zaychik*, wherever he was. I decided to ask.

Unlike other (normal) days when I ran out to meet Papa walking up Sixty-eighth street from his carpool drop off point several blocks away, I didn't hear him come home. I was deep in negotiations with my Guardian Angel and any other Angels who were within earshot on the terms of the safekeeping of my *Zaychik*. I offered to light candles to them in church, which I would buy with my allowance money. I offered to keep a fast on any day they named. I offered to give up stoopball for a week or month, whichever they wanted. I offered to do extra credit homework. I offered to stop resisting the dress code in Russian school. I was so busy praying and offering these things up that I didn't hear any responses. I felt abandoned by everyone. I laid my head down on my desk and listened to the sound of my tears plopping on the blotter, waiting for whatever other punishment would be administered by Papa at Mama's behest.

I could hear Papa's key in the lock, heard the door open and Mama— all sweetness and light—asking him how his commute was, how his day was, what was new. Since I hadn't had my after-school snack, I also heard my tummy rumbling, but I didn't feel hungry. In fact, it felt as though someone had taken all my insides and tied them up into a series of big, huge knots. "Hey, YOU!" I heard Mama throw in my direction, "*Anu-ka, idi syuda!*" The summons. I struggled out from behind my desk, wiped my eyes with my hands and my nose on my sweater sleeve (inner sleeve, so it wouldn't be noticed right away), and walked into the bright light of the kitchen. "Now I'm going to tell Papa what you did. Stand right there." And she did just that, shaming me yet again for an offense that, to this day and try as I might, I cannot recall. As the litany of my misdeeds drew to a close, it was punctuated by the final pronouncement: "And I disposed of the *Zaychik*. He's gone forever." I wondered if my head could hang any lower or if my heart would ever stop hurting. But, after a goodbye kiss to Papa as though nothing had happened and completely ignoring me, Mama donned her hat, pulled on her gloves, and walked out of our apartment and down the stairs.

I was too ashamed and forlorn to even look up at Papa. Instead, I shuffled over to the stove and turned on the burner to warm up the soup. Still looking down, I went over to the cupboard, pulled out two plates and two bowls, and set them at our places opposite each other on the table. I folded two napkins into triangles and set them to the right of the plates. I got two soup spoons, two forks, and two knives out of the silverware drawer and placed them on top of the napkins. I got out the bread and put a few slices into the bread basket for Papa, who had retreated to his chair in the living room, where he was having a cigarette. When the soup was hot, I used the big ladle he'd made in his machine shop to scoop some into his bowl and mine and set the bowls on the table. Head down, I slinked into the living room and whispered, "Dinner's ready."

"Aaah! Well, if dinner's ready, let's go eat!" Papa sounded surprisingly cheerful, given the insurmountable tragedy that had taken place under his roof. We faced the icon in the corner, Papa with his longer (grown up) prayer, me with the child's "Lord Bless" and a quick genuflection. "Well, what did you learn in school today?" he asked, as if nothing had happened.

I looked up at those big gray eyes and felt a tear escape from my left eye and run down my cheek; I sleeved it away. "Uruguay."

"Wow, Uruguay! Such a strange name! And what is this Uruguay?"

"It's a country in South America."

"In South America, you say? Hmmmm . . . that's good to know. You should learn all about it so that one day, if you have to go there, you'll know where it is."

"Mmhmm."

"You're not eating your soup."

"I'm not hungry."

"Not hungry? Why not? Did you have a big snack? Or maybe you had some candy while no one was looking?"

I couldn't believe my ears. What was he thinking? I'd suffered the greatest loss of my childhood today and he was asking about candy. What in the world?

"No. I'm just not hungry. May I please be excused?"

"Well, maybe you'll be hungry later. Why don't you leave the bowl on the table and come back when you're hungry."

"May I turn on the TV?"

"Did you finish your homework?"

"Yes, it was only spelling."

"OK, go watch TV. I'll take care of the dishes."

We watched the news, Papa commenting on Walter Cronkite's comments and the state of the world amid swirls of smoke from his unfiltered Camels, as usual. Then we watched a bit of the *Million Dollar Movie*, but we'd missed the beginning and couldn't figure out what was going on, so I was allowed to get up and change the channels on the old Magnavox black and white until we found something that appealed to us both. The minutes ticked by.

Finally, with a quick glance at his everyday watch, Papa announced the inevitable: it was time to get ready for bed. Bed! How was I going to get to sleep without my *Zaychik*?! Oh, no. I hadn't thought of that. I was sure I'd never sleep again. Nor would I eat again. Those two thoughts were followed by an equally cheerful realization that A + B = C (my death) and the possibility that I would be reunited with my *Zaychik* in the Hereafter. That wasn't so bad. And *then* she'd be sorry she was ever mean to me.

I slid off the sofa and tiptoed into the bathroom to brush my teeth and wash my face. I peeked briefly into the mirror to discover that my eyes were red, my nose was red, swollen and stuffed up, and there was a bit of dried snot on the right side of my face that my sleeve had missed. As I turned the cold water on, I heard Papa tell me that he was taking the trash down to the basement. With a final sniff, I finished my evening ablutions, went into my room, and put on my pajamas. I sat on my bed, feet dangling off the side, afraid to swing them back and forth lest I be accused of "swinging the Devil" on my feet. Superstition? Yes, but who knew? Maybe there was something to it . . . it certainly seemed like old Beelzebub had been running rampant through my life that day.

I heard the key in the locks as they clicked open—even a run to the basement called for a locked door—and then again, as the door closed and the locks clicked shut. I heard Papa changing out of his shoes into his house slippers and start to walk toward my room. He stopped briefly at the kitchen sink to wash his hands and—it sounded like—to wipe down the sink and drain board. My door was ajar since I wasn't allowed to keep it closed, and I looked up as I heard Papa's footsteps outside my room. One arm was behind him as he opened the door all the way and said,

"Look who I found in the trash can downstairs!"

And there he was: my *Zaychik*. A bit worse for wear, with a small mustard stain on his back, but he was all there. Every bit of him, down to his droopy whiskers and flattened tail. I jumped off my bed. Papa lifted me up with his free arm and presented my *Zaychik* "back from the Front" to me. I hugged them both as hard as I could, my little heart beating so fast I thought it would jump out of my rib cage and dance the *hopak* in the kitchen. I didn't know which one to kiss first or most, so I showered my love and gratitude all over both of them.

"*Nu*, this is going to have to be our secret, *detka*. Don't tell Mama I found your *Zaychik*, because she'll only throw him out again. You have to hide him someplace so that she won't see him, but you'll know that he's here and he's safe and he didn't get taken to the trash heap. Now, how about if I warm up a little soup for you?" And with that, he sat me back down on the bed and walked out into the kitchen, where I heard the click-click-click of the burner being lit.

Moods and emotions can swing rapidly in a child's world, moving from despair to elation in nanoseconds; well, at least that was true for me in this instance. I suddenly realized that I was ravenous and with a jaunty step walked into the kitchen, where Papa had already warmed up the soup and was ladling some into my bowl. *Zaychik* was allowed pride of place at the table in the chair next to me—as a Veteran returning from the Front—and sat as a quiet observer throughout my meal. Papa sat opposite me, watching me eat, crinkles forming beside his gray eyes.

One week-end afternoon, months after the Dreadful *Zaychik* Episode, Mama caught me playing with him in my room. There was a long, heavy silence as I saw the steam and anger building. "Oh no," I thought, "now she'll really get rid of him for good." My hands started to quiver as the room turned hazy and my ears braced for the usual assault that started with "Aha! *Where* did you get that thing?? I threw him away, after all!"

Seemingly out of nowhere, Papa materialized and, casually draping his arm around Mama's shoulders, said, "*Ekh, mat'*, it was me who fished him out of the trash can. It's my fault. Let the child have her *Zaychik*, she's not hurting anyone or anything." And just like that, the crisis was averted and *Zaychik* and I could bring our secret rendezvous to an end and live happily ever after, like in the fairy tales I read. Two best friends, reunited.

In case you wonder whatever happened to this *Zaychik,* I'll tell you: he lives in the upper left hand corner of my closet, on the shelf. And every time I look at him, I remember his dreadful deportation and fearless rescue by my hero, Papa. He's still wearing the lace dress and bonnet Mama made for him the year after that, when I was sick and bedridden.

7

Maybe once a month or so, Mama would make a comment to Papa about his hair—or what was left of it—needing some attention. The few pictures we had of Papa in their DP camp days showed him with a thick shock of dark hair either parted on the left or combed straight back with a dashing widow's peak. The Papa I knew had a little sparse hair on top and a dark hedge with glints of silver around the ears and in back. When I asked about this odd discrepancy, I was told that Papa had lost his hair from wearing a hard hat in the German mines. It made sense to me at the time: of course you'd lose your hair if a hat kept it smushed all the time with no room to breathe or grow. I immediately thought of that abhorrent itchy blue hat with spangles that I was forced to wear in the winter and wondered if my hair would fall out, as well. For weeks after learning this, every day as I stood in front of the mirror watching my mother do a quick and mediocre job of braiding my hair for school, I tried to check for emerging bald spots on my head. But I've digressed; back to Papa's hair.

Usually, on a Saturday morning over a breakfast of tea and open-faced sandwiches, Mama started the conversation from somewhere out in left field:

M: We probably should go to church tomorrow.

P: We could.

M: We haven't been in awhile.

P: OK, so let's go. Then we'll have to get up early tomorrow.

M: Yes, a bit earlier than usual.

Pause. Pause. Pause. Pause.

There'd be some talk of chores and errands and, as we finished up, Mama would start to clear the table. As she came over to collect Papa's plate and cup, she'd pause, rub her hand over his neck and collar and then . . .

P: Ah?

M: When was the last time you had a haircut?

P: *Ne pomnyu.* Maybe a month or so ago? Why? Do I need one now?

M: Well, it's not so much that you *need* one, but if we're going to church tomorrow, it wouldn't hurt to clean it up a bit.

P: Well, in that case, I'd better get to the barbershop before it gets too crowded.

Me: Can I come?

And so I'd tag along with Papa, walking to the barbershop down the street from our house, holding his hand. In retrospect, I think it's odd that I never felt out of place in a shop where I was the only little girl. The place would sometimes be filled to overflowing with men waiting for a haircut, looking through magazines, their low voices creating a hum as they commiserated about the Mets or Yankees. Somehow, they always found a place for me to sit and a magazine for me to read, and I never heard anyone say any bad words.

Frankly, I *loved* the place. The wall of mirrors reflecting the bottles of colored liquids shelved in front of each chair, the requisite tall glass jar with a shiny chrome lid of BARBICIDE blue liquid housing different black combs. The sounds of the chairs being raised and lowered—ka-chunk ka-chunk up and then whhhhhhhooosssssssssssssshhhhhh down, the predictable barber's question of "how much ya want taken off?," the clippers' click-click-click, the high-pitched metallic snip-snip-snip of the scissors, the studied shhhhp shhhp of the straight-edge razor being sharpened on a strop, that irreproducible rasp when it was pulled across a man's lathered face, and the flap-flap-flap of a bright white hot towel—it was a symphony of satisfying male sounds that both fascinated and comforted me and sometimes made me wish I was a boy so that I could grow into a "shave and a haircut."

And the smells! So different from the ladies' hair salon Mama occasionally dragged me to when she had her hair permed or set. Those smells were chemically horrific and often summoned the *gonna barf* reflex in me. Mama would deposit me in one of the green, fake-leather chairs in the waiting area, under orders *not to leave* until she was done. Sometimes, when the conflicting stenches of perm solution, setting gel, and hairspray overwhelmed me and even made my eyes water, I'd wheedle permission to step outside the salon door—right outside the glass door where she could still see me—so that I could breathe again.

Women would stroll out of the processing area with every newly colored hair cemented into a teased-up do that made them at least four inches taller, chatting amicably with their hairdressers. Not one of them looked as though she'd had to barf from the stink; they all looked pretty happy as they gently patted their hair, powdered their noses, and reapplied lipstick. When Mama finally emerged with her new set of curls (perm only, no color. Mama never colored her hair. Ever.), she'd thank Dottie, pay her, and we'd head for the door. But, before we could get there, Dottie would come out from behind the counter with a "Hold on a minute, theh, hon" and head toward me. Before I knew what was happening, she'd start pawing through my bone-straight mouse brown hair, telling Mama that she could "chuhn huhintaahreelkewtie." I quickly added another Great Fear to my young life: the fear of Dottie, who wanted to give me Shirley Temple curls.

Life was so much better in the barbershop. First of all, no one even thought about turning me "intaahreelkewtie," I was left blissfully alone. Second, the whiffs of different aftershaves and hair oils that wafted gently throughout the shop and to my nostrils often made me stop whatever I was doing and try to trace them back to their bottles. Lavender to the light purple bottle, some indefinable clean trail to the blue. Sometimes,

Papa would spring for a barbershop shave. When he was done, he'd turn to me, call me out of my chair, and let me pick the aftershave for him. I always picked the light blue one because I knew blue was his favorite color, next to green. Besides, the aftershave he kept at home was a light blue, too. He kept it on the shelf in the medicine cabinet next to his razor and styptic pencil. I did worry somewhat, though, when the barber wrapped Papa's face in a hot towel. For some reason, I was afraid someone else would emerge from under the towel and Papa would be gone. It made for a few minutes of gently simmering panic, so I watched very carefully to make sure there were no substitution shenanigans on anyone's part. The relief that poured over me when the towel was removed and Papa appeared clean-shaven and red-faced was palpable and pronounced.

Freshly spruced up and ready for his weekend chores (and church tomorrow), Papa would open and hold the door for me as I'd step over the threshold and onto the street. He'd stop to light a cigarette, and we'd meander amicably back up Sixty-eighth street, hand in hand. Once in a while, after he'd rubbed out the stub of his unfiltered Camel, he'd give me the raised eyebrow and say,

"Nu chtozh? Kto bystrey?"

And I'd invariably say, *"Davay!"*

He'd count to three and we'd be off as fast as we could go. Although I ran as fast as the wind and my sneakers could carry me, he beat me to the lamppost in front of our house every single time. At the moment that I felt I was about to pull every last muscle in my legs, my arms pumping furiously and lungs about to catch fire, I'd see him pulling up to a slowed yet comfortable step across the invisible finish line. The "run faster" ads about my sneakers rang hollow, indeed. I swore to myself that I'd try harder next time and lived for the day when I'd finally beat Papa fair and square.

And maybe that was the whole point: work harder, don't give up, you'll get there one day.

8

Fourth of July and I'm watching competing fireworks displays: the over-the-top New York City fireworks on my TV and the piddly also-rans of my tiny beach community in North Carolina. I hear the strains of "God Bless America" and my eyes well up reflexively and involuntarily. Did I mention that I am a Yankee-Doodle-Dandy-Do-Or-Die? And how did a first generation American accidentally born to two refugees from the Soviet Union in the 1950s ever get to be this much of a flag waver? Star Spangled, through and through? Simple, I had a great role model.

They say that converts to a religion tend to be better adherents to it than those "born" into that particular faith i.e., more Catholic than the Pope. The same can be said of Papa's allegiance to his adopted country. My hero, my man of steel, stronger than anyone, faster than a speeding bullet, able to leap tall buildings in a single bound, defier of death and defender of children cried every single time the National Anthem was played anywhere. Hat over heart (back in those days all gentlemen wore hats. And not those stupid baseball caps everyone sports now, I mean real hats. Fedoras.)

If we were watching TV on the old black and white for which I had to ask permission to get up and change the channel (hear that, kids? *Get up and manually change the channel.* Click, click, click. Until you got one of the three stations that actually worked. Don't get me started on the sign-off signal), there'd be the occasional broadcast of some random soprano vocalizing "O! Say, Can you seeeeee?" At which point he'd even set his cigarette down in the ashtray out of respect and reverently listen, eyes welling up. "And the hoooome of the braaaaaaaaaaaaaaaave" was always followed by a comment on how beautiful the anthem was. And what a wonderful country—the one that had given them a home when they had none—this was . . . for as long as the country continued to exist. I can't blame Papa for his occasional pessimism; after all, he'd been an eye witness to the collapse of the Romanov dynasty, which had lasted over 300 years.

A survivor of the 1933 famine, WWII, life in the DP camps, and making a new life in a country whose language he barely spoke, Papa knew all too well the Vagaries of Fate. Which is why he loved his adopted country with all his heart—a love he passed on to me by example. In fact, he's the only person I've ever met who never once grumbled about paying taxes—it was the price he paid for living in the USA, and he was happy to pay whatever was due. I, however, have differed with him on this issue every April 15 since receiving my first paycheck. I pay my taxes and fully enjoy the grumble—a native daughter's privilege, I suppose. *Vive la différence!*

9

sssshhhp then CRACK! Followed by an "aha!!!" One of my favorite sounds of summer in a blistering New York City: the sound of a watermelon being cut open for the first time. The cutting board ceremoniously pulled out from its home under the sink, the big knife skillfully honed on the sharpening steel, those moments of anticipation as Papa turned it this way and that to determine the best starting point.

"Mmhmm. Mmmhhmmmm. Mmmmhmmmm. *Nu,* we'll start here?"

It didn't matter where "here" was, the spot was indisputably perfect, whichever he chose. Kssssssshhhhhh the slipping in of the blade, the ssssshhhhp sssssshhhp ssssssshhhhhhp circumnavigating the dark green skin and creamy underbelly, and finally, coming full circle, the *krrrrr-rack* of breaking it open and seeing the bright red interior, spotted with black and white seeds, its juices running all over the cutting board and onto the table. A run for the sponge and kitchen towel and the ritual exclamations: "Oho!!" "Wow!" "It's a goooood one! We picked out a good one this time!"

Actually the "we" was Papa's princely inclusion of my five-year-old self in the whole process. There was no "we" about it, because a decision as momentous as picking out a huge watermelon that would sit in identical halves in our refrigerator, covered with wax paper, for days could not be left to my caprice. Instead, each selection and purchase of this thirst-quenching, cooling *thing* contained a lesson. This one, fortunately, I never forgot: **It's supposed to ring, not thud, when you thump it**. Go ahead, try it: right now (if it's summer), go out to your local fruit and vegetable stand or—if you must—grocery store and pick out a watermelon using the above instructions. See if "ring" doesn't win out over "thud" every single time. Go ahead, conduct the experiment. Buy a "ring" and a "thud," take them both home, set them side by side, and slice them in half, as described above. You'll immediately see what I mean. Then, look up and thank Papa, not me.

That initial cut would be followed by another, this one taking a green-white-red circle off the freshly-cut middle. He'd slide the slice onto one of our everyday gold-blue-white Pyrex dishes and then cut it into equal wedges. (Really, they were all the same size!) We'd take care of the housekeeping first by putting the remaining melon away in the fridge, wiping down the kitchen table, and, of course, getting out the bread. The bread was for Papa: our table had to have bread on it at every meal, a generous serving of it nestled in the napkin-lined straw bread basket. I puzzled over this phenomenon for many childhood years, trying to come to a conclusion as to *why* we always had bread on the table since neither Mama nor I really seemed to eat any. Finally, in a fit of unquenchable curiosity, I blurted out: "*Why* do you always eat bread with everything? Even watermelon?"

The answer was quite simple, really, and came as a result of the 1933 Famine: Stalin's idea to coerce the population into collectivization via starvation; people died in droves. Papa told me, in terms that I could wrap my five-year-old brain around, that the last thing a starving person asks for before he dies is bread. Hence, we always had bread on the table because *we could*. And, given the sanctity of this substance, we *never ever ever never* threw bread out in the trash. If it got moldy, Papa cut the mold off and ate the good part; he saved the remainder to feed to the birds in the park. To this day, I cannot bring myself to throw out a moldy piece of bread because someone, somewhere is starving to death and asking for bread. And because I know he's watching. But I've digressed again.

Back to the watermelon . . .

There was no such thing as polite, sophisticated, pinky-in-the-air watermelon eating with Papa and me. This was REAL eating: chomping into the cold red flesh, not only chewing, but sucking all the cool juices and, before you'd swallowed the first bite, heading in for your second. The pink juice would flow south to my elbows, forming little rivulets on my scraped-up skinny arms. Papa would alternate watermelon and bread bites, smiling and chewing, shaking his head and mmmm-mmm-hhhmmming with each bite. At a time when air conditioning was something only the very rich had in their homes and we'd never even heard of it, this was the closest thing to it—and it worked from the inside out! Our schlurping and chomping and mmmhhhm mmmhing could probably be heard throughout our apartment building and out on the fire escapes where people less fortunate than we were—the poor watermelonless hordes—would go to catch a cool breeze, should there ever be one. We were lucky, and we knew it.

Most of all, it was *fun* to eat this magic fruit that was available only in the blistering heat of NYC summers. The best part, of course, was getting to the very bottom and there was only that cap of red-white-green left. That was when we pulled out the big soup spoons and scraped the last large red dollops off the rind and then sccccchhhhhlllllllurped the remaining drops of juice. I learned many, many years later that this particular phenomenon—eating watermelon with a spoon—was common in their region of the Old Country. And all that time, I'd thought we'd invented a new way of getting every last bit of juicy red goodness out of the watermelon and into our mouths. I'm glad this disillusionment didn't come until long after I'd already gone through my multiple mid-life crises.

10

I talian prune plums are getting harder and harder to find, particularly in my little sand spit of a world. And yet, I love them—have since childhood—so my frustrating search goes on every year at plum season, hoping against hope that one of our two food stores will finally carry them.

Alas, my quixotic quest has not yet borne fruit (ba-dum-BUM!).

Still, like Don Quixote himself, I keep tilting at produce windmills, knowing that somewhere out there lie rows and rows of unblemished Dulcineas, ready for the buying.

I've often wondered what burr gets under my saddle in the summer and forces me to risk my life by merging into height-of-tourist-season traffic in search of these sweet oval deep purple gems. True, they're quite tasty, but so are any number of *other* plums that are readily available. Why not face reality, give up the Quest, and follow a star to any other red, black, or yellow variety? Well because, as that song from the *Man of La Mancha* said, "This is my quest, to follow that Star/No matter how hopeless, no matter how far . . ."

Besides, I do not come from a family of quitters.

Quitting is not in my genetic makeup: I am the product of two (and probably more, if you count ancestors) survivors. When I think of their lives' paths, I sometimes feel like a psychological and emotional ninety-eight-ounce weakling. I suppose Life forced them to be strong: given a choice between lying down and dying of starvation or getting up and risking being shot or blown up and living, they chose the latter. No whining about what they lost, only a solid trudge through the vicissitudes of Fate. They were, indeed, members of the Greatest Generation—the unsung heroes—that Tom Brokaw named and wrote about. However, they were Russian . . . and about those unsung heroes too little has been written. And that casts me and my summer quest for the Italian prune plum in a really lousy light. Alas.

Quite by accident the other day I realized what that burr under the saddle was: the taste of forgiveness and sense of all being right with the world. The taste of being reinstated to full "member of the family" status with all rights and privileges thereunto pertaining. On my way to meet a friend for lunch at a local eatery, I passed a bakery just as someone was exiting the premises. The aroma that wafted through the open door unexpectedly enveloped and enchanted me, prompting a feeling of well-being and a sudden memory bubble that burst like a roman candle into my consciousness. Oh, right.

One of the times Mama had caught me sucking my thumb, out of "lecture topics" and clearly out of patience, she grabbed a couple of things to help her "discipline" me. The Incorrigible Me had her hands tied together with a handkerchief that had pictures of waterfalls and some kind of lettering on it—I hadn't yet learned to read, being pre-K and all. I guess that by tying my hands together Mama had made sure that I couldn't suck my thumb for comfort (either left or right, although my preference was for the right: I've always been right-hand-dominant) while being punished. And, since she was busy with baking and couldn't leave the kitchen, she somehow somewhere found my old potty chair, slammed it to the floor, and slammed me, in turn, into it. I cried bitterly at the humiliation of being seated on the potty chair—I'd been going in the big potty by myself for a long time—and at my inability to wipe my eyes and nose. The colorful hanky got wet quickly from all the liquids exiting my eyes and nose with nowhere else to go.

I don't know how long I sat in the Chair of Infamy, but it felt like forever. There I was, in the middle of the kitchen, crying my eyes out and no one cared. I wondered again if Mama were my real mother; the evidence needle pointed decidedly to NO. I reasoned that a real Mother would never treat her child this way and cried even harder at the knowledge that I was now no different from the poor step-mothered waifs I'd heard about in stories. I felt extremely sorry for myself and wondered if all this crying would change my eye color or even make me go blind. Then, in a matter of minutes, my life changed for the better.

Mama had taken a tray of oval plum *pirogi* out of the oven and had set them on the stove to cool. She turned around, walked toward me—here I started to quiver because I thought I'd be getting spanked on top of everything else—and stopped in front of me. I looked up, but I really couldn't see very well due to the gallons of tears flowing freely from my eyes.

"*Nu?*" she asked, "Are you going to suck your thumb anymore?"

I didn't pause to think it over. I quickly crossed my toes (just in case) and gave my head a sincere "no" shake.

"I asked you if you're going to suck your thumb anymore." Evidently, as in a court of law, the verbal response was required.

"N—n-n-n-noooooo."

Satisfied with my response and apparent penitence and capitulation, Mama untied my hands. I moved my fingers around to see if they still functioned and quickly sat on my hands to avoid any appearance of non-compliance (or the planning for non-compliance). What happened next came as a surprise and set a horrible pattern for the rest of my life.

Mama walked over to the cool tray of *pirogi*, lifted one off, rested it gently on a plate, and cut an end piece off. Then, she walked over to where I was sitting (still on the Chair of Infamy) and proffered the triangle to me, saying,

"Now that you're going to be a good girl, eat this. It'll make you feel better."

As I bit into the pastry, the sweet juices from the plums mixed with the vanilla and citrus-scented pastry and made a happy dance in my mouth. I'd never tasted anything so good *ever* in my life. I swallowed and took another bite. It was absolutely sublime. To this day, I associate freedom, liberation, and the soul-soothing feeling of being forgiven with the scent, taste, and mouth feel of that pastry. And I'm sad that I'll never find it again; I'm sad that I can't re-create it because Mama kept all her recipes in her head. And now her famous memory and she are gone.

I'm pretty sure Mama told Papa what had happened that day, but he didn't treat me any differently than he had the day before. Unlike Mama, who could give me the silent treatment for days, Papa seemed to figure that, once an event was over, there was no sense in dredging it up again. It's over, let's move on. And, in confirmation of that theory, we went for a walk to the park after supper and *not once* did either one of us mention the day's earlier events. Not once. As the light of the day started to dim, we walked out of the park and started toward home.

"*Nu, kak naschyot piroga?*" Papa asked. What about that *pirog*, indeed, I thought. I looked up at him to check for any indicators that **he knew**, but he gave me a quick wink and turned into our apartment building, holding the door open for me.

As I bit into that piece of yeast-raised scented dough filled with reddish-purplish fruit and juice, I realized that it tasted different. Still yummy, yes, but not nearly as good as the piece that welcomed me back into the family. And then a cigarette to aid the digestion. Bliss, family bliss, as I sat on Papa's lap and watched him smoke, pretending that I was smoking, too.

I've been chasing that taste ever since, perpetually without luck. Unfortunately, the concept of food as a reward, food as forgiveness, food as welcome is etched indelibly into my brain. Much to the concern of my primary care physician, who clucks and scolds without a clue as to the true root of the problem.

11

Time had gone by, summer had ended, and fall had arrived. This was a momentous year and my first day of school loomed large. Both Mama and Papa escorted me to school—kindergarten— that's how seriously they took education and the acquisition thereof. I mean, Papa *didn't go to work* so he could walk me to school. I can see, in retrospect, why they might have been concerned: I didn't speak a word of English. 'Twas a rude awakening for me to be surrounded by children who looked like me but couldn't understand or speak to me in a way I'd understand. I was confused for the first couple of months and truly disliked my daily immersion into a foreign world.

It took some time, but I eventually reconciled myself to going to Kindergarten and learned to speak English (gimme dat doll or I'll hit-cha). I decided school wasn't such a bad gig after all. The problem was that it occupied only half my day, which meant that I was left alone with Mama for the remainder of the day until Papa came home and the fun could start.

There was, however, a respite to this: our next door neighbors, Maria Emil'yevna and Yelizaveta Rudol'fovna—a daughter-mother team who adored me. Maria Emil'yevna's husband, Aleksandr Mironovich, a portly former mathematics professor whose cure for insomnia consisted of solving "unsolvable" mathematical equations, worked with Papa at the Jaguar Match Company. Maria Emil'yevna had some sort of heart condition and couldn't have children, so she showered all her unfulfilled maternal love on me. Her mother, Yelizaveta Rudol'fovna, did the same, only from the grandmother's perspective, and I even called her "Babushka." Mama would take me over there when she had grocery shopping to do. In exchange for their watching me, she'd pick up groceries for them. I suspect she thought she was the winner in that trade.

Their apartment was a haven for me. They were always delighted to see me, let me have the run of the apartment, and no matter what I did there, I was praised for it. Patted on the head, praised, kissed, and hugged. Told that I was smart. Given treats. I vaguely remember that one of my favorite activities was peeling the labels off canned fruit and vegetables. Not only one or two cans, but all the cans in the cupboard. Following one of my visits, the Mironovs often got canned peaches or mixed fruit in heavy syrup when they wanted green beans as a side dish. No matter, they only laughed about it and said, "Mashen'ka's been here!"

I remember Maria Emil'yevna as a beautiful, dark-haired lady of infinite patience, grace, and love who wore her long hair in a beautiful twist at the back of her head. She always had a book or magazine for me to look at, cans for me to peel, or other activities to keep me happy. On sunny days, as a special treat, she would bring out her string of amethysts and hold them in the light to make splashes of color appear.[11]

---

[11] The amethysts were a wedding gift from her mother, Yelizaveta Rudol'fovna, who had bought them herself as a young wife. She was on a train to Novosibirsk to join her husband when the train stopped somewhere in the Ural Mountains. A wizened old ragamuffin of a man got on the train, holding something in his hands. When he approached Yelizaveta Rudol'forvna's car, she stepped out to see what he was carrying. He was carrying the string of amethysts and was offering them for sale. Yelizaveta Rudol'fovna had a keen eye for jewelry and precious stones; she stopped the little man and asked him about the necklace. As it turned out, he had mined, hand cut, and strung the amethysts himself. It was a graduated strand with the largest bead in the center, with each of the others in the strand

Even though she was under doctor's orders *not* to lift things, Maria Emil'yevna always swept me up into her arms when I arrived and walked me back and forth through the shotgun apartment, pointing at things and naming them. It was at Maria Emil'yevna's knee that I learned how to pronounce [l] and the trilled Russian [r], two sounds Mama couldn't coax out of or drill into me.

Maria Emil'yevan (ME) would sit on the floor next to me (another no-no for her), much to Yelizaveta Rudol'fovna's dismay, and show me pictures of things that had an L or R in their names, preferably both sounds. Hour after hour. It went on for weeks. While Mama shopped, I peeled cans and stubbornly refused to pronounce what linguists call the liquids.

Maria Emil'yevna: "LLLLLLLLLLLLLLLLLimonad"

Me: "yyyyyyyyyyyyyyyyyyyyyyyimonad"

Maria Emil'yevna: "RRRRRRRRRusskiy"

Me: "yyyyyyyyyyyyyyyyusskiy"

Maria Emil'yevna: "Krrrrrrrrrasnaya rrrrrrrrrrrrrroza"

Me: "kyasnaya yoza"

And so it went. She never raised her voice and never corrected me; instead, she would dissolve into infectious gales of laughter that would set off both her mother and me, and all three of us would laugh and laugh and laugh.

One routine summer grocery shopping day, Mama stuffed my fat little arms through the sleeve holes of a pink sundress, locked all three locks on our door, and rap-rap-rapped on the Mironovs' glossy black door. After the usual exchange of IFF (identify-friend-or-foe)

---

of increasingly smaller size. She asked him, "how much?" He answered, "five gold rubles." Yelizaveta Rudol'fovna dug down in her little reticule, pulled out a five gold ruble coin and a deal was struck. I'll bet that nameless little old man had no idea that his amethysts would end up on a small spit of sand separating the mainland of the USA from the Atlantic. Hell, I'll bet he didn't even know what the Atlantic was. But I think of him, and the story, and the two ladies whom I loved so very much every time I see the flash and sparkle of those beads.

information, Maria Emil'yevna swung the door open to us. She was wearing a floaty white dress and was backlit by the sun beaming in through their kitchen window; for a moment, I thought she was an angel and stood transfixed at the threshold. I came to from a nudge in the back and the words,

"Why are you standing here? Go on in."

Not yet completely in the safety zone, I was still under Mama's control. I stepped over the threshold into Maria Emil'yevna's smiling embrace and hugged her as close to me as I could, burying my head in her flowy skirt. Predictable pleasantries exchanged, Mama asked what the Mironovs needed from the store.

Mama: "Well, what shall I buy for you?"

ER: "Two cans of peas, a can of pears, and two red peppers."

(I perked up at that last item, because I knew it was for me. Other children ate fruit; I was addicted to canned spinach and fresh red peppers. Elizaveta Rudol'fovna always had one or the other—sometimes both—waiting for me.)

Mama: "OK, what else?"

ER: "A pound of chopped meat and a pound of pork. I'm going to make pel'meni."

Mama: "Do you want the butcher to grind the pork for you so you don't have to do it yourself?"

ER: "Yes, please. And tell him to grind both together, it'll make mixing easier. And a French bread. Let me get you a piece of paper and pencil to write it down."

Mama: "No, thank you. I'll remember it."

Mama prided herself on her memory, and rightfully so. She never ever forgot a thing on the grocery list, even when she made multiple stops and detours. In fact, Mama never ever forgot anything . . . for better or for worse.

And so, on this particular day, after a tour around the apartment to check on the plants and see which ones were blooming beautifully (ME: "krrrrrrrasivo!" Masha: "kyasivo"), Maria Emil'evna settled in with me to go through a new magazine (Maria Emil'yevna: "zhurrrrrrrrrrrnal" Me: "zhuynal") with me. Picture after picture, R after R, L after L, on and on until, exhausted by the effort and frustrated by failure, I threw up my fat little arms and bellowed:

"KA—PI—TOO- LEEE—RRRRRRRRRRRROOYOO!!!" to the loud exclamations, applause, and warm hugs from both ladies.

I suppose Maria Emil'yevna was the Henry Higgins to my Eliza Doolittle, Pygmalion to my Galatea, and I adored her. Several hours later, when Mama had hauled all the groceries up the stairs in my old peram- bulator and knocked on the Mironovs' door to deliver them, I was sent to open the door to Mama and directed to say, "Zdrrrrrrrrravstvuy!" I trilled the beejezus out of the R and nearly shocked my mother into tripping back down the stairs.

Once I had conquered the liquids, there really wasn't much for me to work on with Maria Emil'yevna. Instead, she told me stories about her childhood in Imperial Russia and Germany. The stories from Russia were happy ones, and I loved to hear them over and over again. Now that I could ask questions without avoiding words with [r] and[l], our conversations became much livelier and more interesting.

The stories from Germany were much sadder and included stories of Maria Emil'yevna wearing shoes with holes in the winter, getting icy water in them, and then being sick for a long time. Stories of schoolchil- dren laughing at her because she didn't know how to speak German. Maybe that's why she was so patient with me: she wanted to spare me the cruelty she'd experienced as a child. She needn't have bothered: I had an unpronounceable Russian last name at a time when people were still reeling from the effects of McCarthyism. Being called a "commie" by older kids who pretended they knew what it meant helped me de- velop a thicker skin. Especially after Mama marched herself over to their hangout corner and delivered a lecture on communism and why *we* were not—nor had we ever been—communists. And the torment actually stopped, at least temporarily.

In sum, the Mironovs' apartment was my refuge. Sometimes, even while Mama was home, I'd ask permission to go visit our neighbors. The reason I'm giving you all this information is to let you know that, by the time of The Incident, I had developed an outstanding cover story for myself. Like most cover stories, it didn't last forever. But it was great while it lasted.

And so . . .

I developed my thumb-sucking late in childhood. Apparently, it wasn't until I was about three or so that I started sucking my thumb in earnest. While Mama let this behavior slide for a couple of years, by the time I got to Kindergarten and was still sucking my thumb, she was spurred to action. Every time she caught me at it, Mama would blister my ears with a tirade on bad habits and this one in particular. She threatened me with all manner of diseases that I'd get from the dirt under my thumbnail. (I didn't believe her.) She smeared hot mustard on my thumbs. (I discovered a love for spicy food.) Then there was the day I mentioned previously when Mama had stuffed me into my old potty chair, tied my hands together and, ignoring my please for clemency, went on baking plum *pirogi*.

When she released me—having dragged a promise not to suck my thumb anymore out of me—she untied my hands and gave me a warm piece of Italian prune plum kuchen. I'd never tasted anything so good in my life. It tasted like love and forgiveness.

Of course, what Mama hadn't noticed is that I'd crossed my toes (my fingers being otherwise occupied and unavailable for crossing at the time) when making the promise. It's not that I intended to deceive her (well, OK, maybe a bit), but I knew that I couldn't stop sucking my thumb. It was too comforting and reassuring.

After I finished the *pirog*, I still had traces of its sticky yummy gooey filling on my hands, so Mama dragged my footstool over to the kitchen sink and turned on the cold water for me. I rubbed my hands. I rubbed some soap on them. I rubbed them some more, playing with the water cascading down over my fingers. Mama was too busy with the next tray of pastries to pay attention to what I was doing, so I continued playing with the water coming out of the tap. And then I made an incredible discovery.

Archimedes could not have been more excited when he shouted "Eureka!" than I was when I saw that *all* my fingers were now wrinkled. Not just my thumb. *All* my fingers. Ding! Ding! Ding! Eureka!!! I can play in water and disguise my thumb sucking!! And I knew precisely the place where I could get away with it . . .

My visits to the Mironovs came closer together, and I was staying longer than usual. Ever vigilant, Mama checked my thumbs every time I came home but could prove nothing since *all* my fingers were wrinkled from playing in the water. Day after day, water game after water game, successful thumb inspection after thumb inspection, I was lulled into complacency. I truly believed I had orchestrated a terrific work-around to the issue. No one was the wiser.

Pride cometh before a fall, as we've all heard. It's true. One school morning in the late fall, as Mama was rustling around in the kitchen getting breakfast for us, I had wandered to the living room window to count pink cars, a favorite game I played with Papa. Partially hidden by the faded green brocade drapes on my left, still wearing my PJs and holding *Zaychik* in the crook of my left arm, I unconsciously raised my right thumb to my mouth. The noise of the traffic in the street below was loud enough to cover any sounds in the apartment, so I didn't hear Mama come up behind me.

"AHA!! So *that's* what you've been doing over here!!"

I literally jumped straight up, that's how unexpected and scary that voice was. And I knew I was really in for it this time. Uh oh. That tone of voice was never a good thing. It started out high and got higher as she added more and more words and exclamation points to the tirade. The invective was accompanied by some painful swats to my behind that Mama seemed to be using for emphasis.

"I don't know *how* many times I've told you to *stop it!!* [smack] What is it going to take, ah??? [smack smack] I've tried putting hot mustard on your fingers, I've tried tying your hands together, I've sat you on your old potty chair for hours, and *still* you're sucking your thumb??? AREN'T YOU ASHAMED OF YOURSELF??? *Kak tebe ne stydno???* I'm *done* with you!!! [big huge smack] When you get home from school and Papa comes home, he's going to take you away. *Vsyo!* That's it. Now come here and let me get you dressed for school."

That appeal to conscience was the last straw attempt in all scoldings—Russian is a shaming culture. (About fifteen years later, during my tenure as a student at Leningrad State University, my friends and I had rented a rowboat. We were piddling around without approaching the Finnish border or anything, but evidently we got too close to the foreign flagged ship in port, because after yelling at us through a megaphone a number of times, the Soviet Coast Guard resorted to: *"Kak vam ne stydno? Chto u vas, sovesti net?"*[12] Even the authorities used it!)

I remember exactly what I was wearing that day: a white blouse with a Peter Pan collar, a gray skirt with three rows of red ribbons at the bottom, white knee socks, and my brown lace-up school shoes. Because it was still a bit chilly, I also was forced into a white sweater. My hair slicked down, the knots viciously pulled out by a very angry comber, I was shoved in front of the icon of Mary and Jesus that hovered over my crib[13] to say my prayers before setting out for school.

I was summarily marched down two flights of stairs and out of our apartment building, listening to the Fury of a Mother Disobeyed and Deceived all the way to PS 17. I thought my ears were going to start bleeding from the scolding, but I kept my head down in the ashamed-of-myself penitent pose, staring at my shoes and avoiding the stares of my classmates who were being walked to school by younger, kinder, and smiling mothers. I briefly wondered—as I did every time Mama's displeasure was visited upon me—whether she was really my stepmother

---

[12] Aren't you ashamed? Don't you have a conscience?

[13] At the age of five, I still slept in a crib. Really. I guess they couldn't afford a new bed yet. But I really loved my crib because it had pictures of bunnies jumping around patches of grass. My favorite animals. Including my stuffed bunny appropriately named Zaychik, who figures prominently in another part of the story.

and if one of these nicer mothers was actually mine. She let go of my hand as soon as we hit the schoolyard and I dutifully lined up with my classmates. Adriana Salvetti, my new best friend, offered me her hankie for my nose, but I used my sleeve instead—I didn't want her to lose points from Mrs. Zigler for having a dirty hankie during the morning's roll call and nail check.[14]

True, the day had gotten off to a bad start, but I thought everything would settle into place by the time I returned home. The day went by as all school days did back then: The Pledge of Allegiance, the School Prayer, learning a new song, practicing the old song, working on another letter of the alphabet, drawing pictures, learning to share toys and the *rrrrrrrrrrrriiiiiiiiiiiiiiinnnnnnnnng* of the end of school bell. We obediently lined up with our partners, two by two, and, when we were all still and focused on Mrs. Zigler, she walked us down the hall and outside to the schoolyard where the mothers were waiting to walk their children home. I looked wistfully at the other mothers, hoping one of them would claim me, but no such luck. Mama picked up pretty much where she'd left off that morning, gripping my hand in hers and marching me home, repeating with every fifth heel click, "You'll see when we get home. You'll see. *Uvidish!*" I wondered how much worse it could get. I wondered if my guardian angel would step in on my behalf. I wondered if I could somehow get to the phone and call my godmother and beg her to intercede for me . . . or let me live with her family.

---

[14] For those of you who grew up in the tossable tissue age, read and learn how real girls went to school back then: we each had to have a freshly laundered ironed handkerchief folded into a triangle pinned to the waist of our skirt or dress. If your mother pinned it on the left side instead of the right, you'd be ostracized by your female classmates. Not to mention that girls were not allowed to wear pants to school. Dress code? Peer pressure? You ain't seen nuthin', you iphone carrying, earbud wearing, electronics-addicted young'uns. We had our hands and nails checked for cleanliness by the teacher EVERY MORNING. Clean = star; Dirty = note home and demerit. The latter, of course, brought on punishment at home, as well. And yes, this was PUBLIC SCHOOL.

The New York city blocks seemed to drag on forever as we approached home in total silence, Mama's vitriol expended.

In through the maroon door of 107 Berry Street, up the steep, creaking dark stairs to the landing we shared with Mironovs and where Papa would be exiled to smoke when Mama was home. I scooted closer to their door, hoping they'd hear me and invite me in. Yelizaveta Rudol'fovna was the only *babushka* I'd ever known, and I quietly prayed she'd hear us and open the door to let me in.

The key in the top (police) lock turned with a double click. The key in the door handle lock clicked once. Shoulder against the door, Mama gave it a shove and ordered me inside. Oh no. She was really serious this time. Right in the middle of the kitchen on the green linoleum floor that I'd helped sweep two days prior, *it* stood. *It* was a huge flowered brown sack into which Mama had packed all my worldly goods. Everything except toys. (I immediately thought that she was saving them for the next baby she would buy at the hospital who'd be truly hers, unlike me.) The only thing she said to me was, "As soon as Papa comes home, he's going to take you to the park and leave you there." And, despite all my self-defense training and tough tomboy attitude, I immediately burst into tears. I tried apologizing profusely. I promised over and over, through tears and snot and gasps for air, that I would never ever ever ever do it again. Oh, please, please, please don't make me go away. There's DOGS in the park. To no avail and only one response: "It's too late."

I asked if I could take my small icon and my red flute with me. *Noblesse oblige*, I suppose, since those two items were permitted, and I quickly collected them before she changed her mind. I figured that the icon would offer me some protection from the dogs that wandered around the park and scared me senseless.[15] I'd seen people on the streets and in the subways playing instruments and they always had a cup or

---

[15] At the age of 3, I was nearly eaten by a German Shepherd but was saved by Papa. My hero. You'll find the story somewhere in this book.

box in front of them into which passersby threw money. I figured people would feel sorry for a five-year-old homeless girl playing the flute and would give me money for food. If I could survive the dogs, I'd probably be OK. Sad, but OK.

I must have been wailing at a pretty high decibel rating, because there was a knock on our door. As Mama walked by me to answer it, she shushed me so I wouldn't embarrass her with my pitiful howling. The door swung open and, through my tears, I could see Yelizaveta Rudol'fovna and Maria Emil'yevna who looked as upset as I felt.

"Natal'ya Mitrofanovna, please. If you don't want her anymore, please don't send her away. We'll take her," Maria Emil'yevna whispered.

Her mother, Yelizaveta Rudol'fovna added, "We'll be happy to raise her as our own child. Don't send her away. Please."

Instead of taking them up on their offer, Mama escorted them back to their apartment; what she told them, I couldn't hear. I sat down on the floor next to the big brown bag and waited for Fate to deliver its final crushing blow.

I heard Papa's footsteps coming up the stairs—rapid, beating out a happy rhythm. The keys turned in the locks, the door opened, Papa walked in and stopped in his tracks in the doorway.

One howling child, one furious spouse, one very large sack filled to overflowing with little girl clothes. The Unholy Trinity. Mama announced to him that it was his responsibility—since she had to leave for work—to take me to the park and leave me there as a result of my willful disobedience and overall dastardly conduct. She then related the story of this morning's Thumb Sucking Incident in a way that cast an ever more ruinous light on my shameless behavior; my dignity was shattered and disgrace was complete when she stopped talking. Some discussion in German quickly followed. It bothered me to no end that, whenever my parents wanted to discuss something Not For My Ears they did so in a language I didn't understand. At first it was English . . . until I went to kindergarten and, in three short months, was speaking it better than they did. After that, it was German. No wonder I became a linguist—it was my only revenge.

Mama shrugged on her light fall coat and hat, picked up her purse and gloves, gave Papa a kiss, and, giving me a long hard stare, said, "Goodbye." Just like that. *In English.* No hug, no kiss, no suggestions on how to survive in a New York City park with nothing but some clothes and a flute amid packs of roving hungry dogs. Nothing. Goodbye. And out the door. Papa gave me a sad look with those transparent gray eyes.

"*Nu chto-zhe*, we should probably have something to eat before we go." And he lit the burner under the pot of soup that would serve as my final meal at Apartment 3A, 107 Berry Street. He took out the bread and laid it carefully in the breadbasket. Silently, sniffing periodically, I folded the napkins in half and set them at our places, followed by soup spoons, forks, and knife (I didn't get my own knife yet), and dessert spoons. Papa ladled the soup into our bowls with the big ladle he had made during a lunch break in the machine shop where he worked. I couldn't even look up from my bowl as I watched the tears run down my face and plop into the soup, causing little ripples. After the soup, we'd have a piece of the meat used to make the soup with a little hot mustard that Papa made and we always kept in the jolly red-topped mustard jar. After that, there'd be dessert, usually some type of *kompot* Mama made with whichever fruit was seasonal. And then. Then?

Papa stood up, faced the icon in the corner, and rapidly fired off the "thank you for dinner prayer" that I had not yet learned. Because I was still little, I was allowed to simply cross myself and say "Thank you, God" after each meal. I helped Papa clear the table and watched him wash the dishes we'd used. I wondered if this was the last time I'd ever see him doing that and felt the two butterflies in the place where my heart used to be fighting a duel to the finish. I wondered if I was too little to die of the heart problems Maria Emil'yevna and Yelizaveta Rudol'fovna talked about. I wondered if my throat would close up from hurting so much that I'd die from not being able to breathe. I wondered if I'd ever stop crying and if there was such a thing as running out of tears. I wondered if I'd ever be able to breathe through my swollen nose again. I wondered if one of the other kindergarten mothers would walk past me as I played my flute, feel sorry for me, adopt me on the spot, and take me to her house to live happily ever after. On top of all this mental anguish, I watched Papa dry the last dish and put it away in the glass-fronted cupboard above the stove. He gave me a very sad look.

"*Nu, detka,* let's get your sweater on and get going. I'll carry the sack, it's too big and heavy for you. Put on your sweater, it's chilly outside."

I tried one more tear-filled outburst of "pleeeeeeeeeeeeeeeeeeze, nooooooo," but it didn't work. With one more push to the edge of the envelope, I asked if I could take my brand-new neon pink jump rope with me. Wish granted. Papa pulled up my socks, retied my shoes, tugged on my sweater, and gently fixed my flyaway chin-length hair, leaving his left hand on my head while he brushed with the right. I watched him place a brand-new pack of Camels and his *mundshtuk* in his pocket, along with his Ronson lighter and comb.

"*Nu, chtozh . . . poshli?*" As if I had any choice in the matter.

He shrugged on his fall jacket and settled his hat on his head, picked up the heavy sack, checked his pockets for keys and, opening the door, watched me step across the threshold. I took one last look at the kitchen table and the icon hovering over it, the stove with the pot of soup still on the cold front burner, and the kitchen sink where I had learned to brush my teeth all by myself, trying to burn it all into my memory. I remember the red and yellow slashes on the dark green linoleum.

The door closed, the locks clicked, and we walked down the stairs, holding onto the polished wood banister. With one last deep sigh, I walked out the half-glass maroon door and into the sounds of traffic and smells of a working class neighborhood: liverwurst from the sausage factory a few blocks away, the delicatessen smell every time someone came in or out, exhaust fumes from cars and trucks, dog poop and cat pee from around the tree outside our building. I took a deep breath and held it, thinking that if I could remember these smells my nose could find my way home from the park. But as soon as I let out the breath, everything smelled different and I knew I was doomed. Papa softly took my small left hand into his rough right one, turned right, and we started off toward The Park.

I don't remember how far it was to The Park. All I remember from that perp walk was the color of my shoes and all the cracks in the sidewalk. And I remember there being a lot of people out and about, all of whom—I was sure—had come out of their apartment buildings to watch this ultimate humiliation and my last walk into Park Purgatory. Years hence, I thought, they might wonder whatever happened to that little girl in the gray skirt they saw walking toward The Park, dripping tears on the cracked concrete. I was convinced I would have been eaten by a pack of feral dogs, my bones left to bleach in the merciless New York sun . . . and *then* they'd be sorry.

Across one street, then another and, before I knew it, we were at the entry to The Park with its black wrought iron surrounding fence. I wordlessly looked up at Papa, wondering if he was really going to leave me there alone. He didn't look back at me, just strolled into the enclosed area as if it were any other day and we were out for our evening constitutional. It was getting later all the time and the light was starting to change as we meandered along one of the familiar paths and sat on an empty bench. Papa pulled out his Camels and tamped them against his left hand, peeled the cellophane and then part of the metallic wrapper off, and—the way he always did—let me have the first sniff of the fresh tobacco. I loved the smell from my very first sniff ever, out on the landing where he went to smoke since Mama always developed a cough when he smoked in the apartment. It was another one of our rituals that I knew I would miss terribly. I let an audible sigh escape.

"*Nu, rasskazyvay.*" Aha! At least I was going to get to tell my side of the story! The feathers of hope rustled in my little soul.[16] So I let it all

---

[16] Emily Dickinson: "Hope is the thing with feathers/That perches in the soul/ And sings the tune without the words/And never stops at all."

out, in one big gush of words and tears and gulps and gasps, stressing the fact that *I had been snuck up on* and, if I'd known she was coming I certainly would have pulled my thumb out of my mouth in time. I'm not stupid, I pointed out. I made as dejected and beleaguered a face as I could muster at the time and gazed up at Papa with tear-filled eyes, hoping it would work as it usually did.

My pause gave him a chance to light another cigarette, having just finished the first, and gather his thoughts. I waited for him to say something, anything. And then he did.

"What do you mean Mama snuck up on you? Were you doing something wrong?"

Oh, man. How did he do that? I'm the injured party here, for Pete's sake! Sitting on a park bench, watching the light go out of the day.

"Maybe." OK, I'll allow that perhaps, on this one occasion, I may have taken some sort of misstep.

"Maybe. OK. And what was it that you were doing?"

"Counting pink cars out the living room window."

"I don't think counting pink cars would have made Mama so angry. Was there something else, maybe?"

"Maybe. Mama gets mad at me all the time."

"All the time? Think about it: who bought you that little book on Chicken Little?"

"She did."

"Well, she wasn't mad at you then, was she?"

"No."

"So maybe you were doing something you weren't supposed to be doing?"

"Maybe."

"Maybe. Maybe something to do with your fingers?"

I nodded my bowed head and watched a tear roll down my nose and plop onto my gray skirt, making a stain. No one would care because no one would wash my clothes ever again except me. I sniffed loudly and hiccupped.

"Maybe your thumb?"

I sighed. The jig was up. He knew. And now, he'd be ashamed of me. Still, I couldn't make myself say it. A couple of mutts trotted past in the twilight, pausing to sniff around the base of the bench. The hairs on the back of my neck stood up as I pulled my hands inside my sweater sleeves to avoid having them bitten off and scooted closer to Papa.

"Aha," he said, "I see it's getting dark. And I have to get up so early in the morning, you know. I should start thinking about going home."

"*Nonononono*!!! Wait! There are dogs coming out, I'm afraid of them! Wait, don't go yet!!" I could practically taste my fear; I just knew those dogs could sniff it.

"All right, well, as soon as I finish this last cigarette, I'll go."

Overcome with terror at the prospect of what the night would bring, I pulled out my little icon and set it on the bench next to me in an effort to establish a defensive perimeter. Then I pulled out my little red flute and started playing what I thought was an appropriately somber refrain. In retrospect, I suspect it was a peculiarly atonal Bartok-like composition, but it kept me from focusing on my imminent demise. Papa pulled the stub of his cigarette out of the *mundshtuk* and ground it into the grass with his heel.

"*Nu*, I've finished all my cigarettes."

Oh no. Now what? My panicked little brain desperately searched for a delaying tactic but came up empty.

"No, wait, Papa, please. Don't go yet, I'll play you a song."

"OK, I have one of those thin cigars in my pocket. When I finish that, I'm going home, song or no song. But I think you probably haven't said everything you want to say to me yet, eh?"

Damn. Only I didn't say or think "damn" because I didn't know the word yet. Still, I can't help but believe I had a childhood equivalent of the word, probably something to do with bodily excretions.

A large gray dog that vaguely resembled the *seryy volk* wolf of my Russian fairy tales, partnered with an equally large bear-like dog, were trotting across the field in front of us with an eye toward the tasty morsel in white and gray perched on the park bench. My hands started shaking as I broke into a sweat. The music stopped.

Papa lit a second cigarillo, looked over at me, and said,

"This is the absolute last one. When I finish smoking this one, I'm going home and you're staying here. That's it. Are you sure you've said everything you have to say?"

I watched the clouds of smoke rise up and dissipate in the cool evening air. Night was almost upon us. My heart was beating so loudly that I thought everyone within a five-block radius could probably hear it. Finally, convinced that I was in danger of imminent death either from a *"serdechnyy sluchay"*[17] or being torn apart by ravenous dogs, I blurted it out, the whole hideous truth:

"I was s-s-s-sucking my th-th-th-thuuuummmmmmb."

"Ah, I see. And that's what made Mama so mad?"

"Uh huh."

"Maybe it wasn't only the thumb sucking that she's talked to you about so many times. Maybe it was because you were sneaking, too?"

What?! *She snuck up on me* whirled through my head. Oh, man. I hated it when this happened: he was absolutely right. I had knowingly tiptoed into the living room while she was in the kitchen, had half-hidden inside the faded green drapes, and engaged in the verboten activity until she caught me red-handed, as it were. In fact, if it weren't for the rustling of those stupid drapes and the traffic outside, I would have heard her coming.

"Maybe so."

"Well, what shall we do now? I'm supposed to leave you here, but I think if I bring you back home and you call Mama on the phone at

---

[17] "A heart incident" No one I knew ever talked about cardiac arrest, heart attacks, or any other medically appropriate term. In keeping with the superstition that if you name it, it's yours, adults always talked around diseases and never ever ever never showed on themselves what someone else had died from for fear of inviting the same thing into their own bodies.

work and make a very, very sincere apology and promise never to do it again, maybe she'll let you stay. Shall we try?"

The Heavens opened up, the harps played, the angels sang, and I threw my arms around Papa's neck, hugging him close, kissing him on his unshaved cheek over and over and over, galvanized by his Papa smell—the best in the world: my hero. He'd saved me from a horrible, grisly fate!

I hurriedly stuffed my little red flute into the bag and, kissing my icon for coming through for me in a pinch, I returned it, too, to the flowered brown sack. As I moved one of my packed sweaters to the side to make room for the icon, I spotted my neon pink plastic jump rope. Overjoyed by this unexpected turn of events, I pulled it out of the sack and immediately started to jump rope as we turned toward the exit to walk home.

"*Mozhet*, you should stop the jumping—the sidewalk has cracks in it, you could trip," the baritone said.

"Nah, I'm fine."

Skip. Skip. Skip.

"I said, maybe you should stop the jumping and put away the rope. You could fall down and hurt yourself."

"Nah. I'm fine. I know what I'm doing!"

Skip. Skip. Skip. Ka-BAM! The sidewalk reached up and punched me in the chin, scraping my legs and hands along the way. Suddenly, the rope was gone. And then there was the heat across my calves, just one smack.

"I told you not to jump rope."

"I'm sorry. I won't do it anymore," I said, not even feeling the sting of the rope, so ecstatic was I at the prospect of being forgiven and taken back into the bosom of my family. I stuck the jump rope in the bag, took hold of his hand, and skipped the rest of the way home.

Of course, after we got home, I called Mama, played the repentant sinner, and promised to never ever ever never suck my thumb again while keeping two fingers crossed where Papa couldn't see them.

About a year later, when I lost my first two front teeth, I was again standing at the living room window, looking for pink cars. Papa was sitting in his chair with the ashtray on the right arm, reading the latest edition of *Novoye Russkoye Slovo*, the *émigré* Russian-language newspaper. Out of nowhere, seemingly, he remarked,

"Huh! Would you look at that! There's an article in here that says that, according to a recent study by American dentists, children who suck their thumbs when their teeth are growing in get buck teeth. And then they have to get metal braces put on to straighten their teeth. Says right here that they hurt quite a bit. Who could have imagined such a thing? Look at the things they're studying these days. Mmmhmmmhmmm."

I spent the next few weeks surreptitiously pushing on my top incisors as they grew in to counteract any damage I might have done.

And I never wore braces.

12

In case you've started to believe that I was an angelic, perfectly behaved, selfless child, let me put that little illusion to rest right now.
I'm going to narc on myself.

A couple of blocks away from our house, there was a small park that
doubled as the absolute BEST sledding hill around. The entry gate on
Fourth Avenue opened onto a flat mesa-like area. BUT, if you looked
forward, you would see a steep incline down to the benches, followed
by a steep incline up to Third Avenue. Almost ninety-degree angles
on both sides. So, when I said to my progeny that I had to drag a sled
up these *huge* hills *both ways*, I was mostly right. The trick, though, was
to get enough of a running start to propel you down the Fourth Ave.
slope to partially *up* the Third Ave. slope, then turn the sled at the exact
right moment to head back down. It took practice, serious intent, and
a death-defying-devil-may-care attitude about the stands of trees that
awaited us at the bottom of the hill. No matter, we all knew we would
live forever and nothing would hurt us.

My first encounter with this hill froze me in my tracks. Why?
Because I'd never gone sledding *down* a hill. Some of my name-your-
Slav friends had a sled that we'd all pile onto, and the designated adult
would drag us over frozen puddles and ice patches in the local park, but
none of us had ever actually guided a sled down a hill. At first, I was

stunned. And then I sprang into action, begging Papa to somehow get a sled so we could go sledding. I don't remember what happened—probably Papa borrowed a random kid's sled—but I do remember that we went down the hill a couple of times. The first time, I started out with closed eyes, but then, as we gained momentum and the cold air rushed at us, I opened my eyes wide and laughed and laughed and laughed, even as Papa pulled us to a stop and we fell over sideways. WOW! Holy Toledo, what *fun*!!! I was hooked—and hooked in a bad way. Evidently, my need for speed had been awakened, and it was a powerful draw. Naturally, I started asking Papa for a sled on the way home.

I also started priming the pump with Mama the next day as we sat over our usual breakfast of tea and open-faced sandwiches. Slowly, gently, from way out in hell's back acre, I started talking about the weather. And winter. And snow. And how we made snowflakes out of white paper in Mrs. Cassidy's class and then taped them up on the windows . . . Yes, a nice winter-themed introduction followed by an extended narrative on yesterday's sledding activities and how *some boy* let us use his sled because I didn't have one. But we only went down twice because the kid wanted his sled back. Pause. Pause. Pause. Then, the first tentacle eased out of containment,

Me: "Mama?"

Mama: "*Nu, Mama. Nu, chto?*"

Aha. She'd opened the door . . .

Me: "Do you think maybe I could get a sled?"

Mama: "A sled? I don't know, I'll have to talk to Papa about it."

[Aha! Not dead in the water yet!]

Me: "Well, he had fun on the sled, too . . ." [insert winning smile]

Mama: "He did?! Well, that Papa of yours sometimes forgets that he's not a child anymore."

Me: "Haha. That's funny. But we had fun together! Don't you think maybe I could get my own sled?"

Mama: "I said I'll talk to Papa about it and I'll do that. Maybe you could ask Santa Claus to bring you one. If you're a good girl, that is."

Know when to held 'em and know when to fold 'em. I let out a mini sigh and said,

"OK."

What else was there to say? The discussion door had been closed firmly. I thought I even heard the tumblers fall into place on the locks, thunk thunk.

In any event, that snow didn't last. Shortly after I discovered sledding, we had several days of unseasonably high temperatures and all the snow disappeared. Not to be undone by this unexpected meteorological treachery, I kept up the Sled Chinese Water Torture with both parents. A drip here, a drip there, I was convinced I'd wear them down eventually. So focused was I on the acquisition of a sled, that I actually did a little comparison window shopping by pricing sleds in the various hardware stores around our house. Although my memory now fails me on the cost of a Flexible Flyer—I want to say, "about three dollars," but I could be very wrong. In any event, I found the store with the best price and passed this information along to both my parents, in case they were curious, of course.

What was unknown to me in my plotting and scheming was the fact that Papa had been working on a sled for me for weeks. Instead of taking a break at lunch, he would wolf the lunch Mama packed for him and spend the rest of the time crafting a sled to resemble those the rich boys had back in the Rodina. He was intent on finishing it before the next snowfall so that I wouldn't be left out of all the fun in the sledding park.

So, imagine my state of being as the snowflakes started to fall again early one Friday evening. I ran from the back of our apartment to the front to check on accumulations in our back yard and our courtyard. I was so excited that I could barely sleep that night because I just knew, in my heart of hearts, that Papa would come through for me. Mama—I wasn't too sure about her, but I was positive that somehow, some way, Papa would find a way to save the day. I shared this supposition with *Zaychik*, who concurred with my laying odds on Papa.

Saturday morning dawned bright, white, and sunny. I ran to the back windows to assess the sledding prospects and . . . AHA! YAY! Snow on the ground! But wait, I was still sledless. I heaved a deep sigh and dragged myself to the breakfast table, where Mama was starting to clear their dishes—they always let me sleep late on weekends. Except when we went to church, because there was primping and special dressing to be done and an hour-long ride on the subway to get there. Plus, the walk from the subway to the church. But back to the sled obsession.

Mama served up a cup of tea for me the way I liked it, with the lemon slice and sugar smushed together in the cup before she added the *zavarka* and hot water. Not too hot, perfect for drinking. I raised the white Pyrex cup with the blue and gold stripe at the top and schlurped a bit of the tea to check for temperature and sweetness. So far, so good. I took a bite of the muenster cheese sandwich even though I wasn't hungry. I've never really been a breakfast person, especially right after I get up. Starting in college, my breakfasts usually consisted of coffee and a cigarette (breakfast of champions. Hey, don't laugh: I'm a bona fide Phi Beta Kappa magna cum laude graduate of a well-known mid-Atlantic university.) As I chewed my sandwich, I realized that Papa wasn't around. Because he hadn't said anything about picking up some overtime, I didn't think he'd gone to work.

"*A gde Papa?*" I sent out a short feeler to test the waters.

"Papa? He went downstairs for something. And he has to shovel the stairs and sidewalk in front of our house. God forbid someone falls and breaks a leg, they'd sue us and take the house away." And this was *before* we turned into a litigious nation. Just another manifestation of Mama's glass-mostly-empty view of the world.

Hmmmm . . . I almost didn't dare to hope, and so asked permission to turn on the TV (yes, really, that's the way it worked back then) so I could watch the Saturday morning cartoons. Truth be told, Papa and I liked watching them together; in fact, I think he enjoyed them more than I did. He certainly laughed louder and longer.

As the TV started to come to life and I started to settle into my place on the sofa, I thought I heard rattling in the kitchen. Never mind,

Mickey was running around with some fellow Mouses, trying to avoid becoming a toothsome morsel for a feline. Over the sound of canned laughter and Mickey's soprano urging his fellow Mouses onward, I heard my parents whispering together. Then, out of the blue, Papa called my name. A well-trained kid, I jumped off the sofa and stepped lively to the kitchen and . . . oh no. Oh, no. Oh, NO. Oh nonononono.

There stood my parents, beaming at me.

And there was Papa holding out this forest green wooden thing with runners that curled up in the front. It had a rope threaded through the front contraption to help you steer with your feet. Oh dear.

"*Nu? Kak tebe nravitsya?*" How did I like it, indeed. Oh no.

"Aaaaah." I had been struck speechless. Could not think of a single thing to say, except, "aaaaaahhhhh."

Immediately, Mama jumped in with some marketing:

"Look at the beautiful sled Papa made for you! Isn't it beautiful?! Do you know how long he worked on it? He skipped his lunchtimes at work to make this for you! Just for YOU, so you could have a sled! Only the rich people in our town had sleds like this. You're such a lucky girl to have a Papa who loves you so much."

Ouch. And Ouch. And ouch again. Yes, indeed: advertising campaign blended with history, guilt, and shame. A truly Russian gift package.

They were so excited about the sled that I don't think they really paid attention to my reaction. Or, maybe they did, and tried to roll over my obvious disappointment. Instead, Papa commanded that we all get dressed and bundle up because we were going sledding with my new sled and he was going to teach me how to steer it. Another oh no. Oh no, everyone's going to laugh at us. Oh no. I dragged myself into my pink room, got out my warm clothes, and got dressed. Mama tugged another sweater onto me and wrapped my neck in two wool scarves (OMG, the *itching*!!! Worse than frostbite, in my book.), pulled my overcoat and boots on, and declared me ready to sled. Papa was already downstairs, having a smoke while the ladies of the house got dressed.

With a final grand gesture, Mama threw on her long black Persian lamb coat, tied her wool scarf under her chin, grabbed the keys, and ushered me out the door.

I kept hearing funeral music in my head as we trudged to the park, Papa pulling the sled. He offered to let me pull it, but I declined, saying something along the lines of being afraid of slipping, falling down, and breaking it. Yes, OK, so I did lie a bit. But I couldn't bring myself to tell the truth.

The sledding went pretty much as I'd anticipated, with much hooting and hollering on the part of the Flexible Flyer sledders when they caught sight of our Model T sled. Papa didn't speak too much English, so he probably didn't understand much; Mama understood but didn't give a rat's patoot. I, on the other hand, understood every single word and kept getting hotter and hotter in my winter gear.

With Mama positioned behind us in the pushing position, Papa and I climbed onto the Green Machine for its maiden voyage with Papa steering. One push and we were off, the laughter fading into the frosty air behind us. We made it all the way to the bottom, where Papa made a sharp turn that turned us over into some newly fallen snow. His cheeks were rosy red, and he was laughing and laughing so infectiously that I started laughing along with him. Then I laid next to him and showed him how to make a snow angel. I guess they weren't allowed to make angels after the Tsar and his family were murdered and the godless Bolsheviks came to power (spit here). Or, maybe it was a typically American thing to do, I don't know. All I know is that we had a great time finding fresh snowbanks, throwing ourselves in them, and making snow angels together, one large, one small.

Mama reprimanded us for rolling around in the snow and getting cold (we were fine, actually) and said something about her feet getting cold waiting for us. Aha. Got it.

Still, we went down and up the hill a few more times with the Flexible Flyers crossing in front of us and trying to make us tip over. If I hadn't been such a spoiled brat about it, I would have realized how much fun it was and how cool it was to have something so different from everyone else. But Childhood isn't like that . . . at least mine wasn't. As the kid with the unpronounceable name, the parents who "talked funny" and didn't look like anyone else's parents that I knew, my one true wish was to fit in. Be one of *them*. Just be a part of the Norwegian/ Swedish/Viking groups that mixed and matched among themselves but had no room for someone with a last name that didn't end in -sen, -son, or -dottir.

As time went by, the unappreciative spoiled brat in me resurfaced and started petitioning for a Flexible Flyer, building a case by saying that Papa's sled was too heavy for me and was too hard for me to steer. And I always had to depend on someone for a push, whereas, with the Flexible Flyer I could get my own running start. Day after day, the Chinese water torture proceeded, wearing down the parental rocks. Until one fine day, Mama finally said, "OK let's go and get you that stupid sled if it'll make you happy and stop your nagging and whining."

And so we went. Down to the store with the best price where Mama forked over the cash and I picked out the sled that called my name from all the ones that were stacked standing straight up. Bright red runners, the crossboard that moved for me to change directions, and—best of all—Flexible Flyer written all the way down the middle. Now I would be like everybody else, getting a running start, slamming my body onto the sled, and zooming down the hill at top speed. My cup runneth over. I thanked Mama profusely and repeatedly and even kissed her right there at the Fourth Ave. hardware store, on the sidewalk, for all Bay Ridge to see. We stored the new sled in our part of the basement so no one would borrow or steal it (just longer-term borrowing, really). And, when Papa came home from work, I dragged him to the basement to show off my new acquisition.

He was such a Prince, my Papa, he really was.

He looked over the sled, made some comments about how he could see that this one would go faster and turn better than the old one, and how maybe we could go try it out together some time. Jumping up and down with excitement, I threw my arms around his neck and said, "let's go now!" Papa's calmer head prevailed. He mentioned that we hadn't eaten supper yet, and it wasn't a good idea to go sledding without some food in our bellies.

As the Fates would have it, we didn't make it out that night, but we did go the following day, and the day after that, and the day after that. Sometimes we sledded down together, sometimes he went down alone, dragging the sled back up the hill and handing it over to me for a running start and quick run downhill. He never mentioned the other sled again.

Papa had been hanging his green sled on a couple of hooks he'd fashioned and drilled into the brick wall downstairs in the basement near the door, right next to the ones that held our granny cart for shopping. And they hung there, next to each other, being neighborly, for quite some time. When my Flexible Flyer came home, Papa drilled two more holes for hooks and then hung my new sled on them.

It was only in the summer, when I was forced to take the kitchen trash down to the basement trash cans (a terrifying experience. If you've ever been in the basement of a New York apartment building, you'd know what I mean) that I noticed something was different. Without spending too much time staring at the space, I realized that something was missing. I was halfway up the next flight of stairs, taking two at a time, when I realized the green sled was gone. I never asked about it and no one ever volunteered any information about it. It was simply gone as quietly as it had appeared. Just like that.

Fifty-plus years later, as I look at Papa's picture on the table next to my desk, I feel sharp pangs of both guilt (what I did) and shame (who I was). From my perspective today, I was being a spoiled brat, insisting on a conveyer-belt-assembled trinket that "everyone else" had at the expense of a craftsman's gift to his only child. Today, I can think about the hours he spent, the effort he expended, the lunch breaks he missed to make something for me that was so special that only the rich kids "back home" had them. And the greedy little me who wanted what she wanted when she wanted it rejected this gift. And I can't help thinking that maybe I broke his heart a little. And now, mine broke, too.

If we are honest about and with ourselves, we can have 20/20 vision about the past we have created for ourselves. There are no do-overs in life, no rewinds or resets, and we have to live with the things we did and decisions we made *ago*. So, if I had it to do all over again, knowing what I know now, I certainly would have made better decisions about this whole sled thing. Because if I hadn't been such a little self-centered monster, I would now have a true craftsman's creation—an old-fashioned sled that I could give to my grandson. Just so I could see the surprise in his eyes and know that some part of Papa in him rejoices. But I can't.

Instead, all I can do is ask Papa for forgiveness. The way we always did the Sunday before Lent began: on my knees before him, asking him to forgive me for offending or hurting him in any way. Intellectually, I know what his answer would be. It would be the same as it was every year, "*Bog prostit, i ya proshchayu.*" I know that both he and God would forgive me.

Still.

Still, there's a part of me that really wants to hear his response to *Papochka, prosti.*

13

I was sitting at the kitchen table, trying to drink the tea Mama had placed in front of me. She'd cut a slice of lemon, sprinkled sugar over it, and then mushed it all together with a spoon before pouring the tea on it, just the way I liked it. And then she stirred in some raspberry *varen'ye,* a real cure for the ailing. But the tea was too hot, and I was too hot, and my flannel pajamas under the quilted bathrobe were making me hotter. The slippers itched on my sweating feet, but every time I tried to take them off Mama would yell at me about getting even sicker. Every time I took a breath something rattled in my chest and I started coughing. And every time I started coughing, I couldn't stop.

Across the courtyard, our raven-haired Italian neighbor, Mary, had just finished her weekly window polishing and was starting to hang her white sheets on the line between their apartment and ours. She washed, dried, and ironed her sheets every day for some reason I couldn't fathom. Whenever she was working around the apartment—which was always—Mary sang popular songs in her flawless soprano. I cocked my head to the left to hear her better through her open kitchen window as she clipped the linens to the line: "Flyyyyyyyy me to the moooooooon [pillowcase clip clip] an' let me plaaaaaaaaay among the staaaaaaaaaaaaarz. [pillowcase clip clip] Let me see what spring is like on Juuuupiter and Maaaarz . . ." [sheet clip clip clip clip].

Mary had been a nurse's aide before she married Francisco and sometimes tried to teach me neat nurse things like how to make a butterfly stitch and how to press down on a cut to stop the bleeding. I think she liked me not only because I was the landlord's kid, but because I always stuck up for her pariah of a son at school. Back then, fat kids were, as a rule, outcast. Marco's problems were twofold: he was genetically predisposed to obesity (both parents were roughly the size of the tugboats I saw at the Brooklyn shipyards) *and* he loved to eat (thereby aggravating a natural tendency toward blimpdom). I always marveled at the breakfasts Mary served him: bacon, eggs, toast, juice followed by oatmeal with sugar and milk (or maybe cream) and a glass of milk. He was a year younger than I was, so I never got to observe him at lunch to see if that meal equaled the Most Important Meal of the Day. But I've digressed.

It was easy to get lost in Mary's singing: it was almost angelic. Mama once told me that boys' choirs were the best because they sounded angelic; I disagreed (although not aloud) and thought Mary sounded like an angel when she sang. Her voice soared high and dipped low, like birds in flight, and every note was true and good. I also firmly believed that girls' voices were every bit as praiseworthy—if not more so—than boys' and bristled at this first brush with gender discrimination, from a member of my own sex, no less.

I tried to blow on the tea to cool it down but broke into another coughing fit and coughed until I spit blood into the handkerchief Mama held in front of me. For a moment, she looked genuinely sorry for me and even patted me on the head, brushing my hair back from my forehead and behind my ears. I was listening to the rattle in my chest and wondered if she heard it. She held the teacup up to my lips and encouraged me to take a sip. I did, which precipitated another round of coughing. Mary had stopped singing.

A quick knock-knock-knock on our door was followed by Mama's equally rapid, semi-aggressive response,

"Who izz eet?"

And Mary's equally rapid, "Natalie, it's me, Mary. Lemme take a look at Marsha." Mary made the same pronunciation error that all native speakers of Contemporary Standard American English made when saying the diminutive of my name: MaRsha. There is no R in Masha. I fought the **NO R!** battle my entire life and finally gave up about a year after I retired, when no one called me Ma(r)sha anymore.

Mama unlocked all three locks, and Mary swept in past her, moving a wave of bleach-scented air in with her. I tried to hold my head up to say, "hello," but it was too hard. Mary rested her cool hand on my forehead, looked at Mama, and said, "who's ya peeejatrishn?" Mama said that our family doctor was all we needed. There was an exchange of looks that I didn't understand followed by a long pause. Mary broke the silence first, "Marco's doctuh's great. Lemme get his numbuh. Or do ya want me ta cawlim?"

Mama took Mary up on her offer to call, postulating that Mary probably would get better results since the doctor already knew her. Mary bundled me off to my room, remade my bed using hospital corners with me between the sheets and blanket, and swept back to her apartment (2F) to call Dr. Schaumberg. A few minutes later, she came back in, told Mama that we were in luck because the doctor's calling hours were this evening and he'd stop by to examine me around six. The house call would cost three dollars. Right before the room went dark, I remember wondering if I was worth three whole dollars—the cost of a Flexible Flyer—when Papa was making only $1.25 an hour. I felt the heavy burden of guilt descend on my chest like one more stifling blanket. A minor introduction of survivor guilt at a young age. Little did I know that it would become my constant companion in the future.

"Nu chtozh ty, detka, pribolela?"

I caught a whiff of stale smoke and felt a large cool hand on my forehead. When I opened my eyes, I saw that Papa was home and was bending over my bed, stroking my hair back from my eyes.

"Mmhmm."

"Nu, nichevo! Pridet doktor, zavtra budesh'- kak shtyk."

I wondered if he actually believed I'd be better tomorrow, or if he was trying to convince both of us that I would be. And, just like that, he swept me off the bed and carried me into the living room so we could watch TV together. I sat on Papa's lap while Mama made up the sofa with sheets, blankets, and a pillow for me; in a moment of weakness, she even brought *Zaychik* along to sit with me. If I remember correctly, she didn't go to work that evening; I guess one of the other ladies cleaned the twenty-fourth floor of the shiny office building in Manhattan.

Back in the day, doctors actually made house calls. And they really carried black bags with them. At least Dr. Schaumberg did. I tried to peek into the black bag when he made me sit up so he could listen to my chest, and I saw a treasure trove of vials, needles, and other doctorabilia. The doctor smelled like the outdoors and had soft, gentle hands when he felt my throat. He was very kind to me and had crinkles around his eyes when he smiled, which was often. As he wrapped up his heart-listening thing with long rubber tubes, he looked at me again and, smoothing my hair back from my forehead, almost whispered, "It's OK, honey, we'll get you some medicine and you'll be back to playing with your friends in two shakes. But I want you to rest and sleep as much as you can, OK?"

I tried to say OK, but the effort precipitated another coughing fit. This time Dr. Schaumberg held me upright, patting me on the back, and caught the bloody mucus I expelled involuntarily in his snow white hanky. I must have looked horrified, because the next thing I heard after the white noise in my ears stopped, was a very soft,

"See, good thing I had a hanky with me, right? You're going to get better, I promise. But you'll have to take medicine and stay home from school until you're well. Will you do that for me?"

I tried to nod in agreement, but it took too much effort, so I blinked my eyes "yes." And then he did the most kidlike thing: he held up his right pinky and said, "Pinky swear." We crossed our right pinkies into a tight grip, and I started to believe him.

I've heard it said that women make better caregivers than men because they are more sympathetic or empathetic, better listeners, and more compassionate than their male counterparts. While this may be true overall in the general population, my family was the exception that proved the rule. True, Mama was good at the "feeding" angle of "care and feeding;" Papa, on the other hand, was much better at the "caring" part. Maybe because he didn't have to worry about the "feeding" part since Mama had it covered. Especially since he's the one who taught her how to cook. (Yes, really. As the middle child, my mother's responsibilities growing up ran to weeding the garden and hauling water up from the river for watering it. Her elder sisters learned how to cook and sew. On the other hand, she excelled at school and so was allowed to continue on through college, despite her mother's regular diatribes on education being wasted on girls.)

Papa sat down next to me on the sofa, his big calloused hand on my forehead, gently smoothing my brow, telling me how proud he was of me for behaving so well with the doctor and how he was sure that now I'd be getting better really soon. And then he told me about the spring his sister, Marisha, was very sick and how there were no doctors in the village to make her better. But there was an old woman who knew all the grasses, flowers, bushes, and trees and their uses for healing, a woman who brought babies into this world (she found them on tree limbs and delivered them to their families) and could even set broken bones to make them grow back together. So Papa was sent across the village to bring her to their home to help Marisha.

The old woman stood surprisingly straight for her nondescript old age, wore a long black skirt that brushed the ground, and had silvery white hair that peeped out from under a black kerchief. Papa had heard it rumored through the village that she had gone on a pilgrimage to the Holy Land *on foot* and had brought back a large clear stone that she wore around her neck. It was easy to believe the rumor because she seemed to have a glow around her wherever she moved in the house, and her bright cornflower blue eyes sparkled when she looked at him. Although she cut a rather forbidding figure, once she looked at you with those eyes, you felt all warm inside and loved. Not only did she have the healing touch, she had a healing look.

"Babushka Tat'yana, please. Mama sent me for you. Marisha is very sick, please come. Please," my seven-year-old Papa pleaded.

"Sick, is she? Well, what's wrong with her?" Babushka Tat'yana asked softly. And then she ran through a number of symptoms, all of which Marisha had.

"Aha, that's what I thought. Now I know what to bring with me."

And with that, the old lady started to move about the house, pulling a few bottles with colored liquids down from a shelf, selecting bunches of dried herbs from under the ceiling rafters, and carefully, praying softly, started placing them carefully in a sack.

"Ol'ga, I'm going to the Grechenkovs at the other end of the village. I'll be back after the girl is on her feet," the Babushka announced and, turning to the young Kolya,

"*Nu chtozh? Poshli, synochek?*" turned him to the door and stepped over the threshold.

Kolya thought it was interesting and somehow magical that, as they walked, his steps kicked up the road dust while Babushka Tat'yana's did not. He even turned back to look for her footprints a few times, just to make sure they were there and he hadn't been bewitched.

As they walked into the house, Babushka Tat'yana crossed herself three times and then walked straight to where Marisha was lying, swathed in all the blankets the family owned. After a cursory first assessment, the old woman turned to Kolya and sent him out to the woods to bring back some linden tree blossoms for a special healing tea. Babka Tat'yana lived in their house with earthen floors until Marisha was better, dosing her with different teas, putting poultices on her chest and back, praying to the different healing saints and angels, and telling stories to the children. It was from her that Papa started to learn all about the things that grow and how God planted them on this earth to help us.

Babka Tat'yana was Mama's grandmother.

I was listening to his voice—not the words so much, but the timbre and velvety softness of his voice as it rose and fell in waves with the storytelling cadence. It wound itself around me, caressing my ears, until I started gliding slowly into the silky darkness. I felt the sofa cushion move back up as he stood, sighed, and murmured, *"spi, Mashen'ka, spi, detka, spi"* and walked into the kitchen.

I don't remember being moved back into my pink room, but I do remember waking up and seeing Papa next to me. He'd brought in a chair from the kitchen and was sitting next to my bed, watching me sleep. I whispered to him that I wished I could see the stars out my window—someone had lowered the venetian blinds to keep the light out of my room—the way we always used to watch for the first star to appear on Christmas Eve. Stretching as he stood up, Papa moved the five feet or so to the window over my desk and quietly opened and raised the blinds.

The night was dark and clear and at least a gazillion stars were out, dancing against the midnight blue heavens. Papa sat down next to me, quietly took my little hand in his big one, and we gazed at the stars together. Every once in a while we'd see a falling star or a plane with its flashing lights, and Papa would speculate about whose soul had returned to Heaven or to what exotic place the plane was headed, but mostly we just quietly looked up at the blinking stars. Papa told me that you could travel around the world—even at night—if you knew which stars to look for in the sky. And that's how we sat, all night long, with me drifting in and out of sleep, Papa always holding my hand.

Mama once told me that, during the 1933 Famine when people were dying in droves, and during The War, when millions of men lay bleeding and dying on the battlefield, their last word was always "Mama." Papa, on the other hand, had told me that a starving person's last word was always "bread." I secretly believed Papa's story and felt Mama's was a form of self-promotion: you should love me so much that, when you have only one breath left in you, you should use it to say my name. I also knew, in my heart of hearts, that if I only had one breath left, my last word would be the same as my first: Papa.

As the light turned periwinkle and dawn crept in, Papa eased my hand out of his, stood up, and straightened my blanket. I heard him walk to the bathroom and then I heard Mama rattling around in the kitchen,

"Did you get any sleep?"

"Nodded off a bit here and there."

"Maybe you should stay home?"

"*Nichevo*, I'm fine. Just make me some strong coffee and get my lunch together. I don't want to miss my ride."

I remember him coming into my room to kiss me good-bye on the forehead the way he always did. I remember Mama making me take the awful white medicine that made me gag and then, right after, the orange medicine that was almost palatable by comparison. Mostly, I slept.

From time to time, the noise of the sewing machine woke me up. Mama was making clothes for my Barbies and a cross-dressing white lace outfit for *Zaychik*: a dress and hat (with ears) that he wears to this very day. Standing guard against all enemies foreign and domestic, terrestrial and extraterrestrial, on the shelf in my bedroom closet. My oldest friend and keeper of childhood hopes, dreams, and secrets.

14

The first vacation I remember clearly was the summer we spent in the Catskill Mountains of New York. I must've been around five years old. Mama learned about this retreat from the manager of the Polish deli around the corner—the one whose dog tried to eat me when I was about three.

As I recall, we were concluding our ritual Sunday constitutional in our church clothes when, out of nowhere, this 900-pound, eight-foot-tall German Shepherd *lunged* at us, barking his head off and scaring me back into wearing diapers. Papa had just moved me from his right side, where I'd been walking along holding his hand, to between him and Mama. I guess he saw or heard something, but the next thing I knew, Mama had body blocked me to the side, covering me with her body, Papa had a hold on the dog and was yelling something, and Pan Benya was running out of the store, yelling for Papa to please not kill the dog. The menfolk worked things out between them—as menfolk in my world always did—and Pan Benya even offered to buy Papa a new coat since Blitz had shredded the right side of Papa's new spring coat from right below the pocket down to the hem.

Relations between my family and the dog owner gradually thawed and improved and, one fine day over a half-pound of Polish ham sliced thin, he told Mama about his father's "resort" in the Catskills.

Technically, Pan Benya's father—Abel Kozlowski—still owned the store but preferred the verdant Catskills to the old shotgun apartment over the store where he and Esther had spent over forty years building up a thriving neighborhood business. Abel had finally made it to "landowner class" and fancied himself something akin to the old boyars in Imperial Russia, imagining that the renters of his cabins were serfs reliant upon his benevolence. In other words, if he didn't like you, he'd kick you out with no warning, a lot of bad words, and international hand gestures.

Abel's story—which I had overheard while playing at my Polish friend's house as the mothers chatted amicably in a mix of Slavic languages—intrigued me. I could almost imagine myself having enough chutzpah to leave Mama and set off for a totally alien country when I grew up, assuming Papa would be willing to go with me. Abel—Mr. Kozlowski or Pan Abel to us kids—was born into a successful shopkeeper's family in a shtetl somewhere in Poland. Unfortunately for him, he was the third son, which limited his prospects of inheriting wealth since, in addition to his two elder brothers, he had four sisters, each of whom would require a sizeable dowry since God in His wisdom had shortchanged them in the looks department. But Providence is not heartless, and Pan Abel turned out to be his Uncle Ezra's favorite nephew.

Uncle Ezra had married a local beauty named Miriam not so much for her beauty as for her dowry but grew to love her over time. Ezra took Miriam and her dowry on a voyage to America, landed in New York, and never left. He bought first one shop, then another, and settled in the apartment above the first store. Try though they might, Ezra and Miriam were never blessed with children of their own and thought of their nephew Abel as their son. So, it came as no surprise to anyone when Ezra wrote to his brother and asked him to send Abel to America to help with the new business. It helped in the decision-making when Ezra offered to buy Abel's passage. Deal done, Abel packed up his few belongings and hopped on a train to Hamburg where he found the ship waiting at the dock. Two horrifically seasick weeks later, a much thinner and paler Abel staggered down the gangplank and into Ezra's waiting embrace.

That, as they say, was the prelude. The conclusion was far less interesting to Zosya and me. Pan Abel met a local girl named Esther, married her, had three sons—Benjamin, Caleb, and Daniel (continuing the English alphabet)—and brought them all into the business. The eldest now ran the shop around the corner, Caleb had moved to California to grow date palms, and Daniel, much to his father's dismay, had hooked up with a gang of "no goodniks"—here Pan Abel would spit—and was doing time in prison for a crime Pan Abel would neither name nor discuss.

Perhaps because he still felt a twinge of guilt over the Dog Incident, Pan Benjamin (Benya to the adults) told Mama he could wrangle a discount for our family with his father *and* that Pan Abel would even meet us at the bus stop in his car for the ride to the resort. Such a deal! Of course, we'd have to bring our own sheets, towels, pots and pans in addition to any clothes, but it was a wonderful resort. A couple of years ago, Pan Abel had built showers in separate cabins: one for men, one for women. The kitchens were communal and even had dishes, but we'd have to share refrigerator and storage space with the other vacationers. The bread truck came on Tuesdays, the milk truck came on Thursdays, and every Friday Pan Abel drove renters to the local grocery store in town on a resupply run. Still, it was a little piece of heaven carved out of the Catskills.

Mama and Papa discussed this topic in German over the weekend to make sure I'd understand none of it and decided to take Pan Benya up on his offer. I was informed that we would be "going on vacation" this summer and that we were going to the mountains, where I would be able to breathe fresh country air and swim in a lake. I hadn't a clue about how to swim having spent city summers frolicking in opened fire hydrants and city pool sprinklers but, on the face of it, it seemed like a pretty liveable arrangement. I wondered how long it would be until July, when we'd head for the hills. School was in session through the end of June and, even though I loved kindergarten, the prospect of seeing mountains and a real lake made the entire month seem interminable. The days dragged on, the weather getting warmer, then hotter. I told all my classmates that my family was "going away on vacation" after school let out for the summer. Children of wealthier (relatively speaking) and more established parents, they'd been doing this vacation thing all their lives and were most definitely unimpressed.

Finally, one searingly hot New York morning, I heard: "Wake up, Sleepyhead! We're going on vacation!!" Mama had spent the previous day shooing me out of the way and packing all our vacation worldly goods into one suitcase and one carpet bag. All we needed to do this morning was to throw our toothbrushes and toothpaste into the carpet bag and head out on this new adventure. But first . . .

First, we had to say goodbye to Yelizaveta Rudol'fovna and remind her to water our plants and please remember to lock the door when she was done without offending her.

Second, we had to negotiate the steps with all our flotsam and jetsam without crashing down the steep dark steps to end up in a crumpled heap on Berry Street. I'd done that more than once and could testify both to the rapidity of descent and its resultant injuries.

Third, once out on the street, we still had to navigate several blocks to the subway station and the train that would take us to somewhere near the Bahstehrmeenahl and the Road to Paradise.

Fourth, we had to push our way into the subway train—Papa used the well-worn black and red plaid suitcase as something of a battering ram—and claim space and a handhold on the hanging straps for the grownups and the metal pole for me. I clung to Papa's slacks with my free hand thereby ensuring I would get off the train when he did. Holding onto Mama's dress was dicey because I wasn't totally sure I could trust her *not* to slyly place my hand on some other lady's dress and get off the train without me.

And of course, fifth, we had to extricate ourselves from said train when we arrived at our stop. We were sardined between and among other Brooklynites headed for Downtown, all of whom seemed to be carrying some sort of travel paraphernalia. Everyone was sweating, contributing to the overall air of anticipation. I caught a whiff of Palmolive Gold Deodorant Soap that wasn't living up to its appellation. The next thing I knew, Papa had bent down to tell me to get ready since the next stop was ours. He started muscling his way toward the doors which read, across the top, on the left side: PLEASE KEEP HANDS. The right side completed the command: OFF THE DOORS. I mentally started chanting:

Please keep hands! Off the doors!

Please keep hands! Off the doors!

Please keep hands! Off the doors!

I was keeping time with the rumble of the train along the tracks. In no time, I had turned myself into a uniformed drum major in a very tall black fur hat with a whistle in my mouth and a large sparkling baton leading the Macy's Thanksgiving Day Parade past the eponymous department store. My high-stepping march was rudely interrupted by the ear-splitting squeal of brakes as we pulled into the station. The three of us braced for battle as we edged our way closer to the doors. While everyone was still swaying in time to the train stopping, Papa grabbed my hand and threw his weight forward as we lurched out of the subway car with a nearly audible pop, followed closely by the carpetbag and Mama. All things considered, we had emerged relatively unscathed, albeit somewhat rumpled. The first thing Papa did was to check for his wallet, which he'd started carrying in his front pocket since he got pickpocketed on the bus to Easter mass a few months prior. Wallet intact and in place, we could move ahead, ever closer to Vacation.

Sixth, we had to maneuver our way through the pungent New York City underground haze and maze with all our belongings until we finally reached near-Nirvana: the Bahstehrmeenahl. I'd heard Papa speak about this place every single day since his factory had moved to New Jersey and he had to take a bus in addition to the subway to get to work. However, I'd had no idea it was so huge, so swarming with people, filled with a constant din and loudspeaker announcements about gates and destinations; I was fascinated by the spectacle and immediately spellbound by the entire experience. My mouth hung open as my head spun faster and faster from side to side to catch everything going on around me.

Papa sent Mama to handle the ticket purchase because she spoke English better than he did, while we killed time by speculating what Kozlowski's Kabins would be like. You could feel the excitement bubble expanding. Mama came back with our tickets (I checked to make sure there were three and not just two) and information on where to catch our bus—leaving in twenty minutes!!—on one of the upper levels. My job was to be quiet and not get lost. I kept my eyes on the suitcase and firmly held onto Papa's hand all the way up the escalators, plotting a possible escape from home to the Bahstehrmeenahl, where I would blissfully spend the day riding up and down the escalators, maybe even in the opposite direction.

There it is! I can see it!! Gate 309! And there's a shiny steel and blue bus with a dog painted on its side parked there! Already, people were lined up waiting to board. Oh, no! What if there were no seats left?! I started to rush the line, tugging on Papa's hand, hoping we weren't too late to claim three seats. What if we couldn't get on the bus?! What would happen to our vacation?! Pan Abel would be waiting for us somewhere at a bus stop in the mountains. What if we didn't show? Would he ban us from the Kabins for life? How would we ever vacation again? How could I look my schoolmates in the eye after all that bragging I'd done? My world started to crumble around me as I came close to experiencing the first panic attack of my life. My breath came faster and faster until Papa smoothed my hair and spoke the most reassuring words I could have hoped to hear:

"Mashen'ka, *detka*, they won't sell more tickets than they have seats."

"Really?"

"*Chestnoye slovo.*"

And, since it came from Papa, I knew it was true. I could almost feel the fear and worry lifting from my shoulders as he smoothed my hair and lit a cigarette. Ah, relief and reassurance swathed in smoke from unfiltered Camels: it didn't get any better than that moment. I secretly breathed in the smoke and pretended I could make smoke rings.

As the bus driver in his neatly starched uniform opened the door and the crowd started moving forward, Mama produced a little yellow pill and told me to swallow it. I asked for water, but there wasn't any nearby. My mouth was still dry from housing all the fear about bus seats, but she made me take the pill anyway. I desperately tried to muster up some spit, then felt the little pill start to lose its coating and melt on my tongue. It was, by far, the worst taste I'd ever experienced in my life, and I felt that involuntary *gonna barf* reflex kick in. Oh no, not this! Help, somebody, please help, I'm gonna ruin our vacation!! Miraculously, Mama found a Life Saver in her purse and gave it to me. Green. Not my favorite, and a bit of tissue stuck to it, but it would have to do for now. And it did. Barf avoided. We inched toward the bus door, baggage in hand, Life Saver on tongue.

Those of you who grew up riding in cars almost certainly have no idea what that little yellow pill was. Here's a hint: I used to get seriously barfingly sick on long bus, train, or car rides. I was perfectly fine on city buses and subways; it was the longer distance and comfortable seating that made me sick. An over-the-counter solution to the "motion sickness" problem. Like most OTC medications, its effect on me was marginal, at best. Still, I guess it was better than retching for a couple of hours and ruining the trip for everyone else.

I chose a window seat so that I could see *everything* as we left the city, Mama wedged in next to me, lacquered straw purse on her lap, carpetbag stowed on the shelf overhead. The door closed with a whoosh, the driver put the bus in reverse, backed out of the space and, before I knew it, we were inching our way out of the breathtaking Bahstehrmeenahl redolent with gas fumes, inhaling the final whiffs of citysmell.

I really don't remember the ride, trying as I was not to barf the entire way. I tried looking out the window, Mama tried opening the window for air, Papa tried not to smoke and, finally, I was instructed to close my eyes and try to sleep. I tried, really I did, but I was so afraid that Mama would get off the bus and forget me that I kept opening my eyes every few minutes to make sure she was still there. (I was unconvinced that she'd gotten over her attempt to be rid of me in the Great Exile Episode and lived in constant fear of being "forgotten" somewhere.) The churning of the wheels underneath my seat matched the roiling of my stomach. I prayed that we would arrive soon, since I didn't know how much longer I could keep swallowing all the extra spit (where were you when I needed you?) forming in my mouth.

The bus stopped at a nondescript shelter on a nondescript blacktop somewhere "in the mountains." Pan Benya had told the truth: Pan Abel was there in his worse-for-wear off-white station wagon with fake wood paneling on the sides to meet us. The hood was up, and Pan Abel was bent over the engine, wiping the back of his neck with a faded plaid neckerchief. The bus door opened with a whooooooosh, the driver got out to help Mama down and to retrieve our suitcase from the bus' bowels. After shuffling the baggage around, he and Papa identified our well-worn plaid behemoth and, with a combined effort, managed to pull it out from behind a brand new light blue suitcase that landed on its side and acquired its first battle scars. The driver said something about the owner being able to recognize it better, he and Papa had a laugh, shook hands, and with a jolly "Enjoy your vacation!" he was off to deliver the other passengers to their versions of Shangri-La.

After I finally had escaped the confines of the bus by jumping from the second step onto the gravel, I was astonished to find that the air really *did* smell different here. I couldn't identify the smells because they were new to me, but I determined that they were decidedly different and pleasant, maybe even clean smelling, if there was such a smell. I had a few moments of panic when I realized that I'd have to get back into a vehicle again and run the risk of barfing in Pan Abel's car—an egregious sin of commission I was sure would get us banished from the mountains before I'd even figured out what they were.

Papa lit a much-deserved cigarette and walked over to where Pan Abel was trying to coax Avishag ("father's joy") back to life. I trailed behind Papa on the gravel and stood to his side as he ducked under the hood. Papa tightened a couple of what looked like screws and held down a couple of plugs, then asked Pan Abel to start the aging Plymouth wagon. After a couple of anemic coughs, Avishag came roaring to life, spurting dark smoke from her tail pipe. Pan Abel, Mama, and I applauded, gave a hearty "uuuurrrraaaaaaaaaaaaaaahhhhhhhhh!" and walked back to the open car doors.

With a wink and a head pat, Papa wisely sat me near a rolled-down window in the back seat while he lit a second Camel in the passenger seat next to Pan Abel and asked him how far the cabins were. I quickly and surreptitiously crossed my fingers and toes, hoping to influence the outcome.

"Ah, eez just couple meenoots, no more," Pan Abel fired out. He was about to become the first "fast talker" in my world—I'd never heard anyone speak so fast that it sounded like the machine guns in the war movies Papa and I watched together.

"Here, look, I show you! Here is sign I make myself for people with car, to find reezort: KOZLOWSKI KABINS. You like?"

We all liked very much, of course, because it was a *great* sign. Hammered onto a telephone pole, the white sign with blue hand-painted lettering and a huge red arrow indicating the turn was a sight to behold. No, I thought, with a sign like this you certainly couldn't miss the turn if you were lucky enough to have a car to take you places. My parents—despite the fact that Papa was a first-class mechanic—never owned a car,[18] and I blamed my wretched motion sickness on these

---

[18] Alternate street parking in NYC made having a car a nuisance, apparently. That, and the threat of auto theft. My parents preferred the stress-free non-own-ership of automobiles, which sentenced us to public transportation. Somehow,

carless circumstances of my young life. Still, as all the trees whizzed by, I stuck my head out the window like a golden retriever and let the wind blow my hair back. Mama gave my pink flowered sundress a sharp jerk, hissing "*sidi po-chelovecheski!*"

So much for vacation. There it was, the inescapable "*po-chelovecheski*"—like a human being. Evidently, Mama carried it in her purse wherever we went lest I forget myself and behave like a kid. Sit down and eat like a human being, who eats standing up? Speak like a human being, I can't understand you. Eat like a human being, take smaller bites. Walk like a human being or you'll trip and fall. That last one usually was followed by a trip and crash on my part, resulting in perpetually skinned knees and arms and the firm belief that I was secretly being cursed for returning from Exile. Just because you're paranoid, doesn't mean they're not out to get you.

I sat like a human being with my head down and my hands folded in my lap until Pan Abel stopped the car in front of a large white house with steps up to a wide front porch with rocking chairs. I'd only seen pictures of such houses in books and had always wondered what it would be like to be inside; now, it appeared that I would be *vacationing* in this princely palace. I started imagining my room in shades of pink, a four-poster bed with a canopy, a rocking chair, and a trunk full of dolls and stuffed animals . . .

I never missed what we didn't have. I just waited impatiently for the day when my parents would have to purchase a token for me to ride the subway: the tangible proof that I was no longer a baby. There's a story about that, as well, buried somewhere in this tale. But I've digressed again. Still, there's nothing like that blast of pungent tell-tale New York smell when you descend into the bowels of the city to take the subway. I miss it like I miss the pizza, bagels, and Sabrette's hot dogs with mustard and sauerkraut. Like I miss skating at Rockefeller Center under the ENORMOUS Christmas tree in my matching skating skirt and skate pom poms. Like I miss our annual trip to Radio City Music Hall on American Christmas Eve to watch the Rockettes and the Christmas spectacular. Like I miss Coney Island in summer—the end of the subway N line.

"One sekundochka," Pan Abel said, "I get key to you kabin. Ein moment."

What?! Wait, what was that?! Did that mean that THIS wasn't our vacation home? But what about my canopy bed? My stuffed animals and dolls and a rocking chair for daydreaming? Oh, no . . . this was not looking good. I consoled myself by gazing at the different trees, their leaves in varying shades of green rustling in the slight breeze. Off in the distance, there was a large field edged by little white houses. Papa turned around and winked at me,

"We're almost there! I wonder which one is ours?"

"Which one what?" I asked back.

"Which of those little white houses; there, just beyond the field."

"You mean we're not staying in this house?" I squeaked out.

"No, that's Pan Abel's house. We'll have our own little house to ourselves. Of course, we'll share the kitchen with neighbors, but maybe they'll have children your age to play with."

Ah-ha. Children my age. The thought of playmates helped ease my despair over losing the big house and all its fantasy delights.

I studied the front porch carefully, wondering if I'd ever be allowed to go up there and rock in one of the chairs. Before my brain could fly off into one of its perpetual imaginary excursions, a commotion at the front door grabbed my attention. There was Pan Abel, followed closely by a stout woman I assumed to be his wife, who was berating him for something while wiping her hands on her faded floral apron. The dark knot of her hair net sat firmly in the center of her forehead as she eyed me suspiciously through her black cat's eyeglasses. I realized at that moment that sitting on one of their big white rockers on the front porch was not something I'd be doing any time soon. I shrank down on the leatherette bench and tried to become invisible.

Pan Abel came trotting down the front steps of the big house, brandishing the key to our Kabin as if it were the key to Paradise itself. "Look, see? Nahmbehr tree! Is good luck number!" the Pan chuckled. It looked nothing like any of our house keys. In fact, it looked like something a witch would use to lock a princess in a tower the way it happened in one of the stories Mama had read to me recently. The hairs on the back of my neck stood up as I saw myself, flowered sundress and sandals, being thrown into a tower with hungry German Shepherds guarding the only exit.

AHA!

This was it, then: Mama had finally managed to find a way to get rid of me! And poor Papa had been duped into believing this was a vacation!! If he asked where I was, she'd probably tell him I was off playing with new friends . . . until he stopped asking. No one would know where I was, the dogs would get meaner and hungrier while I got smaller and weaker until, one day, I would simply die of starvation and a broken heart and the dogs would tear apart my tiny shriveled remains. I felt a tear start to roll down my cheek and quickly brushed it aside—I couldn't let Mama know I was onto her and her dastardly scheme. I'd make a break for it as soon as I figured out the lay of the land. I wasn't sure where exactly I would go, but I had no intention of allowing myself to be cast away and forgotten before I even figured out what mountains were and how to swim in a lake. Well, at least I was onto her and could keep my eyes and ears open and radar on alert; I was at DefCon 3.

This time, Avishag started up without complaint, and we rolled slowly down the beaten gravel path toward the little white squares at the end of a field of tall grass. As we got closer, I could see that each little square had a front porch with two rocking chairs on it—a hopeful sign. As Avishag's wheels scrunched to a halt in front of Kabin Nahmbehr tree—it was the third from the left and had a big black number three painted on the door above the knocker—I started to notice the minor details. Yes, the Kabin had once been white, but the paint had peeled in a number of places, revealing the gray wood underneath. The shutters had probably once been painted a navy blue but had now faded to a steely color with pockmarks—evidence of the bare wood under the missing paint. The rocking chairs were a light weather-beaten gray. I would discover the hazards of weather-beaten wood after I blissfully threw myself onto one in my bathing suit. I got splinters in places I didn't even know existed, much less were part of me.

Pan Abel, having suddenly remembered something about genteel manners that he'd read in an etiquette book Esther kept for reference purposes on the top shelf of their bedroom bookshelf (you never knew when a displaced Count or Duchess might decide to breathe some fresh air courtesy of Kozlowski Kabins), jumped out and ran around the back of the car to open Mama's door.

"*Lehdeez fyurst! Lehdeez fyurst! Proshe Pani!*" The Pan even clicked his heels together and bowed slightly, revealing a bald spot catching the sunlight on the top of his steel wool covered head.

By this time, Mama had managed to sweat through the multiple layers of de rigeur 1960s garments—longline bra, girdle, underwear, stockings, full slip, and dress—and had become glued to the scratched brown leatherette bench seat. She acknowledged the Pan's courtly gesture with a nod of her head and a smile and then started to rock in an attempt to both unglue herself from the seat and escape the innards of the car. I watched silently as a new Olympic sport came into being: sumo long jump. After a couple of grunts and flailing her pump-clad size sevens around in search of ballast or propellant, Mama launched herself forward and smack dab into the slight and shriveled Pan Abel. It was a sight akin to the clown being shot out of a cannon in a variety show I'd recently seen on our black and white RCA ("his master's voice"). Only the clown had been followed by a volley of confetti not in evidence in the Catskills. Both Mama and Pan Abel miraculously remained upright, albeit slightly tousled and embarrassed. I managed not to laugh, pretty much because I knew what the consequences would be. Papa twisted another unfiltered Camel into his *mundshtuk*, flicked his lighter once, and inhaled deeply. I saw his lips lift into a half-smile as he turned away.

The inside of the little cabin actually had some redeeming qualities to it. Pan Abel was nearly beside himself with excitement as he ran from pillar to post (so to speak), pointing out all the special features of our new home. Not the least of these was the interesting phenomenon of opening the windows—which he demonstrated by coaxing, banging, and threatening the windows open—and then leaving the second door slightly ajar to catch a breeze. I immediately proceeded to practice leaving the door ajar by placing the large rock left there by previous residents between the door and the door jamb. It worked! I tried to catch Papa's eye for approval; however, I was ensnared by Mama's glare and immediately retrieved the rock and carefully closed the door. *Po-chelovecheski.*

True, it was only one room, but it had two beds in it: a big one for my parents and a slightly smaller one for me, with a large enough gap between the two for us to walk through sideways. It also had two doors: the one through which we'd entered from the front porch and a second one on the far wall that opened onto a small field bordered by woods. Pan Abel's pet goats—which he proudly pointed out to us—kept the field both neatly mowed and fertilized. The yellowed lace half-curtains on the windows were not only aesthetically pleasing, they also trapped mosquitoes and other flying varmints that tried to get in through the holes in the screens. Two chairs rested in the corners, ready to receive either our suitcases, clothes, or us. Pan cautioned us about the left one, which had a tendency to rock a bit due to one leg being shorter than the other three—an unfortunate reminder of the fire from which it had been rescued.

There were braided rugs (Pani Esther's efforts at beautification) that slipped and slid all over the faded and scratched wood floors, threatening entrants with bodily injury if trod upon too swiftly. And, although the chenille bedspreads had seen better days, their washed-out appearance seemed to round out the room nicely—all the faded and muted shades of gray created an atmosphere of quiet repose. There was even an empty vase with a chipped lip on the little table for any wildflowers we might pick in our many leisure hours. The bare light bulb in the center of the ceiling lit up the room nicely, and the long dark yellow shiny strip of paper with dead flies stuck to it was the only detraction from the overall theme of genteel loving use. But the absolute best feature of this room, in my view, was the fact that each wall had been papered in a different print. The North wall had some sort of blue Chinese-y drawings on an off-white background; the South wall had pink and red peonies bursting into bloom. The East wall was covered in climbing English ivy, while the parts of the West wall that I could see had my favorite flowers on them: yellow-centered daisies and black-eyed Susans. Wow. What a feast for the eyes!

The familiarization tour of the room complete, Pan Abel ushered us out through the door to the front porch and on to a couple of considerably larger buildings. As we got closer, I could see that one door had a lady painted on it in what used to be pink paint, while the building next door had a man painted on it in faded blue. I thought the blue resembled the color in the KOZLOWSKI KABINS sign we'd seen upon entry into the compound, but couldn't be sure, given that the paint on this sign was peeling while the paint on the road sign had looked pretty fresh.

"*Ein moment! Proshe pan, pani, ein moment!*" the Pan fired off in his staccato delivery. He straightened his faded red shirt with cars, dice, and ladies in bathing suits on it, smoothed his SOS pad hair with his hands and, with a great deal of dignity and aplomb, knocked on the door with the pink lady on it. No response. He knocked again. Again, no response.

"Ah! *Ausgetseichnet,* excellent, *otlichno!*" proclaimed the Pan as he flung open the door to a dark, dank room that immediately assaulted my nasal passages with unfamiliar and overwhelming soapy odors. The wood floors were damp, even wet in some spots. The whole barn-like structure appeared to be divided into small wooden cubes equipped with doors that had handles and hooks on the inside. Interestingly enough, I noticed that it was the interior of the cubes that was wet. The wood plank walkways between the cubes were a damp dark gray, slick, and with patches of green. I also noticed that you could see the dirt underneath the floor planks, a couple of inches down. I thought I heard a frog ribbet.

Pan Abel graciously opened one of the cube doors and, with a flourish of his hand, ushered Mama inside. He pointed out the conveniently located little triangular chrome shelf for soap and the two silver handles, one for hot water and one for cold. And, once Mama was done marveling at this convenience, Pan Abel allowed Papa to have a look-see for himself, pointing out that Papa would be using the building with the little blue man painted on the door.

To the right, in an add-on to the building that I'd completely missed, was a door with a white hand on it. As we were shepherded into this structure, we discovered that it was the toilet-and-wash basin place. Apparently, when you woke up in the morning, you grabbed your towel, toothbrush, and soap and marched yourself through the dewy grass from your Kabin to this place. It really wasn't that different from my routine back home, where I had to get hauled out of the crib I still slept in—there being no room in our apartment for a "big girl bed"—and drag myself to the toilet at the far end of the kitchen.

Tour completed, Pan Abel ran through the litany of "conveniences" Pan Benya had mentioned: bread truck, milk truck, grocery run. Pan Abel shuttled all the week-end Dads to the bus stop on Sunday evening for the return to New York and their jobs. He made two runs on Friday evenings and two on Saturday mornings to pick non-car-driving Dads up from the bus stop for the weekends. If Papa missed the ride, he'd have to walk to the reezort and Kabin by himself. (I didn't think this was a problem, given that my parents had walked through most of Europe at the end of the War. Mama's calves remained taught and muscled until the day she died at eighty-eight—the age the gypsy had predicted when she read Mama's palm somewhere beween the Soviet Union and war-torn Germany.) With that, the Pan whirled outside, revved Avishag a couple of times, and was gone with a crunch of gravel. We were on our own. Vacation had begun.

While Mama was left to unpack, Papa and I went out on our first reconnaissance mission of the compound and its surroundings. Much to my surprise and delight, I discovered that quite a few of my little Slavic friends from New York had made the journey to Kozlowski Kabins.

We quickly bonded into a motley crew of five- six- and seven-year-olds that rolled screeching all over Pan Abel's fields, plaguing his goats and scaring the chickens that ranged free at one end of the property. It was the first time in our urban jungle lives that we'd been allowed to run free, without parental supervision, all day long. We didn't have to watch for oncoming cars or elude the older kids who hung out on corners, waiting to shake us down for our lunch money. There were no streetlights, so we meandered home when the light started to dim. We were breathing and living free and it was glorious.

Our arrangement was that Papa would stay for two weeks, then go back to the city to work. He'd come down on the weekends until Mama had to go back to work. Then, he'd come and stay with me in the mountains while Mama returned to the city. Mama would come for one final week before we all packed up and returned to our apartment in Brooklyn. In other words, I would spend most of the summer in a place where the omnipresent and all-powerful *po-chelovecheski* would recede into the background. I could blissfully stomp my feet on the floors without getting yelled at about disturbing the people who lived below us. I wouldn't have to wear those horrible Sunday dresses with all that tulle that scratched my legs and made holding still *(po-chelovecheski)* impossible. *You* try wearing one of those pieces of frippery to church and see how long you can stand still, much less sit. I wouldn't have to speak in hushed tones so as not to disturb the neighbors. I could yodel, shout, bellow, scream, and not be reprimanded (too often). My friends and I were *na svobode* in a way we'd never been before, and we reveled in our new-found freedom, happier than pigs in . . . well, you know.

This was the summer when I first really saw Papa's wealth of knowledge about the natural world. Sure, he'd shown me plants and weeds in the parks we visited, but now, surrounded by so many different trees, bushes, grasses, and plants, he returned joyously to his natural element and his own childhood that had been carefree for such a short time. I don't know whether the actual chronological children (of whom I was one) or Papa reveled in their surroundings more.

He was a shaman of sorts. Having grown up at a time when Russian rural medicine consisted of dried roots and herbs, an occasional laying on of hands, prayer, or incantations, he knew all manner of things magic, mysterious, and fascinating to a child. His knowledge of these mysteries had come from need: when you're ten and poor, your father is dead, and you have a mother and sister to support, you find substitutes for just about everything. Which unprepossessing white flowering grass could be used as a substitute for soap; which tree leaf made the best whistle sound; which tree's twigs would make the best carved flutes, and—most important to me—how to weave long grasses into furniture and random flowering weeds into hair wreaths for me.

Unlike the other adults I knew, Papa was the absolute best at understanding why I was arranging the grass furniture a certain way—and why my clumsy little fingers couldn't make themselves reproduce what he'd showed me. And, unlike the others, he had the infinite patience endemic to a soul that loved me completely regardless of what I said or did. I know, in my heart of hearts, that if St. Exupery's Little Prince[19] had asked him to draw a sheep, he would have done exactly that, right on the spot. I worshipped him. Little did either one of us know that I'd spend the rest of my life chasing that unconditional soul-level adoration. Unbeknownst to him, he'd unintentionally set an impossibly high bar for the entire XY population of Planet Earth.

The Pied Piper. Except that Papa loved children of all ages, perhaps because he remained a joyful child at heart despite—or perhaps as a result of—the horrors he had witnessed, experienced, and survived. Early on a Saturday morning, while all the other parents were sleeping in, he'd corral the mangy sleepy-eyed lot of us and cajole us into the communal kitchen where we spread peanut butter on Wonder Bread slices while he wrapped the sandwiches in wax paper. (The *real* kind of wax paper, the nearly see-through kind that smelled of wax and made

---

[19] Antoine de Saint-Exupery, *Le Petit Prince*. One of my very favorite books, even in (chronological) adulthood.

crunching noises when you folded it. Technological progress has led to a thinner, less transparent version. Still, when I pull a sheet of wax paper off a roll, I can't help but smell it in hopes of reconstructing those sun-dappled days in "the mountains.") Loaded with sustenance and a couple of thermoses of Hawaiian punch—and tea for himself—we marched up up up into the hills, Papa swinging a walking stick he had whittled out of a fallen branch. We learned the names of flowers and plants and their medicinal or fun uses and learned never to pull the plant up by the root—both why and or else. He showed us tracks of animals and had us guess which animal had left them and which way the animal was going. By the time the sun had climbed to its apex, we would have conquered the summit, played king of the mountain—usually, though not always, without casualties—and had our lunch. Dutifully placing our detritus in his waiting fishing/mushroom basket, we commenced our ritual whining and pleading for his carved flutes.

Ah, the flutes. These were not just *any* flutes, these were special! They smelled of the tree from which they'd been carved and still tasted sweetly of the sap running through the tree's veins. Each one hit a different note, subtly proving to us that each one of US was unique and very special and had his own voice. Once everyone in our impromptu woodwind section of the orchestra was properly equipped, we'd race down the mountain, blowing full blast on our new instruments and vexing beyond description all the adults nursing a hangover lakeside or on the cabin porches. Alas, by the end of the day, the wood would dry out and we could toot no more, much to the delight of the aspirin-popping and highball-swilling adults.

From about the age of four, I started self-defense training with Papa. I had no idea it was self-defense training, all I knew was that it consisted of learning to make a proper fist (and remembering to spit in it like I meant business) and then hauling off and punching the palm of his hand as hard as I could in order to make it move. (After a lifetime of hard manual labor, Papa's arms were solid muscle and his hands strong and rough but gentle.) Again. And again. And again. Until I'd land one of sufficient ferocity and oommph to get some positive feedback, "*There*! Just like that! That last one was a good one! *Molodets*." And I'd be RoR'd until the next session.

I didn't have to wait too long for an opportunity to see if the training would hold up under the pressures of the real world. Seven-year-old Lyova, after pledging his undying love to me and proposing marriage in a musty spiderwebbed corner of Kozlowski's storage cabin, attempted to kiss me. For field expediency's sake, I dispensed with the spitting and popped him a good one right in his puckered lips. He ran off crying for his Mama, and I ran off to tell Papa of how I'd used his training in practice. This little spat probably could have gone on for the entire summer, except for one small glitch in the system: I didn't know how to back down "like a girl."

While Papa was laughing out loud at my story of the Lyova punch, Lyova's father was reading Lyova the riot act on the other side of the Kozlowski Kabins compound. From what I could hear, it went something like this:

"What's wrong with you? What are you crying about?"

"My mouf huhts. She punched me!" *Snivel, snivel, sniff, sniff, whaaaaaaaaaaahhhh.*

"What do you mean *she* punched me?! A *girl* punched you? What's wrong with you?!?! You go back there right now and punch her back! You show her who's boss! What kind of a man are you to let a girl punch you? Get over there right now!"

Silence.

A little nudge in the back from Papa as if to say "Go on. Show him what you're made of—you're the Grechenkov breed. *Grechenkovskoy porody*." Bouncing up and down in my Keds ("Run faster! Jump higher!"), I skipped over into one of the mowed fields we ran around in with the others, pretending sweetness, light, and innocence as I stopped to pick a random dandelion or buttercup. Still, you could feel the tension starting to build as our little cohorts—all of whom had not only heard the wailing but had overheard my version of the Great Punch in the

Kisser—started to trickle off their respective cabin porches. Even the adults—mostly the fathers—came out to pretend to read their Russian or Ukrainian or Polish newspapers on the humble verandas.

I saw him coming before I heard him:

"Hey! You! Marya! YOU! Come here! I have business to finish with you!" The use of the pejorative diminutive *Marya*, emphasis on first syllable, clearly was meant to intimidate me.

"Oh yeah? What kind of business is that?"

I saw Papa stand up from his chair and walk to the front of the porch, obviously ready to intercede should I fail to defend myself properly. But he needn't have worried, because I was pretty sure I could take the scrawny blond Lyova if push came to shove.

"C'mere!" I heard him yell. I could swear his voice was higher than mine.

"What for?"

"I said c'mere because I got somethin' for ya."

"Oh yeah? Lemme see." And as I swaggered toward him, I saw that he was trying to do something with his hand. The closer I got, the more I realized that he was trying to form a fist . . . and had no idea how to do it. And he was a lefty—an unexpected development that might prove significant in my defense strategy.

"Whaddaya want?" My voice dripped defiance and contempt for this pitiful example of the male of the species. Even my checkered yellow sundress seemed to develop starched pleats.

"Get closer. Right now!!"

I walked within arm's length of Lyova and noticed that he had started to circle me with that little left paw formed into the biggest example of a sissy fist I'd ever seen. After he'd circled me once, I lost patience with him:

"Whaddaya doin'?"

"I'm trying to figure out a good place to hit you!"

Perhaps it was some version of the "fight or flight" syndrome, or maybe it's true what they say about moments in life when your brain freezes and your body kicks in and takes over all the action. That's exactly what happened to me: before I knew what had happened, I heard a buzzing in my ears, the entire field had gone bright white, I'd formed a REAL fist and popped him in the nose (again, minus the spitting, but time was of the essence). It wasn't really my best shot because there'd been no blood spurt. Lyova took off crying for home and I skipped back to the front porch, followed by my cohorts in crime who had now become a crowd of cheering fans. Yes, sometimes the best defense is a good offense.

Another part of my training was being told how *else* to defend myself against unwanted attentions or pestering from a person of the male persuasion. We never actually practiced that one—for reasons I couldn't understand yet never bothered to ask—but I was pretty sure my skating- and stickball-playing legs were more than up to the task. In retrospect, my fuzzy memory drags up something that must have happened on the subway—something I missed but Papa obviously hadn't—because it was somewhere between DeKalb Avenue and our transfer to the RR train on the Fifty-ninth Street stop when he gave me my first lecture on how and where to kick a boy. Education in life skills and self-preservation on the Brooklyn-bound N train.

Summer days flowed smoothly one into the next, punctuated periodically by rainy days that forced us all into the communal kitchen to play board games. The youngest among us huddled together and made up games of our own while the older six- and seven-year-olds were corralled by their parents and forced to read quietly. Every once in a while, when we got a bit too rowdy, the Mother On Duty would yell at us to calm down; but, apart from that, we were left to our own devices and imaginations. Cooped up but still *na svobode*.

One of the things about the mountains that I discovered was that mornings tended to be cold. However, as the sun climbed higher into the sky, it got warm and then even hot, so I was forced into a sweater in the mornings despite my protests that *I am not cold*. Besides, I hated the lavender sweater. Not as much as I hated the blue spangly hat in the wintertime, but I felt that lavender was not a true reflection of my perky (and occasionally warrior) self. Still, it was the only Mashasweater that Mama had packed, so I was doomed to wear it in the mornings, much to my chagrin. I waited impatiently for the sun to climb higher in the sky so that I could ditch the sweater and trade in my long pants for a sunsuit or bathing suit. Unfortunately, Papa wasn't much of a help in pleading my case since he deferred clothing decisions to Mama.

One morning, after breakfast, Papa announced that he was going to walk around the lake in search of a good fishing spot. Fishing?! Really?! Wow!! I'd never been fishing before!

Papa: "I'm going to walk around the right side of the lake to the opposite side. I think I saw a pretty good fishing spot the other day when we climbed the mountain."

Mama: "You don't have a fishing pole. How are you planning on catching fish? With your hands?" sarcastic smirk smirk smirk.

Papa: "The way I used to back home. I'm going to find a suitable stick, tie a line to it, add a hook and some sinkers, and maybe a float."

Mama: "And where do you expect to get the line and other paraphernalia? There's not a store within miles of here."

Papa: "I brought it with me."

Me: "Can I come?"

Before Mama could say anything, I took off my sweater and ran outside to wait for Papa.

And so we set off, just the two of us, because the answer to "can I come" almost always was "*nu konechno*," of course. The walk turned out to be longer than I'd anticipated, but I trudged along, trying to match my smaller steps to Papa's longer ones without actually breaking into a trot. Not too long after we set out, just as we hit the woods lining the right side of the lake, I remembered that I'd forgotten to use the bathroom before we left. And I remembered it in a most urgent way.

"Papa!!"

"Ah?"

"Papa! I have to go to the bathroom!!"

"What? Right now?"

"Yes!! I forgot to go peepee before we left!!"

"So? Go peepee."

"Where? Here?"

"Where else? Of course, here."

"But what if somebody sees me?"

"Who's going to see you? The rabbits?"

"I don't know. Somebody. I really have to go!"

"Don't you know how to peepee outside?"

"Noooooooooo!!!! "At this point I was jumping up and down with my legs crossed—no small feat.

"Ah, so that's the problem. OK, let me show you how."

And so I discovered the true freedom of peeing in the wild, with no one to see me, feeling a light breeze on my behind. It was later in the walk when Papa taught me how to do my other business outside—especially the part about selecting leaves to use as toilet paper. A bad choice there could have very serious and unintended consequences, he told me. The obvious choices were maple or oak leaves—always better to pick from a tree than from a bush or vine you didn't know. And how to deal responsibly with what I left behind. As it were.

We meandered through patches of woods, through sunlit grassy spots, Papa looking for the ideal place from which to fish. At the same time, we were both keeping our eyes open for a stick or branch of appropriate length and thickness, sturdy but with a little give on one end, to craft into a fishing pole. After what seemed like hours, Papa slowed his steps and gradually came to a stop. He looked around. He looked down at the lake. And then, he made the pronouncement:

"This is it. This is where I'm going to come fishing tomorrow."

"Why here?"

What followed was my first lesson in the art of fishing: selecting an appropriate spot. It couldn't be out in the sun because it would get too hot. Trees not only made shade, but they served as camouflage for you from the fish. Papa explained that certain fish were so smart that, if they saw you, they wouldn't take the bait on the hook. Trout, for instance. If a trout saw you, you might as well pack up your fishing pole and go home.

So, the spot he'd selected had trees behind him, a nice grassy spot to sit on, and reeds in front of him to hide him from the smart fish in the lake. Perfect. We started in earnest now to search for the fishing pole.

First, we looked around on the ground for downed branches that Papa could whittle down to the right size, but we couldn't find any with give on one end. (If it doesn't give, it could break off when the fish hit and then you'd lose part of your pole, your hook, your sinkers, your float, and most of your line, I was told.) Left with no options—and an unyielding desire to go fishing—Papa found a branch on a tree, broke it off, cut the leaves off with his switchblade, and we set off on the return journey to the Kabins.

Rather than horsing around with my cohorts that morning, I watched intently as Papa made his fishing pole come to life. First, there was the whittling and carving guides into the pole. Then there was the intricate tying on of sinkers, hook, and float. Papa explained that real fishermen didn't use floats and simply watched the line, but he wanted to be able to relax, maybe read something, and not have to worry about the line. When the float started to dance, he'd know a fish was nibbling on the bait. What followed next was, of course, inevitable:

"Can I come?"

"You? You want to come with me?"

"Uh-huh."

"But I'm going to get up really, really early in the morning. Just as the sun is coming up."

"I wanna go."

"It's going to be cold."

"I know. That's OK. Can I please come?"

"OK, you can come, but you have to be quiet or you'll scare the fish away."

"OK."

"I mean it: no talking. Not even on the way there. *Absolyutnaya tishina.*"

"I can do that. I won't talk, I promise. I promise I'll be quiet."

"OK. I'm going to wake you up very, very early, so don't complain."

"I won't, I promise."

Deal.

I ran off to tell my cohorts that I was going fishing with my Papa tomorrow morning before any of them woke up and that we were going to bring back so many fish that everyone could have some. Yes, leaning forward a bit on that last part, but I hadn't yet reached the age when my sense of optimism had been beaten out of me by life.

After a day of running, eating, and playing "HORSEFLY!" in the lake—a game we invented wherein someone would scream "*horsefly*" and we'd all dive under water to avoid those enormous nasty biting flies—left me more than ready for an early bedtime. Sleep was slow in coming, however, because of all the anticipation of tomorrow's fishing expedition. I must have fallen asleep eventually, because the next thing I knew, Papa's hand was on my head and he was whispering my name. I sat bolt upright, "I'm awake, I'm ready."

"You're not ready yet," he whispered, trying to let Mama sleep. "Let's get you dressed and then go brush your teeth and wash your face, *rybak.*[20]"

I quickly dragged on the clothes Mama had laid out for me last night, grabbed my towel and toothbrush (but not the soap, hoping no one would notice), and ran for the toilet room. I splashed water on my face, brushed my teeth—I even used toothpaste in case there was an unannounced check—and raced back to our cabin. By this time, Papa had made his secret fish bait recipe and was outside Kabin Number Tree with his fishing pole, a basket with the bait, our breakfast sandwiches, and my lavender sweater. Discretion being the better part of valor, I decided *not* to argue about the sweater and to simply submit to having

---

[20] fisherman

it buttoned onto me for expediency's sake. I could always claim to be hot and take it off later.

We set off quietly, hand in hand. No talking. Only the crunch of our sandals on the gravel, followed by our soft footfalls on the dewy grass. I remember that morning as being cool and foggy, and how it felt almost fairytale-like to walk through fog as if walking through clouds. I remember the smell of the woods as we cut through on our way to The Spot and the crunch of fallen leaves under our feet. I remember the stillness of that morning, as if Nature herself was obeying the *absolyutnaya tishina* dictum. I remember the tall grasses on the banks of the lake and a few cattails here and there, standing straight up in the still morning air. And I remember coming to our secret fishing spot and how the bank on the left side was covered with grass both short and tall, how Papa gingerly set down his basket and fishing pole, and how he pulled a clean pressed handkerchief out of his pocket and laid it down on the grass, making a special place for me to sit.

While Papa was otherwise occupied, I decided to step over to the right side and have a peek at the lake, just to see if maybe I could see some fish in there without drawing unnecessary piscine attention to my presence. I was having a bit of trouble seeing through the tall grasses, so I decided to maneuver over to the patch of dirt I saw slanting down into the water. Oh-so-quietly and delicately, barely breathing, I slid my feet, one by one in tiny baby steps, closer and closer to the reddish-brown dirt. A little bit more and I'd be able to look into the lake and determine if the fish would come to us. I wondered what a real fish would look like, whether it would be bigger than I was, and whether it would be scary or not. I set my right foot on the patch of dirt and then quickly brought my left foot over, trying to maintain my balance. Only, something happened.

Before I could say or do anything, that reddish brown dirt surged forward and threw me into the lake, lavender sweater, sandals, and all. I didn't get a chance to yell or call for help, I just wound up face down in the water. I think I remember Papa yelling something but can't be sure whether I actually heard it or imagined it later. But what I remember most clearly is Papa's hands grabbing me and pulling me out of the water. He didn't even bother to wring out my sweater, only bundled me up close to his chest, water soaking both of us, and ran back to Kabin Number Tree, where Mama was sitting on the porch, reading a book.

After many shouts of *"Ay, Gospodi,"* Mama ripped my wet clothes off me, rubbed me down hard with a towel, stuffed me back into my pajamas, and tucked me into bed. I fell asleep right away and woke up some time later—the sun was up, and I could hear my friends playing outside—after a nightmare about a huge purple dinosaur with pink spots trying to eat me. As I sat up to make sure that there were no dinosaurs in the vicinity, I noticed that Mama was sitting in the saved-from-the-fire chair, watching me.

"I had a bad dream," I started to say, but nothing came out except a croak.

Mama came over to the bed and felt my forehead.

"Well, that's where your fishing's gotten you: now you're sick. I told you to let Papa go by himself, but you wouldn't listen to me. So, no playing outside today. You're going to stay in bed until you're better. And no more fishing." Wow. No playing outside, no fishing, no getting out of bed. I might as well be back in the city. So much for my vacation. I still was unclear as to how I'd landed in the water but figured Papa would tell me when he came back from collecting his fishing gear before somebody could swipe it. After that pick-pocketing incident, he'd grown particularly cautious and suspicious of others.

Mama hustled off to the kitchen to make me some tea (the Russian cure for whatever ails you) with strict instructions *not* to get out of bed or go outside. I nodded my head to show I'd understood and would obey, since my throat hurt too much to talk. Zosya came running over and knocked on our door, but I couldn't tell her to come in since I was, like the Little Mermaid, temporarily voiceless. A warrior in training like me—only a bit more aggressive—Zosya tried the door and, finding it unlocked, let herself into the cabin, where she found me tousled and sitting in bed in my bunnies PJs.

"Hey, what are you doing in here? Come on out!"

Croak. Gack.

"What? I can't understand you. What did you say?"

Gack. Koff-koff-koff-koff. Ugh.

"Are you sick? Can you come out? Come on, it's hot out, we're going swimming after lunch. My Mama said you can come with us."

And, of course, at that moment *my* Mama walked in, bearing a cup of hot tea.

"She's not going anywhere, and especially not swimming. She's had enough swimming for one day—pathetic fisherman that she is. She went fishing with her Papa early this morning and managed to fall into the lake and nearly drown herself. And now she's sick. So she can't play with you today." With that, she opened the door for Zosya and, when my friend crossed the threshold on her way out, shut the door firmly. My humiliation was complete, much like my enforced isolation. My hands shook a little bit as I took the cup of tea. I'd had no idea that nearly drowning could get me killed by Mama. Life is full of surprises, and not all of them are pleasant.

I spent most of that day—when I wasn't sleeping or being plied with tea—staring out the window at my friends running around *na svobode*. It got quiet in the afternoon, after I watched them in their bathing suits, carrying various and sundry swimming accoutrements, head toward the lake and multiple rounds of "HORSEFLY!!" I closed my eyes, clutched *Zaychik* close, and opened a conversation with God. I believe this conversation/monologue was the first instance of my deal making with God, and it went something like this:

"*Bozhen'ka,* please hear me. I don't want to be sick on vacation. Please make me better, please. I want to go swimming with my friends, please. Please make me all better, please. Please let me be all better tomorrow so I can go outside again, please. And please let Mama not be mad at me anymore. And please let Papa take me fishing again, please.

I promise not to fall in the lake again, if you'll please let me go fishing again with Papa, please. Thank you for listening to me. Amen."

I drifted off to sleep, hoping, praying, and believing that God would make me healthy by the next day. Because, even then, I believed in miracles and the unending mercy and grace of God. Not without reason, either, because when I woke up the next morning, my voice was back, my throat didn't hurt, and I was feeling pretty darn perky. Still, until I'd successfully passed all of Mama's health assessments, I wasn't allowed to join my friends. In other words, I was checked for fever, my throat was checked for redness, my eyes were checked for I-don't-know-what, and I was forced to sit down and eat breakfast, my least favorite meal of the day.

I truly detested having to eat in the morning because my mouth wasn't ready to receive anything: all the textures (no matter the texture) were wrong, tea on an empty stomach made me nauseated, and even the smell of eggs frying was enough to trigger the *gonna barf* mechanism. Even so, I forced myself to sit *po-chelovecheski* and slowly chew and swallow whatever was set in front of me. After clearing my plate, Mama made me sit still for a couple of decades to "digest my food." OK, it felt like an eternity but was probably closer to the thirty-minute "no swimming after eating" rule. (Whoever came up with that, anyway?) Eventually, I was released to go play with my friends with Mama's parting caution: "Don't run around so much, you were sick yesterday." Right. The kitchen screen door slammed behind me (sin of commission) as I raced across the field to join my buddies in a never-ending game of tag or hide-and-seek or whatever was in play at the time, relishing my re-claimed freedom.

In addition to all the pastoral and mountain pleasures I discovered that summer, two things stand out in my memory. The first was the appearance of the Peddler's Truck.

Picture this: Middle of the week. Mothers sitting on porches doing needlepoint, reading, knitting. Urchins running free through mowed and unmowed fields. Children's laughter ringing through the air. All of a sudden, a car horn starts beeping in a "shave-and-a-haircut-two-bits" rhythm. Mothers look up from their pastimes, urchins fall silent and cluster together. Along the long gravel path from the main road, past the lake, and down to the cabins lumbers an ancient farm truck with wooden slats on the back. What in the world?!?

Naturally, the cluster of cohorts runs as one to greet this dust-raising, gravel-crunching, blissfully beeping rusty old rattletrap of a truck. It's not a regular bread, milk, or groceries day, so what could this possibly be? We were transfixed and a tad afraid of what might come out of the cabin or bed of the truck, trading whispers, speculating on who or what this could be.

What we saw when the old man with a three-day stubble gray beard got out of the truck and opened the locks to the truck bed was so astonishing that we all fell silent. Pause. Pause. Pause. In unison, we exploded with "WOOOWWWWWWWWWW!" and ran to our respective cabins to drag our Mamas to this astounding sight. Absolutely everything in the world to improve the quality of the vacation experience could be had for mere pennies from that truck!

Games of all sorts; balls of different sizes and for different sports; penny candies and gum; pedal pushers and pants for kids and adults; sweaters (ugh); ribbons; sewing and embroidery supplies; hooks and needles and yarn for the knitters; pretty barrettes for girls' hair. You name it, the gray-bearded, shabbily clad Mr. Luca Jilks had it, and for mere pennies. None of us had ever seen such a glorious assortment of goods, and we marveled not only at the variety, but at all the brilliant colors. And, of course, begged as one or in unison for our mothers to spring for this game, that ball, or wax lips.

The mothers gathered 'round the truck and, clutching their wallets to their chests with one hand, started fingering the clothes with the other and whispering among themselves. One after the other, the Mamas started negotiating prices with Mr. Luca until the babble around the old vendor reached an unheard-of decibel level. The women's voices, the whining of the children vying for their mothers' attention, combined with the acrobatics of older children climbing onto the truck for a better view of the merchandise created a mini tornado in the dust around the entire living tableau.

Experienced though he was in price negotiations, Mr. Luca clearly was overwhelmed by the activities and sounds around him. The Mamamob, each proferring numbers far below asking price, the ceaseless high-pitched whining of the youngsters, as well as the loss of merchandise that was disappearing over the top of the truck bed with the older children put Mr. Luca at a clear disadvantage. Overcome by the overall commotion and ado, Mr. Luca capitulated and yielded to the women's price demands. He even threw in some extras like ribbons and barrettes for the fiercest negotiators . . . which is how I came to own a couple of pink bow-shaped barrettes that never really stayed in my hair. (Poor Mr. Jilks. Mama was a veteran black-market trader from her DP Camp days in post-war Germany.) Still, it was the thought that counted.

Once the truck was gone, the mothers of girls pulled us all aside to lecture (and threaten) us on *tsygane* and why we were never ever **never** to get close to one of their trucks or wagons and especially not to one of *them*. Most of us didn't see what the big deal was, considering how decrepit Mr. Luca appeared to be, but we all nodded our heads in understanding, mentally telegraphing each other that the sooner we nodded, the sooner we'd be released to play. Personally, I found it grossly unfair that the girls were singled out for a boring lecture while the boys got to run off and play—especially since I'd already demonstrated my ability to deal with unpleasant forward boys. Still, I had to admit that it was pretty cool to meet a real *tsygan*, even though he was nothing like I'd imagined.

There was one other Truly Stupendous and Memorable thing that happened that summer: I had a real, bona fide American birthday party. With cake, ice cream, party games, party favors, and gifts!

OK, by now you've realized that I didn't come from a "normal American family" . . . whatever that is. Define "normal," to start with, if you're in that kind of mood. Birthdays *à l'américain* had simply not been part of my world. On my birthday, every year thus far, I had been stuffed into a gorgeous store-brought dress from my Godmother, lace-topped anklets, white patent leather mary janes and matching purse, topped off with a straw hat with a ribbon and white lace gloves, and trotted off to church, where I would take communion. My Godmother's family and my Godfather's family would all be there and then every-one would come back to our house for a celebration. There was no cake, per se, certainly no American type cake. There was tons of food, plenty of vodka for the grownups, soda for us (cream soda being my particular favorite for festive occasions), and the first toast was always for the *vinovnitsa torzhestva*, the culprit of the celebration, i.e., me. Then to Mama, then to Papa. Everyone would eat and drink and eat and get happier and louder and pretty soon we'd be released to play in the living room while the grownups had their fun.

One of my most favorite desserts that Mama made was a rice *babka* with strawberry *kisel'*. All that rich, buttery, eggy, ricey goodness with a coating of *kisel'* to provide the fruity counterpoint and ease the bite's journey from my mouth through my throat to my stomach. Oh, yum. No one sang "Happy Birthday," there were no candles to blow out and make a wish, no ice cream on the side. Just a piece of deliciousness. And, after everyone was done eating (for the first round), all the grownups would come into the living room to watch us play. Some of them—my Godmother and Papa, if you really want to know—would get right down on the floor with us and play along. And they made our fun even funner, and I know that's not a word, but you know what I mean.

So, imagine my surprise when one of Pani Esther's daughters-in-law (Pan Benya's wife, Gilda, up in the Catskills for the summer) asked how many children had August birthdays. I raised my hand while looking around at my cohorts to see if I had any company; alas, I was the only one.

"That's GREAT!" shouted Pani Gilda, "We'll have a *birthday party* for you!" and gave me such a huge hug that we both almost toppled over. Pani Gilda was one of those women whose hair color changed from week to week, so we never knew what to expect and made kiddie bets—anteing up our best candy samples—on what she'd look like on a Saturday morning. Pani Gilda performed her hair tinting and setting mysteries on Friday night in the recesses of the Big House, trying to stay out of sight of the Urchin Pack (and probably The Pani). However, one of the older boys managed to catch a glimpse of her in her room, where she was sitting on the bed, reading a magazine with pink curlers in her hair and some kind of white goop all over her face. (Remember those pink curlers? Gotcha, you've just revealed your age!) Saturday morning, Pani Gilda—all dressed up in bright colored shorts and shirt, usually coordinated to accent her new hair color—would come running down the front steps of the house as her husband, Pan Benya, came roaring into the compound in his fancy black car. As the car came to a stop, he'd throw open the driver's side door, jump out, and grab Pani Gilda, spinning her around and around and around as they both laughed and laughed. If the Pani was in a position to see this, she'd usually emit a loud harrumph, turn her back on the couple, and walk away. We all agreed that the moustachio'd mean Pani was an adult to be avoided at all costs. Some of us even believed her capable of casting an evil eye, so we'd spit three times over our left shoulders, just to be safe.

Pani Gilda wore bright pedal pushers, tight blouses, lots of make-up, and reeked of a perfume that reminded us of musty potting soil, but she was fun, fun, fun and created all kinds of games for us while the menfolk were away. She claimed that she wanted to give our poor mothers a break and corralled us for games like seeing how many of us we could fit into her VW bug before she went careening all over the Kozlowski Kabins compound at a high rate of speed, doing donuts around the trees, all of us screaming and laughing. Invariably, we'd scream for more, no matter how squished we were, and she'd oblige. I believe, though, that all that driving made her dizzy because when she got out of the car, she'd hold onto the hood and sway a bit in the Catskills breeze. Maybe it's because she wore those fancy high-heeled mules that she had trouble with balance; after all, it's tough to stay upright when your heels sink into the gravel at uneven depths. Be that as it may, we loved Pani Gilda despite the fact that Pani Esther seemed to dislike her intensely. We figured this out pretty quickly because, the first time we unscrambled ourselves from inside the VW bug, we caught sight of The Pani standing on the front porch, hands on her hips, her lip curled under her faint moustache as she watched the spectacle. And then, in a true display of disgust, she spit in the direction of the car. Evidently, there was no love lost between them . . . which may go a long way toward explaining why Pani Gilda chose to hang out with us: we were her only defense and refuge.

But back to the Birthday Party. My five-year-old buddies were as confused by this as I was, but the older kids—the ones who'd been to *real* birthday parties—hooted and hollered and carried on like this was the greatest thing since sliced bread. As a horde, we approached the older kids and started to pry birthday party information out of them. Pani Gilda had woven her arm through Mama's and was walking the two of them up the front porch steps . . . ostensibly to plan the party. I suspected that Pani Gilda was using Mama as a defensive shield, the way she played with us to create a barrier between her and her monstrous mother-in-law.

For such a momentous occasion in my young life, it's odd that I have almost no memories of what actually happened during the party. What I do remember is that the pile of presents next to me on the bench at the table under the oak tree was almost as tall as I was: boxes on boxes on boxes. And I remember the cake, of course. It was so big that it almost covered half the table, and it was gorgeous. Pure white with pink frosting roses in the corners, green frosting leaves and vines swirled around the outside. And **Happy Birthday Maria** written across the entire cake in pink icing, in Edwardian script. And candles! Pink candles—six plus one to grow on—to make a wish and blow out. I don't remember what I wished for, but I remember taking a really, really deep breath (all that training playing the HORSEFLY game finally paid off!) and blew as hard as I could at the neatly grouped six, saving a final puff for the seventh candle. Everyone cheered and clapped, and Pani Gilda gave me a huge knife to make the first cut in the cake. I'd never held a knife so large before, but I didn't have to do it for very long—just the first cut, and then Pani Gilda took over, professionally slicing the cake and doling out scoops of strawberry ice cream for everyone.

And, when the ice cream had melted and there were only crumbs left of the beautiful cake, Pani Gilda turned a radio on very loud and showed us all how to dance the Twist. If you don't believe me, there's a picture of Zosya and me—party dresses and all—dancing the Twist in front of one of the Kabins. We're smiling despite the dresses.

It had been a truly banner summer.

15

I believe it was Heraclitus who told us that you can't step into the same stream twice. Wolfe said you can't go home again. You get my drift. But that sort of thing urges the inner rebel in me to rampage forth yelling, "Oh YEAH?! Watch me!" The sane, logical part of my brain knows these no-return facts to be demonstrably true. My heart refuses to accept it and yearns for a return to the same home of sweet memory. The connection between those two organs is faulty and results in misfires wherein one or the other is dominant, at least for a time.

So, it should come as no surprise that the siren song of the house on Sixty-eighth Street called my name for decades. And yet, I never went back to my old stomping grounds, not for years. The reasons were myriad and changed over time, as did my life circumstances. At first, when the need to go back was most acute and painful, I didn't have the resources (or permission) to do so. Then I was young and free and more worried about mid-terms and finals and financial aid than about a childhood not-too-long past.

Then I was in love, engaged, in grad school, getting married, having children, having a career, having a husband who was physically present (for the most part) but emotionally absent (for the most part). I was drinking too much, beating up on myself for the failure that I perceived myself to be (having forgotten my achievements as a bona fide magna cum laude, Phi Beta Kappa university graduate), gaining weight, losing weight, drinking still more in an attempt to fill all the holes in my heart and life, then not drinking and turning my life around . . . perhaps too late for some, but just in time for myself.

And then the house on Sixty-eighth Street called my name louder still, until my friend Christine heard it too, and insisted on going with me. And, because she was one of the only people I trusted to understand whatever my reactions might be, I agreed to go.

As we flew into LaGuardia over the Statue of Liberty, I felt that same flip of my heart that I'd felt every time I'd gone back to New York City (but not my home). I'd returned for conferences, professional meetings, and so on in Manhattan, but had never crossed either river or bridge to Brooklyn. I guess I kept it, much like the rose in *Beauty and the Beast*, under an imaginary glass dome, unchanged, in my heart. Except that now, accompanied by my dear insistent friend, that was about to change. I was about to step into the whorl of time-space continuum to be whipped out on a subway platform once as familiar to me as the palm of my hand.

After our taxi deposited us in front of our hotel, Christine and I stowed our luggage in our hotel rooms and walked a few blocks through rain and then sleet of mid-town Manhattan to a nearby subway station, where we waited for the R (formerly RR) train to carry us back to my childhood. For some unfathomable reason, the trip seemed much shorter on this day than it was in my memory. It used to take *forever* to get from Manhattan to Brooklyn, but now it took under an hour.

Are the trains faster now?

Maybe it was that phenomenon of time creeping when you're young and then accelerating as you get older?

I don't know.

What I do know is that when I heard the announcer's voice declaring that we were on the "Brooklyn bound" R train, I felt like he'd nailed my state of being right between the eyes.

That was me: Brooklyn Bound.

I also know that when we emerged from the train and I headed instinctively—like a salmon swimming upstream—for the exit, I took in a long deep breath of subway air. It smelled like home.

It also immediately gave rise to a memory bubble of some sixty years' vintage.

In the days before magnetic cards and digital everything, your ride on the subway required a *token*. But only if you were six years old or older; under six, you rode for free. All my life I'd ridden for free, but so obsessed was I with becoming a Big Girl, that even this apparently insignificant-to-others aspersion cast on my status as Little Girl had been eating away at me for a year. I longed for the day when I would be six years old and have a token ("toyken" in native Brooklynese) of my very own to drop into the slot of the turnstile.

As I may have mentioned previously, throughout my childhood I suffered from an acute truth-telling affliction. Part of this truth-telling affliction manifested as my a) ability to sense deceit, followed immediately by b) inability to tolerate lying or deceit on anyone's part. Anyone's. Something would happen inside me when I heard a blatant lie told or someone would try to cheat on a test or in a game, and it was uncontrollable. Almost like the Hulk—although my personal preference was Captain America—I would start to twitch and breathe faster and, if I didn't catch myself soon enough, true words would fall out of my mouth and cause unpleasantness. I didn't mean to do it, it was only that I appeared hard-wired to be intolerant of prevaricators and their messages, to expose cheaters and always to root for the underdog. Quite possibly, that last character "flaw" may have been directly correlated to my own feelings of underdogedness, but I was too young for psycho-analysis. At least back then. Nowadays I'm surprised that overachieving Type A parents don't condemn their toddlers to personal shrinkdom as soon as they begin talking, the way they get their offspring-to-be onto waiting lists for exclusive private schools even before they're born. But I've digressed (again).

My family did not own a car. We used public transportation, like almost everyone else we knew in New York. Everyone rode the subway. Everyone took the bus. Unless you were rich enough to ride in a cab, of course. Every time I saw a yellow cab go by, I'd look at the rates painted onto the side and wonder how in the world people could afford to go from one place to another when a ride could cost them the equivalent of what we spent on weekly groceries. But New York was, of course, the Land of the Free and the Home of the Brave, not to mention the Land of Opportunity. Apparently, some of those who had been brave enough to seize the Bull of Opportunity by the horns had become quite rich and lived on Park Avenue in Manhattan. I'd see them as we came up out of the subway en route to Russian School on the upper East Side, so I knew those people were real and impeccably dressed.

So, back to the subway.

All my life up to a certain point, I'd ridden the subway for free. I don't know what the rules are now, but back then children up to the age of six were a freebie for the parents. Whichever parent claimed you as you approached the turnstiles was the one who shoved your head under the turnstile arm and propelled you forward before dropping the unique brass token into its proper slot and proceeding through the (now-moving) turnstile. I guess that I had some sort of minor inflated ego problem the summer I turned six, possibly because I'd smacked the snot out of that would-be Romeo at Kozlowski's Kabins.

Having a late-summer birthday ensured that either a) everyone would come to the party because there was nothing else to do, or b) no one would come to the party because they were away on vacation. My parents wisely chose to celebrate my sixth birthday deep in the Catskills, *chez* Kozlowski Kabins, where there was a captive audience. And, of course, Papa had primed the pump by taking our entire ragamuffin crew on various and sundry adventures up and down hills and through woods.

In case I didn't mention it previously, I'd like it noted for the record here that Papa was the absolute BEST at playing Horsefly: a game that was free, fun, and required only that you be in close proximity to a body of water. Someone would scream "HORSEFLY!!" and the entire crew would rush into the lake (in this case) and duck under the water to avoid being bitten by the eponymous airborne beastie. Once in the water, each urchin would take it upon himself (that's the grammatical "he," for you feminazis) to scream "HORSEFLY" as soon as we all came up for air. No one drowned, no one even swallowed any lake water, although I did, from time to time, either get it up my nose or stuck in my ear where it sloshed around until I hopped on one leg long enough to get it out. As I think back on this game with the clarity born of separation by time, I realize that it was a great way to get us away from our long-suffering mothers. In retrospect, I bet it was one of the mothers who started the whole thing. Too late to check on that now.

Back in the city, though, I was stuck in that interminable time-space continuum between the end of summer vacation fun and the start of the new school year. Stuck in a sweltering city where the sidewalks continued to radiate heat long after the sun had set and the streetlights had come on to illuminate our half-hearted games of freeze tag or stoopball. So the day that I woke up and Mama announced that we would be going to buy my school shoes, I felt a frisson of excitement. Not only would I get new shoes, but I'd get to ride the subway, where the temperature was at least twenty degrees below that outside. The added bonus was when you were going down the steps and a train was pulling into or out of the station, you got a huge WHHHHOOOOSSSHHH of air rushing up at you, cooling you off even more. There was always the hazard of it blowing your dress or skirt over your head (à la Marilyn Monroe), so it was important to hold onto the railing (and to wear clean underwear) and to wear shorts if at all possible.

While I went through my morning ablutions in our one bathroom, Mama and Papa were quietly discussing today's outing, how long it would take and whether they'd be able to accomplish anything else on the trip. I came out of the bathroom and slid into my usual chair opposite Papa and to the right of Mama. All of a sudden, I was struck, absolutely gobsmacked, by a thought out of the wild blue yonder. So stunned was I by this "vision," that I let my guard down and blurted out the first words that came to me:

"I'm six years old already!"

Mama gave me the raised-eyebrow look while Papa smiled and said,

"*Nu da!* Of course you're six years old! Did you forget? How could you forget after that big party where you all danced the Twist?"

"No, no, I mean, yes, of course I remember. But I mean *I'm six*. That means you have to get *me* a token to ride the subway! I'm too old to go under the turnstile!"

"*Akh, von ono chto!*" Papa laughed.

I pointed out that this wasn't funny, that we'd be breaking the rules if I was forced to duck under the arm of the turnstile, and pointedly stared at Mama for as long as I could before the raised eyebrow cowed me into submission.

"*Nu, èto yeshcho posmotrim . . .*" Mama sighed and started to collect the breakfast dishes. We'll see, indeed, I thought to myself and started to go about plotting a way to ensure that I'd finally get my own token—the symbol of adulthood.

The subway station was only a block and a half away, so I had to come up with something pretty quickly. I asked *Zaychik* as I was getting dressed, but he was enigmatically silent on the issue. Clearly, I was on my own and I had to think and work quickly. I took the brush off my dresser and walked into the kitchen to have Papa brush and braid my hair for me.

You might think it strange that I'd ask Papa, but there was really nothing odd about it. Papa had been bossed around mercilessly as a boy in the Old Country by an older sister he both adored and feared. Marisha taught him how to braid her hair in all kinds of fancy ways, ensuring she always had a hairdresser at her beck and call. In fact, Papa was much better at doing hair than Mama. He even did her weekly set—with both pink curlers and bobby pins—after she finished her Saturday evening bath.

As soon as I stepped into my usual hair-braiding position in front of Papa's kitchen chair, he sent me back to my room for the comb. I'd been so focused on how to get a token purchased for me that I'd forgotten a key element of the coiffing procedure. At least I'd remembered the ribbon—lavender, to coordinate with the little flowers on the dress Mama was forcing me to wear—and the ponytail holder. To force the maturation issue a bit, I'd opted for one braid rather than two: one of the telltale little girl indicators. Or Pippi Longstocking, for whom I never could develop a liking, no matter how many Pippi books I read.

Dressed, braided, and shod (with anklets), I was ushered out of the apartment and down the stairs. I heard Mama turning her key in the first of the three locks while Papa started after me. I ran along the first-floor hall black rubber runner, flung open the curtained foyer door, took a step onto the tiled foyer floor, and jumped onto the stoop. I estimated the temperature to be at least three hundred degrees on our sunny side of the street. Really. The shady side of Sixty-eighth Street was always at least thirty degrees cooler, in my opinion. And yet, we almost never played with the kids across the street, despite the fact that their stoops were much cooler. Every once in a while in winter they'd venture across our one-way street to thaw out, but we never were able to develop an ongoing working relationship. They were, however, a necessary evil when we were counting heads for stickball.

I'd been tugging at Papa's hand to get a head start to the subway ever since his feet had hit the stoop, but for some reason he insisted on waiting for Mama. I'd been hoping to get to the cashier before she did so that I could announce to everyone within earshot that I was *six* and needed a token of my own. Alas, I was trapped in the overheated doldrums of our stoop, watching Papa make smoke circles from his unfiltered Camel. It never occurred to me that I wouldn't smoke when I grew up; indeed, it never even occurred to me that someone would try to stop me, given that Papa had been smoking since he was seven years old. I did, however, wonder about which brand I'd select: Winston ("tastes good, like a cigarette should")? Marlboro ("come to where the flavor is, come to Marlboro country") with its rugged cowboy and horse? Tareyton (whose "smokers would rather fight than switch" to another brand) with its magazine models sporting one black eye? Or maybe the menthol Newport brand ("tastes fresher") with their smokers engaging in what I imagined were upper class activities: sailing, snorkeling in clear blue Caribbean waters? Or maybe a Kent ("you've got a good thing going") in its classically simple packaging? So many to choose from it could make a girl's head spin.

My smoking reverie was interrupted by Mama's appearance on the stoop, preceded by a brief cloud of perfumed cool air from the foyer and her pulse points. *Krasnaya Moskva* again. The bottle was much more pleasant than its contents—it had an onion dome stopper—but Mama wore it religiously when she went out, maybe because Papa had bought it for her at one of the Russian stores they frequented in search of "real bread" or *kolbasa* that reminded them of "home," the *Rodina*. With a final drag on what remained of the Camel, Papa lifted himself off the stoop shelf, zipped down the steps, threw the Camelstub into the street, and secured his *mundshtuk* in his shirt pocket next to the half-pack of cigarettes. He went back up the steps to help Mama come down (after all, she was wearing heels) then slipped her arm through his as they turned to walk toward Fourth Avenue. I watched them for a few seconds, wondering what they were talking about and if they'd notice that I was missing. Then I remembered the Exile Episode in my life and decided not to chance it; I caught up with them before they got to the intersection.

Mama grabbed my hand as we headed across Sixty-eighth Street "on the green, not in between," past the bar on the corner of Sixty-eighth and Fourth Avenue, next to the Chinese restaurant which was next to the deli next to the Swedish bakery that had somehow added salt, rather than sugar, to the whipped cream frosting of my birthday cake one year and lost our business forever (especially given that Papa took the offending cake straight back and forced the ladies behind the counter to eat a piece).

As we neared the subway entrance, I heard a train pulling into the station and tried to scoot over to the grate to benefit from the whoosh of air but was thwarted by Mama's relentless hold on my hand. Mama never walked on the grates, and I don't think it was because she was afraid of her dress blowing over her head. I think she was afraid of either falling through or getting her heel stuck like she did one year at Macy's, where she'd taken me to see Santa Claus. The event turned memorable and nearly tragic when her heel got stuck in the escalator step and it took several beefy guys to free her and her shoe, nearly preventing us from seeing Santa. After much ado, a near faint on Mama's part, and me getting shoved into the glass perfume counter and rattling some precariously perched expensive creation of Jean Patou that caused the saleslady to blanch, we dusted ourselves off and turned the corner into a magical place.

Enormous Christmas wreaths, fake snow, colossal red, green, and gold bulbs, twinkling lights, sparkles seemingly floating through the air, beautifully dressed ladies in their hat-glove-purse finery, and the endless stream of carols all contributed to an aura of wonder and anticipation. There was simply nothing to compare with Macy's at Christmastime. Nothing. Gimbel's always was an also-ran until it closed its doors and shuttered its windows one last time. But I've digressed. Again.

So, back to the subway.

Mama finally let go of my hand so she could hold onto the railing while going down the stairs. I held onto the railing, too, but I made sure to get in front of her and to go down at a rapid clip so I'd be waiting for my parents (like a good girl) at the bottom of the stairs, not far from the cashier. After a cursory check of pockets (Papa) and purse (Mama)—as Fate would have it—my parents discovered they had no tokens. (AHA!) Mama announced that she'd go get them and turned toward the cashier's office. I saw Opportunity, knew She wouldn't knock twice, and quickly caught up with Mama, pretending I only wanted to see what was going on. For once, Mama didn't suspect me of any wrongdoing and simply held out her hand for me to hold. I complied.

I felt my heart starting to beat faster as I breathed more rapidly.

I watched Mama pull a one-dollar bill out of her wallet and slide it under the cashier's window. I knew that if I didn't do something now, I'd likely have to spend another year ducking under turnstiles. I gently nudged Mama to the side while I pulled myself up to the change counter and stood on my tiptoes, pretending to see what was going on.

Sometimes the Fates can be cruel. At other times, they can look upon our dilemmas from the dizzying heights of Olympus, smile, and give things a gentle nudge in our favor. On this particular day, I suspect that Lachesis took a break from deciding other people's lots in life and floated down to the Sixty-ninth Street station cashier, because what followed could only be explained by Divine Intervention.

The grumpy old cashier in a transit uniform he'd outgrown three sizes ago took one look at me and said,

"So, how old are ya, liddle goyl?"

The Heavens parted, the angels sang, and harps played. And, just as Mama started to answer with "She'zzz . . ." I took advantage of my bilingual superiority and belted out the truth: "I'M SIX! I just had a birthday and *I'm six!*"

I could feel Mama's glare on the back of my neck and at the place that eventually would become a widow's hump. However, in case I hadn't made myself sufficiently clear, I added a bit more information:

"There were *seven* candles on my cake, *six* for me and *one* to grow on!"

Yes, I was breaking many rules—including the "don't talk to strangers" rule, but I was not about to be outdone or overruled, so determined was I to walk proudly through—not under—the turnstile.

"Dat right?"

I nodded "yes" so fast I nearly hit my chin on the change shelf.

"Ya gotta buy her a toyken, lady, she can't ride fer free no more."

And that, as they say, was that.

Eager to demonstrate my law-abiding nature, I stuck my right hand out, palm up, to receive my very first subway token. Wow. There it was: round dull brass with raised lettering on one side reading NEW YORK

CITY TRANSIT AUTHORITY, a carved-out Y in the middle, and GOOD FOR ONE FARE on the other side. I closed my fingers tightly around it so as not to drop it before I got to the turnstile where Papa was waiting.

"Did you hear?" Mama immediately turned on Papa.

"What? What was I supposed to hear?"

"Your daughter."

"Why? What did she say?"

"She told the cashier that she's six!"

"*Nu I chtozh*? She *is* six."

"Now we have to buy her tokens. She can't ride for free anymore."

"*Akh, von ono chto!* So she told the truth?"

"*Nu, da, nu . . .*" Mama retreated into mumbling something *sotto voce* to Papa as she passed a token to him.

"Good girl! *Molodets!*" and here Papa punctuated his remark with a pat on the head that smoothed my flyaway hair. "Always tell the truth, no matter how bitter it is. A lie, no matter how beautiful, is far worse than the ugliest truth. Remember that."

And I did.

Still do, as you can see.

I walked with my shoulders back and with as much adult grace as I could muster to the first turnstile on the right, dropped my token into the slot, and listened to it as it found its way down the chute, ending with a muted metallic clink at the bottom. I took a deep breath and, leaning hard into the metal arm of the turnstile, pushed forward. It moved! And spit me out on the platform that led to the stairs down to the trains! I was on the other side! I'd done it! I'd used the turnstile for the first time in my life! I suddenly felt very mature and much older. I slipped my hand into Papa's large calloused one and we proceeded to descend the stairs, Mama trailing behind us with her lacquered straw purse over her arm, to await the next RR train to Manhattan.

For some reason, I'd always liked the strange smell of the subway—the mix of mechanical, industrial, with peoplesmell. A truly odd combination, but one that always felt like home to me. On this particular day, as we stood on the platform waiting for the local, I took a deep breath and smiled. Now it smelled like victory, too.

16

If I remember right, it was the summer I was to turn seven. We had moved into apartment 2R in our own house in Brooklyn, I had been enrolled in the local school—a mere six city blocks away from home—and first grade was coming to a close.

My parents had launched their discussions about vacation, but conducted their negotiations in German, so I was totally clueless about the where-and-whenness of our escape from New York's brutal egg-sizzling-on-the-hood-of-a-car summer. It was mid-June, so I knew decisions had to be made pretty soon, but no one, thus far, had asked my opinion on the subject. I maintained a low profile and eavesdropped on every Russian conversation they had while pretending to read, play school, or while brushing *Zaychik*.

One weekend evening, after watching the news on our old black and white RCA, Papa suddenly came up with a brilliant idea. Out of the blue. Got up from his chair, switched off the TV, and turned to our new Hi-Fi that we'd carried home from the store a couple of weeks ago. Flipping through the three or four records we owned, Papa selected one and lowered it onto the turntable. Then, he moved the coffee table from our living room into their adjoining bedroom and rolled up the rug in the center of the room. Mama was watching all this activity with a noncommittal air while reclining on the sofa; I sat up and took notice.

"Why are you moving all this stuff?" I asked the Mover and Roller. "Because."

"Because why? What for?"

"What for? You'll see in a minute."

I waited to see.

"*Nu!!* Get up off the sofa!"

"Me? Why?"

"Why? Because I'm going to teach you how to dance."

"Really?!?!?"

My heart exploded with joy. I had watched Papa dance with ladies when we had company or at other people's houses and had always thought he looked particularly debonair and sophisticated (although I didn't know those words at the time). And now, he was going to teach *me* how to dance!! My cup runneth over.

The first thing he did was make me listen, really listen, to a waltz. I believe it was "The Blue Danube." As the first strains hit our ears, a smile came to Papa's face and he softly started "ta-ra-ra-ing" to the music.

"Ta-ra-ra-ra-RAH-bum-bum-bum-bum

"Ta-ra-ra-ra-RAH-bum-bum-bum-bum . . . " tapping his foot for emphasis.

"Sing along with me," he said. So I did, just as softly,

"Ta-ra-ra-ra-RAH-bum-bum-bum-bum

"Ta-ra-ra-ra-RAH-bum-bum-bum-bum . . ."

"Now tap your foot like I'm doing."

"OK. Like this?"

"Perfect."

He took both of my hands in his and started to sway in time to the music. I found that, not only was this fun, but it was very easy. Even after Papa showed me how to move my feet, I didn't think it was very complicated and simply moved in time to the music and the internal rhythm I seemed to have inherited from him. Before I knew it, we were spinning in circles around the living room. We practiced waltzing over and over again to the same "Blue Danube" strains until we were comfortable with each other, I no longer stepped on his feet or tripped over my own, and I had learned how to associate the way he pressed his hand on my back with how I was supposed to turn or move.

Every evening, after dinner, Papa and I would finish watching the news and then practice our dancing. I graduated from the waltz to a variety of polkas which we both thought were much more fun. Once in awhile we'd get the sillies, and Papa would do a little soft shoe on his own or teach me how to do the hopak, traditionally a men-only dance. Well, actually, that's not completely true: the men did the fun type of physically exhausting dancing while the women circled around them in mincing steps, waving colorful kerchiefs. I never learned that part, nor did I want to, because I couldn't picture myself prancing around in a brightly colored *sarafan* with a *kokoshnik* on my head. I simply wasn't that girlish.

It's interesting, from my perspective now, how Papa only taught me the boys' parts in dancing and instructed me in boy things. Back in those days, toys and activities were definitely segregated by gender, and our roles were clearly defined along those lines. I'd like to say that it was because Papa was so ahead of his time, but maybe it was simply because these were the things he knew and enjoyed and he wanted me to know and enjoy them, too. In any event, my being a girl was never an impediment to any of our activities. In fact, it was never even an issue. Except the time that Papa told me he'd wanted a girl and not a boy and how happy he was that I was me.

Papa had been ruled in his childhood by an older sister whom he adored despite the usual sibling torment. He was forced to learn girl things like the different ways to braid hair (Marisha's was raven black, thick, and fell all the way down her back to her waist), how to braid ribbons into hair, how to make hair wreaths out of flowers, and other strictly girl secrets. So, after another story about Marisha, I declared that I was going to grow my hair long so Papa could teach me how to braid it properly. And every night after that, as Papa brushed my hair before bedtime, he'd give the ends an extra gentle tug, pronouncing the magic incantation,

Rosti kosa do poyasa

Rosti kosa do poyasa

enchanting my hair into growing all the way to my waist.

And, over the next few years, that's exactly what it did.

Never discount the power of Papamagic, be it in braid growing or polkaing.

Even now, half a century later, I close my eyes and remember how it felt to have those powerful callused hands gently brush and braid my hair. I remember the feel of the gentle tug to the end of the braid centered carefully down my back, and of the gray eyes that twinkled into mine in the mirror.

If I close my eyes, I can imagine myself, fully grown and young, in a forest green fitted and flared dress with a sweetheart neckline and sparkles, my hair raven-colored and full of luscious curls, skipping across the Pavilion to grab Papa for a few turns on the dance floor to the tune of *Korobushka*. He's wearing a light blue short-sleeved summer shirt and I can feel his shoulder through it as I rest my right hand lightly on it. He stubs out his cigarette, blows the smoke into the air, his chair scrapes the floor as he moves it back to stand. I slip my right arm through his left one as the two of us walk, in time to the music, to the edge of the dance floor. My right hand in his left, we wait for a few beats to go by as we orient ourselves to the music and the dancers.

"*Nu?*" he asks, the way he used to when we'd race.

"*Davay!*" I answer, laughing up at him, still shorter than he is. But the angle is almost nonexistent; I just have to lift my chin a bit.

And we stomp off, Papa whirling and twirling me in a dance to which we know all the words. We don't sing, because we're having too much fun dancing and laughing together, especially at the two fat ladies dancing together and occasionally bopping their bellies together and propelling each other into exoplanetary orbit.

So many women dancing together—they're the ones who have no

men to dance with. Unlike me, forever whirling, stomping, and laughing in a dream that feels too real to let go of—the images, the smells, the lights dancing on the dark lake, the feel of Papa's shoulder under my left hand, and the reassuring feel of my smaller pampered hand in his large callused one. Can you roll elation and security into one feeling? Elacurity? Seclation?

And the whiff of his aftershave commingling with cigarette smoke.

Just one more turn around the dance floor.

Just one.

17

The quality of mercy is not strained;
It droppeth as the gentle rain from heaven
Upon the place beneath. It is twice blest;
It blesseth him that gives and him that takes . . ."[21]

The summer I turned seven my parents found a new place to vacation: the area around ROVA farm, a Russian emigré resort in New Jersey. For some reason unknown to me, we never actually stayed on the compound. We stayed with other families of our socio-economic status in "cottages" (actually, rooms in cottages) that belonged to an elderly couple named Serdyuk. The rooms were almost exactly the same as the ones in the Kabins of fond memory when it came to wallpaper and furnishings—prompting questions in my mind about their decorators—and were located in converted chicken coops. While some buildings had porches, the room we stayed in did not, but it was blissfully close to the washroom. I say this because our little chicken coop housed anywhere from seven to ten people, so if you were late getting out of bed, you might have to make a dash to the woods behind the building for your morning pee. All the rooms opened onto a common

---

[21] William Shakespeare, *The Merchant of Venice*

kitchen—great room furnished with table, chairs, and moldy sofas that poofed out dirt and dead bug parts if you sat down a bit too forcefully.

The interiors were Spartan, but outside we had fields to run through, woods in which to pick mushrooms, the old man's remaining chickens to terrorize, and a slow-burning dump at the very edge of his property to explore. It was perfect for kids. It was perfect for Grisha and me, a friend I met our first day there since his family was in the room next to ours. Grisha was a year or two older than I was, but we hit it off splendidly—no surprise, given my tomboyishness—and actually remained friends for years.

However, not every day of vacation was filled with sunshine and petrified chicken squawks; sometimes, it rained. Rainy nights at the Serdyuks' so-called cottages invariably prompted a fiercely competitive game of BINGO. As soon as a few drops of rain hit the screen door, vacationers would run around closing all the windows and doors lest a flash of lightning bolt through the open window and electrocute one of us. Someone in the crowd always had a story about someone in the Old Country getting fried by a bolt of lightning just as they were sitting down to supper because *someone had left the windows open* and a draft had sucked the lightning in, straight for . . . a) the family's *babushka* or b) the baby in the family. Whether it hit the *babushka* or the baby, the results were the same: hair sizzled to a crisp, lurid details on what happened to various body parts, as well as vivid descriptions of the odor. Yet another cautionary tale from among our resident Mothers and Fathers Grim: another story that generated a round of adult head nodding and mmmmhmmmming. As for us, the intended audience, we accepted it with a grain of salt and filed it in the backs of our brains under G for gavno. [22]

Safety and security of all thus ensured, an adult would be designated (usually by voice vote) to pull the Bingo set out of its secret hiding place. After all, something so precious as the sole game provided for

---

[22] S★&%

the amusement of the renter population couldn't be left out in the open where some misguided child(ren) could decide to play with it unsupervised and lose a critical piece like B12 or N33. The possibilities were too devastating to contemplate, evidently, so the location of The Game was a tightly held secret among the adults. There were a few times when someone would break out a set of dominoes and pull together a foursome for some impassioned tile slamming on the table, but it was *adults only* and we were allowed to sit, observe, and learn as long as we sat still and didn't make a peep. But the domino set was something you had to bring with you, along with many other things that did not come with the rented rooms and common areas, like a decent knife or sheets that didn't smell moldy.

The Bingo routine was always the same, with the kids—usually just Grisha and me—allowed to sit in and play as long as they were quiet and didn't fidget or do anything to distract the serious players from the business at hand. Our parents told us that this game could sharpen our number and money management skills (really? Future Rockefellers out of twenty pennies?), so we were to pay attention and not horse around. Grisha and I usually sat next to each other and communicated via a makeshift improvised language consisting of knee nudges, light foot kicks, and an occasional elbow jab. The jab, however, as a rule, drew a reprimand for Grisha with a warning to "leave Masha alone! Why can't you sit still like she does? Look how nicely she's sitting." Depending on how egregious the offense (or a parent's perception thereof), the warning might be followed by a smack to the back of the head (Grisha's) for emphasis. Especially if someone had brought out a bottle of "the good stuff" and shared it with the other grownups in a few rounds of highballs or shots to encourage conviviality and a sense of community.

Après reprimand, I made sure to sit up straighter on the sticky repainted rickety wooden kitchen chair, straightening my braid in the process and tucking my flyaway hairs demurely behind my ears. Not once in all those years did I mention that it had been one of my flipflopped little kicks that had prompted his elbow jab response. I just sat there like butter wouldn't melt in my mouth, looking as innocent as possible, with a tiny Mona Lisa smile playing on my lips. After all, I had a reputation as a "good girl" and paragon of virtue to maintain while his was shot from the get-go simply because he was a boy and misbehavior was expected from him. I pretended to study my two cards while surreptitiously surveying the Barbarians at the Gate, i.e, the other players at the table. I knew that I was outgunned moneywise and that my ability to remain at the table and in the game depended heavily on my winning at least a couple of rounds. Having been trained to be the "best in class" by my parents—through both encouragement and terror—I naturally expected to win at least most of the time. In retrospect, this was a good initiation into Life and Karma: 1) you can't always get what you want (just like Mick Jagger sang) or expect and 2) both good and bad deeds come back around to you as either reward or retribution.

The most ferocious players were the old ladies with tightly curled hair in shades of apricot, lavender, and blue. Once a week, they would prevail upon Old Man Serdyuk to drive them to the local hairdresser for a "set and comb out," where they dutifully left their twenty-five cent tips and complained about the service in a language no one but they understood. Since they smiled while doing it, everyone in the salon thought they were "just the *nicest* ladies" and treated them like the royalty they claimed to have been in Mother Russia. For Bingo, they chose their seats at the table with an eye toward both luck—if one of them had sat in a "losing" seat one night, she'd never sit there again—and keeping a close eye on the caller to make sure there were no shenanigans with the numbered wooden barrels in the linen bag with a drawstring closure. *Doveryay no proveryay*, as the late President Reagan tried to say. Trust but verify.

The caller—a rotating honor—was selected by public acclamation, with the choice usually falling to someone who either didn't need, or who remembered to bring, glasses. The other requirement was a loud voice to accommodate some of the more mature players who managed always to have water in their ears from swimming or showering. The caller would announce the never-changing rules to refresh everyone's memory: five cents per card for the initial ante, one cent per card thereafter; five matches in any direction; no yelling "BINGO!" unless you were positive; and, most important: the caller had to read aloud all the drawn numbers to verify that a) the win was legitimate and b) no one else had won. In the unlikely event there was more than one winner, you split the pot per stirpes.

The stack of cards would be passed ceremoniously from one player to the next for selection. Oh! The anticipation! I could barely sit still, fearing in my little heart of hearts that that nasty Auntie Sonya would take my winning card. I just knew she did it to be evil and to torment me in yet another way. The nasty old baggage made it a daily practice to rat me out to Mama for some real or imagined offense, prompting an immediate disciplinary response that usually resulted in my forcible detention inside on the musty and dusty old sofa in the common area while my cohorts romped outside. A cloud of dust motes and dead bug parts would poof into the air as I plopped my detained self onto the couch every single time, leading me to wonder on one occasion how many gazillions of dead bug pieces lay buried in the cushions and beneath them; it was a gruesome prospect. Auntie Sonya never complained about me to Papa, but I figured it was because he was considerably bigger than she was and took grief from no one, ever. The protective Papa Wall stood tall and strong between me and the rest of the world.

This wicked old hag Auntie Sonya also had the habit of waking up first and commandeering the only available toilet for what seemed like hours, forcing the other vacationers to stand in line outside with their feet in the early morning dew on the grass (said to keep your feet from being stinky), towels over their arms, soap, toothbrush, and toothpaste in hand. I secretly thought she brushed every single one of her nasty clicking false teeth one at a time just to make us all wait in line like the peasants she deemed us to be. More than once I'd had to make a run for it to the woods where I was terrified of being bitten on my privates by a snake. It never happened, but you never know: it's that one time that you're not watching . . .

The Aunties Klava and Varya were slightly more benevolent. Slightly. One childless widow and one old maid took it upon themselves to instruct all the parents in that cottage (or any other, for that matter) on the fine points of raising their children properly, so they would grow up to be *kul'turnyye lyudi* (i.e., civilized and tamed to the Aunties' liking). They took upon themselves the obligation that every single Old Person in Russian society shoulders: the duty to reprimand the young at each step. Out loud, in public, so that their words would serve as a lesson to everyone within earshot. They smelled of old face powder, mothballs, and the cheap dime store perfume they seemed to bathe in. We hated all three of them with a purple passion, but knew enough to apologize—whether we'd misbehaved or not—and to look meek in their presence. If you could fake humility with them, you had it made. Another Life Lesson packaged in Old Lace (and arsenic, no doubt).

With a great deal of shoulder scarf flapping, poofs of powder, and snarky *sotto voce* comments on the state of the table, these Erinyes would select their cards and seats and nestle onto them very much like the Rhode Island Reds we saw ranging free near the perpetually-smoking dump at the edge of the Serdyuks' property. One final, pointed stare at us through their cat eye glasses, the counting out of the transparent red hard plastic circles we used to cover called numbers, and some throat clearing from the Caller and we settled in for combat.

I must admit that I preferred male voices to female voices, even at that early age. For some reason, men's voices were more solid and reassuring while women's voices tended toward the panicked and shrieky, especially when they were urged by the Aunties to speak louder: "*Gromche!* I still have water in my ears from that horrible lake!" (My little brain typically was ready with a retort along the lines of "Well, who told you to go swimming, you old *ved'ma*?[23] You nearly scared the babies off the

---

[23] Witch

beach" but my instincts toward self-preservation outweighed the urge to speak my mind. So I'd kick Grisha under the table. For the results, see above.) Of course, I always liked it when Papa was the caller. I sat either right next to him or directly across from him because we had our own little language, too. That, and I felt very protected from the Aunties when he was there—they didn't pick on me (as much) when he was around.

And so, the Game would begin, with Grisha's father, Uncle Yura, calling the numbers out in his slow, methodical, professorial way: O . . . 6. Pause pause pause. O . . . 72. Pause, pause, pause. I . . . 25. (Usually by this time, one of the Aunties would have asked both for repetition of at least one number and then a translation of it into Russian. I unobtrusively nudged Grisha. See above.) B . . . 15. On and on in that monotonous drone until finally someone—not me—would yell BINGO!!! The numbers would be re-recited and the loot pushed toward the winner. We'd ante up our penny per card and made ready to do battle with the Forces of Chance again. On and on and on, with everyone winning except me. With each new round, my stash of pennies would grow smaller, as would I. I started sinking into my chair and my eyes started stinging while I tried to be very grown up and not cry. Usually, right around the time when my nostrils started to flare and the room started getting hazy, Papa would offer to call the numbers for Uncle Yura, who was always delighted to be rid of the authority and responsibility conveyed by the stained linen bag that held the worn wooden numbered barrels.

Papa made a great show of shaking the bag with both hands—in front of him, to his left, to his right, above his head, and again in front of him. The barrels clacked in rhythm with the Aunties' teeth as the B12s ran into the N44s into the G59s, over and over, to demonstrate to everyone that everything was honest and aboveboard—no stacking of numbers or of the odds here! Round one would go as the previous rounds had, and I'd sink still lower in my chair. Round two—ditto. By this time I was sitting on my braid—the one Papa had so diligently braided a colored ribbon into earlier that evening. But I soldiered on as valiantly as I could—no quitter I, no matter how beaten down. Luck clearly was *not* being a lady that night, no matter how many times Frank Sinatra asked. And again, G 55 . . . I 17 . . . Hey! Wait! I have those! I'd miss the next two or three, then—as if by magic—I'd land two more in a row. Four. I had *four in a row.* Now, if I could just . . . And then, miraculously, there it would be: N 33! BINGO!!! That's me!!! I won!!! Of course, one of the Aunties would call for a repeat of the numbers, which Papa would dutifully call out . . . except for the last one, which he had absentmindedly thrown back into the sack right after he called it the first time. Having learned a very good lesson from Mama's Unforgiveable Colossal Gambling Loss during their DP Camp days, I would smugly rake in my winnings and leave the table to pursue other interests that didn't cost me any of my hard won money.

Years later, Mama—in one of her less controlled moments—told me that Papa used to fake the number to let me win. According to her story, when he'd see that I was losing all the time, he'd offer to call the numbers and would orchestrate the win for me. At first I was stunned by this little revelation: the man who taught me that the truth, no matter how bitter, is always better than the most beautiful lie? The man who never let me win a race *intentionally cheated* and let me win at Bingo? Why? What could he possibly have been thinking? I chewed on this dilemma endlessly, until my agitated, restless brain finally came to the following conclusion: in games of skill, you have to keep working at it; in games of chance, Fortuna occasionally needs a helping hand. Especially if the child you love is about to cry.

Aha! Got it.

The quality of mercy is not strained, indeed. It blesses both the giver and receiver.

18

Ekh yablochko, kuda katishsya?
V NKVD popadyosh—ne vorotishsya!

Other kids had "ring around the rosy;" I had the above dit-
ty—a cautionary couplet sung to a jaunty tune warning the
little apple to stay out of secret police hands lest it not return.
Charming. Our little family had good reason to sing it: at the beginning of WWII, Papa had nearly been shot for desertion by an NKVD
colonel in a *rasstrel'nyy podval* or shooting basement. Just another false
accusation in a Soviet Union swimming in the blood of its countrymen.
Not since the Albigensian Crusade had a tyrant been responsible for so
many deaths of his own people.

Over the years, Papa told this story in increments, never from
start to finish, but I managed to piece it together over time. Also,
over time, I observed in that magnificent generation of survivors, an
almost eery bravado mingled occasionally with a near-indifference to
the horrors they had experienced. Over shots of vodka (for Papa the
self-imposed limit was three) followed by numerous *zakuski*, my parents
and their friends would relive episodes from their past *na rodine*, in the
Motherland. Invariably, the final sentence would be something akin to
"*Ekh, zachem byloye vspominat'?*"—a twist of the head, a tear in the eye,

a duck-call-sounding *"ekh!"* and the briefest of pauses while everyone's nerves settled back down. Cigarettes would come out, lighters would be flicked, and the smoke would curl toward the ceiling, taking the words and memories with it.

The women would click open their purses and take out their embroidered, laundered, and pressed hankies to wipe their tears and blow their noses. Widowed, deserted, orphaned—or some combination of those—they cried so easily back then. Everyone had at least one tragedy in the family—most had more than one—and so they were able to empathize with each other in the fullest sense of the word. And then, as if by magic, someone would start singing a song from the War Years or even the revolution-civil war-famine-purges years—their youth. And everyone would join in. Whatever started as sad, invariably led to happy songs and those, in turn, inspired people to dance. The rugs would be rolled up, furniture moved, and an impromptu ballroom created. Some singing, some dancing, everyone Enjoying Life. After all, they had survived against unspeakable odds in inhumane conditions.

As I look around at my generation, I wonder if, in our sheltered, protected lives, we haven't lost a measure of empathy or sympathy toward our fellow humans. It seems as though we've forgotten how to truly relish Life; perhaps, because we were given so much in peacetime by parents who had lost everything in The War or during the years of terror that preceded it. But, again, I've digressed.

So, you need to hear Papa's story about his encounter with the NKVD colonel. However, before you do so, here are a couple of brief asides:

1. Mama told me the part about what Papa said; and,
2. She actually used the *really bad language* when she told the story. This was a shock to my system, because I never ever never heard either of my parents use bad language. Ever.
3. Years later, Mama told me that Papa was something of a legend in his use of bad language in Russian *and* English. Well, knock

me over with a feather. And I always thought he didn't speak English well. Go figure. The things we don't know about our parents. [24] In his poem *"There are no uninteresting people in the world . . ."* Yegeniy Yevtushenko mentions this strange phenomenon of knowing someone really well and yet realizing that you know nothing about them. That's where I was in that moment when Mama told me the story: *". . . I pro otsa rodnogo svoego/My, znaya vsyo, ne znayem nichego."*

So, here's how the story went:

Papa and two of his fellow soldiers were the only survivors after their unit was encircled by Germans and massacred. I don't know whether they faked death to survive or got buried under their fellow soldiers' corpses or what, but their unit was sacrificed so that the bedraggled remains of the division could fall back.[25] Cut off from their own division, these three survivors had to find their own way back with no weapons or protective gear, although Papa had managed to hang onto his *pilotka*, or garrison cap, somehow. (Based on how poorly equipped the Soviet army was in their region, Papa must've figured he wouldn't be issued another one.) And, in the spirit of "if I didn't have bad luck, I'd have no luck at all," they were discovered by Soviet recon, captured, and dragged back to answer for the crimes of desertion and treason. It's amazing they weren't shot on the spot, actually.

The three were separated so they couldn't collude on their story. (I wish I knew the names of the other two, but I'm not sure Papa ever told me. Names were a sensitive issue among immigrants since many changed their names along the way to protect families "back home" from Soviet retribution.) One by one, they were shoved into separate

---

[24] See the seventh stanza of Yevgeniy Yevtushenko's poem, *"Lyudey neinteresnykh v mire net . . ."* (There are no uninteresting people in the world . . ."). The last two lines, *"I pro otsa rodnogo svoyego/My, znaya vsyo, ne znayem nichego"* (We, knowing everything about our father, know nothing at all [about him].)

[25] Iosif Stalin: "One death is a tragedy, a million is a statistic."

rooms in the basement of what had once been an elegant pre-revolutionary palace. In each room, an armed uniformed interrogator was sitting behind a table, his back to a wall. The desk was clear except for a couple of official-looking documents and a handgun. In retrospect, I suspect Papa's interrogator was a member of military intelligence, but to Papa's way of thinking, they were all NKVD and *vsyo odna svoloch'*—the same bastards. I guess if you've just escaped with your life from near-certain death at the hands of the enemy and are suddenly thrown into another near-death situation (from your own people, no less), you might be forgiven for lumping them all into the same odious dung heap of assholes.

Papa was shoved into a darkened room that was hot, stuffy, and smelled like someone had butchered an animal in it a few days ago. It seemed as though that smell and the stench of *makhorka*[26] cigarette smoke started to permeate his skin and clothes; a wave a nausea hit him and he swayed on his feet. He couldn't remember the last time he'd eaten something and he said that the room grew dark in front of his eyes as he tried not to vomit. (Ding! Ding! Ding! *That's* where I get my "stomach issues" from—Papa. Maybe neither of us was cut out to stomach Life's injustices and vicissitudes of Fate.) As his eyes adjusted to the light, Papa saw that the walls were pockmarked with bullet holes and blood smears. He also realized that the reason his feet were sticking to the floor was that the floor was covered with a thick coat of congealed blood, fresh puddles here and there flickering with reflected light from the sole suspended light bulb.

A fat, balding full colonel was sweating through his uniform behind

---

[26] Makhorka is a rough cut home-grown tobacco used in hand-rolled cigarettes. Any paper available—including newspaper—was used to roll the cigarette. Unless, of course, Comrade Stalin's picture was in the paper. If you used THAT for a cigarette you'd be arrested and tried for any number of crimes. I am not making this up. Mama actually knew someone who was arrested for using such a newspaper to wrap herring to carry home from the store. She never made it home. Neither did the herring.

the desk. He'd wedged a scrap of wood under one of the legs to keep the table from rocking. A thin folder sat on the lower left side of the desk. The colonel took a filthy rag out of his pocket and started polishing the gun. All you could hear in the room was the colonel's heavy breathing and the clicks and spins of the gun. He'd load the gun, spin-spin-spin, take aim at Papa, set it down, unload the gun. Light a cigarette and blow the smoke in Papa's direction. Then again. And again. And again. For what seemed like hours. And then the interrogation began. I can only imagine what was said back-and-forth during this process, but I only know what was said verbatim toward the end of the ordeal.

Papa was a man of many fine qualities. Patience, however, was not one of his virtues. After the seventh or twentieth retelling of his story, after having the gun pointed at him repeatedly, after listening to the colonel call him a liar and traitor, after hours and hours, Papa's patience ran out. He told me that he figured he'd be shot anyway, so he wasn't going to keep his mouth shut anymore. With valor outrunning discretion by miles, Papa threw his *pilotka* at the colonel's head, missing by inches, summoned up what remained of his voice and barked, "Shoot! Go ahead, shoot me, you mother*&%ing kike!! Shoot!! What?! Not enough Russian blood has been spilled for you? SHOOT!"

And, after a final spin of the revolver, the colonel spit on the floor, stamped out his cigarette, looked at Papa, and told him to get the f*&% out. Just like that. I guess the officer figured that, Papa's momentary anti-Semitism notwithstanding, he must've been telling the truth or was crazy, because no one would ask to be shot if he were lying or sane. So why waste a bullet on a psycho? Besides, Comrade Stalin's order applied to each Soviet soldier: save the last bullet for yourself.

The Life Lesson I took away from this was: don't back down. Stand your ground. Stand for the truth, even if it costs you everything. Be willing to lay down your life, but do the right thing. So, where were you and what were you doing at the age of thirty-three? Uh huh. Then you see my point.

All three men (oddly enough, from the same village) were released to what remained of their unit to fight another day.

And I never found out what happened to his *pilotka*.

I suspect that most American children grew up hearing stories of princesses, knights in shining armor, frogs, ogres, and witches that roasted children who strayed too far from home. The stories on which I was raised were stories of the horrors of revolution, civil war, dekulakization, starvation, and World War II. Stories of escape from the Nazis, from the Soviets and—unbelievably—the Allies and repatriation. Stories of families torn apart; stories of the Purges and how people disappeared into Black Marias[27] in the middle of the night never to be seen again; stories of families being dispossessed and exiled during Stalin's dekulakization campaign; stories of women stepping off mountains into the river Drau near Lienz, clutching their babies to their chests, rather than face repatriation to the *rodina*. Stories of my family members being tried on trumped-up charges, jailed for no reason, executed, sent to the camps, or simply dying in jail. Mama's father was jailed on trumped-up charges and literally was squished to death in a jail cell meant to hold three but had over forty men crammed into it. My maternal great-uncle, as another ferinstance, was sentenced to seven years hard labor in the camps for corresponding with a foreign national. He signed his name with an X. His illiteracy, apparently, was no hindrance to this evil anti-Soviet correspondence. The day after his wife gave birth to twin boys, she got up from the childbirth bed to make a sack full of rusks for him to take into exile. She handed it to him as the convicts were being marched under armed guard through the village to the waiting rail cars headed east.

I come from sturdy stock.

---

[27] A type of black sedan used exclusively for these purposes. And for senior members of the NKVD to go girl hunting at night: they'd spot an attractive woman walking alone, stop the car, grab her, rape her and sometimes let her go. Other times, they'd keep her for a few days and then shoot her to complete the fun. No witnesses, no problem.

To say that my world view was shaped early and firmly would be to understate the case: my ogres were human beings whose actions revealed the worst aspects of man's inhumanity to man. Much like the witches in your stories, the humans in mine could be nice-as-pie to you one day, and then rat you out to the secret police the next day on some phony charge just to get your square meters of living space reassigned to them. Danger lurked everywhere, and it looked "normal." It looked just like you. But the point is that you never knew when they'd show up for you, why, or if you'd ever see your family again.

The reason I'm telling you all this is so that you'll understand what happened on a clear July day lakeside in New Jersey and its aftermath. Because the story is worth telling, and because you need to understand how unending and pervasive fear—not for yourself, but for your family—can be when you come from the Workers' Paradise.

It was a particularly lovely crystal-blue-sky July day at the lake. Grisha's, Iuda's, and our blankets were next to each other, which was convenient to running out of the water and communally begging our parents for money for burgers, ice cream, name-your-treat. Even though we always brought food and drink with us, everything tasted better when you paid for it and someone else made it. The sound of a gaggle of children, voices merging into an Alban Berg-like atonal high-pitched cacophony, aimed at parents who wanted only to be left to doze in peace, is incredibly effective. Our parents barely grumbled when they handed us our dimes and sent us on our way to Dunya's Diner—a dismal pea-green shack (a color dubbed *"caca d'oie malade"*[28] by one of my adult friends) with peeling paint, perched precariously at the edge of the lake near the rent-a-rowboats.

Ah, the Diner! It was a diner in name only, since there were only three patched stools to perch on—only two of which actually spun around—and the menu was limited to shoe-leather burgers that leaked grease onto the bun, decades-old hot dogs, three types of soda, and

---

[28] French for sick goose poop.

six tubs of ice cream that varied depending on what Dunya could buy cheapest. Not high on quality, but we weren't exactly clients with discriminating palates. Still, when you only had one dime to spend, you were wise to take your time making your selection, looking for the tell-tale ice crystals that screamed "melted and refrozen!"

Old Dunya was her usual *ved'ma* self, cigarette hanging out of her mouth, gray hair (or what remained of it) restrained by a hair net, sweat trickling down her forehead and temples, her basso profundo repeating the same mantra: *"Nu?* Vaht you vahnt?! I no have all day. Vaht? Hooory ahp!"* Bathing suits dripping on the worn green tile floor, we milled around the ice cream tubs, shoving each other out of the way to get a better look, wondering sotto voce whether she had dripped sweat or ashes into the ice cream and, if she had, which tubs were affected. *"Nu?!* Make up yoor maynd or gitout! Hooory ahp! Yooo are making mess on floor. I no have all day mop up for you. *Nu??"*

Couples were out on the lake in rowboats, the Pavilion had just been opened, and local teens were sweeping, mopping, and setting up tables in preparation for that night's festivities. The sunlight danced on the liquor bottles lined up on shelves in the bar. Live music, dancing! I mentally started rehearsing the steps for *korobushka*, the dance I'd tried to learn the previous week-end. My reverie was interrupted by Iuda's not-so-gentle shove.[29]

"Hey! Lookit what's goin' on!"

Not only was Iuda a liar and a snitch, she was the biggest gossip around, having inherited her overweight-undereducated-pockmarked-redheaded mother's worst traits. While I tried my best to avoid her, I was nevertheless consistently counseled by Mama to "be nice" to Lyudochka (she even used the diminutive!). I wasn't even allowed to

---

[29] *Iuda* was what I secretly called my overweight, freckled, and obnoxious god-sister. It was left over from my learning to talk days when I couldn't pronounce "L." It fit her personality to a T: it's the Russian version of Judas. More on her and her clan later. But I've digressed. Again.

bite her back after I came home with bite marks from Iuda's nasty sharp teeth up and down my left arm. Don't ask. Did I harbor resentments? Like I said, don't ask.

Her greasy left palm slapped my arm as she flailed her burger with her right hand. In her hurry to draw my attention to the action, Iuda had forgotten the "don't talk with your mouth full" rule and was spitting burger bits left and right. My stomach started to do mild flips in preparation for full-on nausea.

"Lookit it! Fight! It's your Papa! I'm gonna go look!"

"I think you should probably stay here . . ." I mumbled as my stomach started to twist itself into its long-distance bus ride *gonna barf* position.

"Shaddap. I'm gonna go see."

From a distance, as though through a haze, I saw something akin to a scuffle and heard grown-ups yelling. I noticed that it took about four big men to hold Papa back, and there was a lot of yelling of Russian words I'd never heard and didn't understand. The crowd was growing thicker as rubberneckers peeled themselves off their blankets and beach chairs to get a closer look at the goings-on; Iuda wormed her way through the scrum of grown-ups to get a better look, clutching the ragged remains of her burger. I heard a male voice yell, "*Ty chto?! S uma soshol?!*" which led to a renewed effort on Papa's part to break the hold. If there was one thing you never, ever said to Papa, it was any form of the word "crazy." That was the only thing he hated (and maybe feared).

By this time, the Barfing Band was playing loud and proud in my stomach, and the tell-tale light sweat had broken out on my forehead. My ears felt as though they were full of lake water, my eyes started to water, and I was having trouble breathing. Even Grisha noticed, but he thought it was the Dunya effect and dragged me over to the picnic table side where I could sit and look at the water lilies while trying to breathe normally again.

"Hey, are you OK?" Grisha's concern was fueled by his never-ending and futile crush on me. I jumped when his hand touched my left shoulder.

"Uh, yeah. I think Dunya's cigarette made me kinda sick," I lied.

"Yeah, I know," laughed Grisha, "she has that effect on me, too." Because Grisha was two years older than I was, he liked to throw around adult words and phrases to impress me. Little did he know that by third grade, I was reading at the ninth grade level and could out-word him on any given day. I simply chose not to rub his nose in my lexical superiority. After all, he was my buddy and ally against Iuda and you couldn't buy that kind of loyalty.

We could hear the volume subsiding in the swimming area with the exception of a few choice phrases we could recognize, like "*sukin syn*" and "*ubil by tebya—podonka*" and some other expressions I couldn't understand but that involved someone's mother. We batted around a few theories on what might have happened, but neither Grisha nor I had any facts at our disposal, so mostly we were just talking to cover the scary sounds coming from the direction of our parents.

I remember how peaceful the water lilies looked. I remember thinking that there was nothing anyone could offer me to make me swim among them. I was happy to admire them from a distance, but you'd never get me to step off the dock into their midst. Who knew what horrid thing might be lurking there? I've had a lifelong fear of stepping into murky waters (literally and figuratively) in which whoknowswhat lurked, waiting for me to slip into its domain and drag me into the muck. (The ocean was different. There, I waited to be eaten by a shark or swallowed whole by a whale and had an escape plan ready should the latter ever come to pass.) The only safe place to swim was a pool, where you could see *everything*; unfortunately for me, I got pink eye every time I swam in one of New York City's finest pools. (Of course, if Papa was with me in any of those *natural* venues, I felt perfectly safe. Probably because I'd climb on top of his shoulders.)

The sounds had stopped, people were shuffling back to their beach blankets and chairs, and I saw the rather portly and disheveled Leonid

Petrovich from a couple of weeks ago leave the area with his wife. I saw about six people on our blanket, Iuda in her snooping mode, prancing around the periphery, pretending to practice dance steps while annihilating the remains of her burger. Finally, I saw Papa light a cigarette and blow out a whoosh of white smoke. I sat on my hands to keep them from shaking. Disagreements, arguments of any kind, raised voices always sent me into a terrified paralyzed state. It wasn't so much that I always thought things were my fault and punishment would follow swiftly and painfully (thanks, Mama), as the disruption to the smooth flow of Life that upset me.

Eventually that day, things went back to the way they'd been before the Bol'shoy Skandal (as I would henceforth refer to this episode). Grisha made me get the mint chocolate chip ice cream (which I didn't like but pretended to) instead of the peach, and we finished up the cones as the gooey mess ran over our hands. Sticky and dirty, we raced to the water and dove into the brown lake, leaving Iuda to sit out the mandatory "no swimming for thirty minutes after you eat" rule on the blanket with her mother. When we got tired of each other, we raced to my family's blanket and persuaded Papa to go with us to the Big Humongous Tree whose branches hung over the Really Deep Part where older kids were climbing the tree and jumping into the lake. The trick was NOT to go over the falls, which lurked dangerously close to the prime diving spot.

I was quite proud of the fact that my papa was the only adult climbing the tree and jumping off it. In fact, he seemed to be having more fun than the rest of us. I had a flash of embarrassment when one of the kids accused Papa of wearing his underwear (he had a light-colored bathing suit with some sort of pattern on it that could easily have been mistaken for boxers) but it was quickly forgotten when he gave me a boost up to the first branch and I launched myself into the Very Deep part of the lake. I was the only girl climbing the tree and jumping, but it never occurred to me that there was anything strange about that circumstance. I regarded all boys as friends or potential friends and felt much more comfortable with them than with their frilly-bathing-suited moon-eyed female equivalents. Girls told tales about you while boys, if they had a problem with you, just socked you. I've always preferred the direct approach.

Later that day, after we'd gone back to the Serdyuk compound to eat dinner and prep for the evening's dancing at the Pavilion, both Grisha and I tried to wheedle information from our parents on what had happened that day. Both of us were told in no uncertain terms that it was none of our business. We huddled on the mildewed singing-spring sofa in the common room to strategize. Naturally, we decided to redouble our efforts and pledged to conduct espionage anywhere and everywhere we could. We figured that Iuda's cabin was the best place to start: Gossip Central.

Iuda's young Aunt Zhenya[30] had just arrived for the week-end from New York City and doubtless would be catching up on local gossip from her older sister, Shura—Iuda's mother. Grisha and I figured that if we hung around the water hand pump by their cabin, we might be able to catch some news on the breeze through the open windows. We brought along a ball to kick around to further mask our clandestine collection activity.

Zhenya touched up the flaming red color of her sister's hair and then carefully started to roll her own blonde strands onto pink curlers. Grisha and I quietly speculated between kicks as to which Miss Clairol variant Zhenya would be sporting this week-end. She'd clearly fallen

---

[30] Many years later, I learned that Iuda's father—my godfather (about whom there are many stories, maybe one will make it into this book)—had been in love with Zhenya, who was the prettier and livelier of the two sisters. When he went to her Old Believer father to ask for Zhenya's hand in marriage, my godfather was told that the elder sister had to marry first, according to their traditions. If he was intent on marriage, my godfather could have Shura, the elder sister. Intent on marriage, my godfather settled for the pockmarked, sullen, red-haired Shura and regretted the decision for the rest of his life. The worst part was that, in keeping with Russian tradition, the groom paid for everything. Little did poor Vasya know that he'd keep on paying all the days of his life.

for either the "The closer he gets, the better you look" or "Blondes have more fun" advertising ploy hook, line, and sinker because she modeled a different shade of blonde every week. There was, of course, the visual disconnect between her [name your blonde] locks and her brunette eyebrows, but the fire engine red lipstick she wore seemed to pull the whole look together somehow.

So, Grisha and I kept kicking the ball around and around the cabin, trying to get closer in case there was an inadvertent spilling of the beans. He'd kick it to me as I backed up to the cabin, forcing me to "chase the ball" as it neared the house. I'd dribble it for effect past the windows, then kick it back to Grisha, who had rounded the north side of the cabin. And so it went until we'd covered all four sides, worked up a sweat and a thirst, and heard nothing except gossip about which man might be back this week-end to dance with Zhenya, whose prospects for marriage were fading with every lighter shade of blonde she chose for her hair.

After a quick several shlurps at the hand pump—that water was the coldest and best tasting we'd ever had (probably because we had to cup our hands to catch it and then shlurp from them like random aborigines)—we'd return to our intelligence collection mission. We heard nothing about what interested us, but we did hear quite a bit of "oooohhhh"ing," "oooooooooooooyyyyyyying" and "*da-ty-chto*"ing from Zhenya as she interrogated Shura on this or that man from last week-end. From a distance, we could hear our mothers calling us in and blissfully ignored them, figuring that we had a good ten minutes until they marched down the field to catch us. And then I heard the distinctive "feeeeeew-wheeeeeet" of Papa's whistle, turned on my heel, and beat feet toward our cabin, leaving Grisha behind to listen for any information that might spill out of the Ivanovs' cabin. Ignoring that whistle could have had dire consequences like being forced to sit out tonight's dancing, so I knew better than to risk it.

Shura and Zhenya's family claimed to be Leningraders in the hopes that the legendary beauty of Russia's imperial capital would lend them the polish and caché they naturally lacked. However, we all knew that they were born in Leningrad as much as I was born Scarlett O'Hara and secretly snickered behind their backs at this improbable stretch toward gentility. True, they had the distinctive (uneducated) speech of Northern Russian marked with heavily accented O's (as in "OH, aren't you vile?). In Slavic linguistics this phenomenon is called "okan'je," in case you were wondering if I made it up. However, all that meant was that they originated somewhere north of the Fifty-eighth parallel; it said nothing about education, upbringing, or sophistication. They were not, in my eyes, *"kul'turnyye lyudi,"* particularly since their offspring chose to malign and even bite me whenever the opportunity presented itself. And I was unable to defend myself, unable to cross the red line my parents had drawn in insisting that I be nice to my godsister no matter what.

Here's an example of how offensive it is to the non-northern ear. The verb *GOVORIT'* (spelled as transliterated here), "to speak" or "to say" is pronounced as follows in Contemporary Standard Russian:

[*GUHVAHRIT'*] (first O reduced to an "uh," second O reduced to an "ah")

Unless you're Iuda's mother, aunt, grandmother, grandfather, or uncle. In which case, you pronounced it this way:

[*GOVORIT'*] (both Os given "full value" as OH)

Say a couple of words and not only will I tell you where you're from, I'll also tell you whether you can read anything beyond a primer. Just sayin'.

Grisha and I (not necessarily in that order) were sent—towel and soap in hand—to the shower room to scrub the grime off our sweaty selves so that we could be turned into respectable representatives of our families before we all set off for the Pavilion. I returned to find both of my parents ready to go and quickly threw on a dress that allowed freedom of movement and wasn't too foofy. While Papa finished braiding a ribbon into my hair, Mama was trying to wear me down with her insistence that I take a sweater for later in the evening. I was pretty sure I wouldn't need one, since I could feel the heat radiating off my sunburned shoulder blades. I'd gotten a bit "overdone by the sun" while snooping and was now paying the piper with every move of the sundress' straps. The worst part was, of course, that I was suffering in vain: we had learned absolutely nothing.

I learned—many, many years later, when all probability of danger had passed—what had set Papa off that day. Here's how the story went:

One Saturday afternoon, while Mama and Papa were sitting on their blanket at the lake, a man and his wife had walked past my parents. They stopped, turned around, and stared at them. Then they walked back and stopped at the blanket.

The man said, "Nikolay?"

Papa said, "Nikolay."

Man: "Grechenkov?"

Papa: "*Nu, a chto?*"

And then, a flicker of recognition from both Mama and Papa: it was Lyonya. From their village in Russia.

Imagine this: you're living in a country thousands of miles away from home, among strangers. Suddenly, out of nowhere, appears a guy who lived down the street from you "back home." Your parents knew his parents; you two knew each other. How would you feel?

So you understand that the reunion was a joyous one, with much hugging, backslapping, crying on the women's part, and so on. I was "feeeeeew-wheeeeeet"ed out of the lake to come and meet these *zem-lyaki*[31] of my parents. I gave up trying to race Grisha from the diving board to the boat ramp and obediently dragged myself out of the water and to the blanket, where I proceeded to drip and shiver until Papa threw a towel over my shoulders. I dutifully and respectfully gave both Leonid Petrovich and his missus, Klavdiya Ivanovna, a firm (wet) hand-shake, a smile, and a *"zdravstvyute, ochen' priyatno"*[32] through chattering

---

[31] Roughly translates as "fellow countrymen"

[32] Hello, very nice to meet you.

teeth. After a brief interrogation on my age, which grade I was entering, and how I was doing at school (Papa answered that one for me, saying I was an *"otlichnitsa"*[33] in everything), I was released to continue my swimming exploits while the adults returned to their reminiscing and catching up.

Fast forward a couple of weeks.

Leonid Petrovich and Klavdiya Ivanovna have descended again upon the Russian *émigré* resort in the wilds of New Jersey from their New York apartment. They have rented a room somewhere on the other side of the woods from where we are staying and are walking down the hill to the lake in search of my parents, for whom they have a Big Surprise. I spotted them coming down the walk through the two enormous cedars and told Grisha that, if we wanted treats from Dunya's, *now* would be the time to ask for money—before Leonid Petrovich and missus arrived and we'd never get a word in edgewise. We left the non-swimmer Iuda in the shallows in front of the life guard and raced to our parents' blankets (see above).

The couple's arrival at our communal blankets was greeted by much ballyhooing on the part of the adults, or so it appeared to us from the perspective of Dunya's diner. You know how the visit went, so I'm going to tell you *why* it went the way it did.

There's also a reason I told you the story about Papa's interrogation. Serious readers and the people who know me (not that those two groups are mutually exclusive) will realize that I'm laying the groundwork for something else. So, here goes another bit of a tale:

When the Germans overran my parents' village, my mother was a German teacher in the local high school. (See earlier in this chapter for comments on luck). Papa had managed to somehow get back home and was busy getting his mother and sister onto a train heading east. To the Urals and beyond. His hope was that he could save them by getting them out of occupied territory and beyond the Urals—the

---

[33] An excellent pupil

mountains presenting a formidable challenge to the seemingly un-stoppable Wehrmacht which, unlike Alexander the Great, had not yet resorted to using armed war elephants in this conflict.

As the cannons were booming, the earth was shaking, and pande-monium was the order of the day, Papa got his mother and sister Marisha onto the last Soviet cargo train headed east from the nearest railroad sta-tion, forty kilometers away from their village. In keeping with Russian tradition, they all kissed each other three times, his mother made the sign of the cross over her son, and they sat down on their bundles in the corner Papa had secured for them for one minute of silence. As the train started to move, Papa walked over to the open cargo doors and, before jumping out, said to his mother and sister,

"*Yezzhayte, ya vas naydu!*"[34] and jumped off the train, walking alongside as long as he could, watching his mother's and sister's forlorn faces, trying to memorize every detail and wondering if he'd be able to keep his word about finding them. He heard the women keening in that peculiar Russian way and, even after he no longer could keep up with the train, he thought he could hear their voices calling his name. Papa said that the strangest thought popped into his head as he watched the train carry his sister away: Who's going to braid your hair now?

He never saw them again.

Once the Germans overran that particular part of *Rostovskaya Oblast'*, they discovered through earnest and convincing chats with a few of the locals that a gifted mechanic lived there. Since supply chains weren't always reliable and equipment malfunctions were a daily occur-rence, it didn't take them very long to dragoon Papa into being their star mechanic. It did, however, take him quite some time to earn their trust.

Mama, on the other hand, had been "relieved of her duties" as the high school German teacher and presented with the opportunity to work as the commanding officer's translator/interpreter. To make sure you understand the circumstances (and before you start calling either

---

[34] Go, I'll find you.

one of my parents—or both—collaborators with the enemy) the option to decline these job offers simply did not exist. And, if you didn't care much about your own life, there was always your family—in Mama's case, her parents, sisters, brother, nieces, nephews—who made convenient valuable hostages. It also took a long time for the enemy to trust Mama.

In both cases, once the *fashysty* trusted my parents, the latter had the opportunity to help their fellow countrymen. Papa, by having access to all kinds of machinery, parts, and deficit industrial items was not only able to "expropriate" them, but to deliver them where they were needed by taking "a car that's not running right" out for a test spin.

Mama, on the other hand, was the first to know when someone was about to be arrested or executed and was able both to warn the families (if not the targets themselves) and to stash official German Marschbefehl (travel permission) for the Kommandant's signature in among the other papers she stacked neatly for him.

Russians in forced labor positions did that sort of thing at great risk to themselves. Like the telegraphist of legend who "misplaced" a punctuation mark, turning an execution order telegram into one of pardon.

None of us ever found out how many people they had saved.

As students of WWII history know, the Soviet Army eventually was able to turn the tide of the war and force a German retreat. Both Mama and Papa knew what Fate awaited them when the Soviets returned to their village. The hangman's noose would be the best option for two *izmenniki rodiny*—traitors to the Motherland. So, as chaos once again reigned, Papa strode over to his supervisor and told him that this particular car he'd been working on *still* didn't sound right, and he'd like to take it out for a test drive before turning it over to them. After all, they wouldn't want the car to break down in a few kilometers, right?

Ja, ja, Nikolay, aber schnell, schnell.

Schnell it was.

Meanwhile, Mama had prepared travel orders for them both and, with the papers signed by the commanding officer (unbeknownst to him) folded neatly and squirreled into the middle of a dictionary, walked quickly from German HQ to her parents' house, where a locked trunk full of her documents and other possessions stood quietly awaiting her departure.

A few minutes after she had walked in, Papa pulled up in the car and, leaving it idling outside the stone wall around the house, knocked briskly on the door and walked in. Now, mind you, Mama had been preparing for this moment. She'd packed anything of value into that trunk. Diplomas. Awards. Clothes. Pictures. You get the gist.

One thing I came to learn about Mama over the years was that she was a phenomenal panicker. And, when she panicked, she went immediately into seeing the worst possible outcome. Having read the above, you shouldn't be surprised by the following. Mama looked over at Papa, burst into tears, said to her mother and remaining sisters and niece "*Vsyo! Ya uyezzhayu!*" that she was leaving, and that "*my bol'she mozhet nikogda uzhe ne uvidimsya*" they may never see each other again. And, with that, she opened the trunk, dumped everything out, slammed the lid shut, and dragged it across the earthen floor. Papa grabbed it, threw it into the trunk; Mama kissed her family good-bye and got into the passenger seat. Two car doors slammed, and they left in a cloud of dust, with only the clothes on their backs.

She never saw her family again.

Their story of escape and evasion is fraught with adventure and misadventures, near-misses and near-connections. But it's a story unto itself and requires much more attention, pages, and different treatment. Not to mention the fact that it's not really a part of this book. Suffice it to say that they drove as far as the car could go and then walked, got horses and a cart, drove that, slept in barns, begged for food, and eventually wound up in a DP camp in Germany administered by the US Army.

In case you've never heard about a particularly ugly part of WWII, lemme introduce you to a horrific five-syllable word: repatriation. The US had struck a deal with "Uncle Joe" Stalin to return "his people" to their country. Americans—born free, live free, die free—could not imagine how or why one wouldn't want to go back home. Exiles, DPs, emigres-to-be elected their own representatives to explain the facts to the US Authorities. Suffice it to say that while they may have been heard, no one really listened. Or, perhaps, they were unwilling to create problems for their ally in the east.

Once word started trickling out and throughout the DP camps of forced repatriations and what happened to those forcibly repatriated, Mama and Papa vowed that they would never try to find or contact the families they had left behind. There was no reason to inflict punishment on them—both families had suffered enough. With no news or contact from them, their families would naturally assume that Mama and Papa had been killed during the war. And that would be that. No one would look for them, there would be no consequences for anyone. They would simply be two more in the countless millions who died before, during, and after the War.

So, figure from 1945 until that unexpected meeting of the *zemlyaki* in 1965, my parents had neither seen nor heard anything about anyone from their parts. For twenty years, they had maintained a determined silence, hoping fervently that those left behind had mourned their passing and moved on in life. Every time we went to church, Mama would diligently fill out the piece of paper "*O zdravii*" with a long list of family members' names and a piece of paper "*O upokoyenii*" with a shorter list of family members' names in her perfectly perpendicular script—for those who had died while Mama and Papa were still "back home," i.e., confirmed dead. You wouldn't want to write a living person's name on the "repose of souls" list, for example, and somehow, inadvertently, cause his demise. As I've said before, we are a superstitious and mystical bunch.

So, back to the Bol'shoy Skandal. See, I knew we'd get back here eventually.

After the initial overjoyed greetings, hugs, and kisses were exchanged, Leonid Petrovich, fairly bursting with good news, made an announcement:

"Nikolay! I've done you such a favor! You'll thank me for the rest of your life!"

"Favor? What kind of favor? I don't remember asking you for anything."

"No, you didn't, I know. And that's why this is such a Big Surprise!"

"A surprise you say? And what kind of a surprise can this be?"

"You'll thank me for the rest of your days."

"*Nu, davay, rasskazyvay,*" Papa egged on the Surprise Giver.

"*Nu, vot.* As soon as Klavka and I got home after we saw you, I sat right down and wrote a letter home."

"*To yest'*, what home?" Papa wanted to know.

"Home home—*na rodinu!* I've been corresponding with my family for years now."

"You did what?!"

"Yes! Exactly! I wrote to them and told them that you and Natasha are alive and well, live in your own house—I even wrote down the address—and have this little daughter named Masha."

And that, apparently, was the last straw for Papa, who jumped up from the beach blanket and was about to add Leonid Petrovich to the "*o upokoyenii*" list next Sunday with a couple of well-placed, bare fisted punches. (That Papa could do this is undoubtable: he once felled an obstreperous horse with a fist to the head. They were best friends after he helped the horse up.) So, this was what all the loud words were about. And this is why a number of men got involved in restraining Papa and making Leonid Petrovich apologize and sue for peace.

We never saw Leonid Petrovich or his wife, Klava Ivanovna, again.

But the effects of this Big Surprise on Mama and Papa were significant and long-lasting.

For the record, I learned all the above many years later from Mama, not from Iuda. Evidently, my godsister had missed the most noteworthy part of the incident and had to make do with having learned only a couple of new words. Grisha and I overheard her using one of the words to her mother a day or two after the Bol'shoy Skandal while we were conducting espionage around their cabin. The word was followed by a loud slap, lots of yelling from Shura, and some impressive howling by Iuda. Grisha and I headed over to the trash heap—that day was trash burning day—and chased a few chickens around for kicks. In other words, summer vacation seemed to be back on track.

Except that it wasn't. At least not for my parents.

19

Zatem, chto i v smerti blazhennoy boyus'
Zabyt' gromykhaniye chernykh marus'[35]

The weeks following our return to Brooklyn that summer after the now-infamous Near Death Experience of Leonid Petrovich found us a somewhat changed threesome. Well, maybe only two of the threesome were changed. Me, I was milking the last hours of freedom by racing around with my block buddies, checking the sewer grates for dropped coins—you could make a fortune those days with a piece of string and a little well-chewed gum—and spending our findings at the Fifth Ave candy store run by an old stooped woman with a hawk nose and short temper we not-so-affectionately referred to as Mrs. Crabeeappletree. Even though we all secretly believed she turned into a bat as soon as the sun set and the street lights came on—the store closed promptly at 6:00 p.m. and *no one* ever saw her enter or leave—we continued to patronize her establishment for two reasons:

1. It was around the corner, so we didn't have to cross Fifth Avenue, and

---

[35] Anna Akhmatova, *Requiem*

2. She sold wax lips at three for one penny and Mary Janes (the dentist's friend) at two for a penny. You really couldn't beat the prices.

Still, there seemed to be something amiss in apartment 2R. It was as though an unseen force of some kind had moved into our apartment: my parents spoke to each other in very low voices and stopped talking whenever I walked into the room. I figured they were up to some scheme to be rid of me—Mama agitating for it, Papa arguing against it—so I assiduously watched my Ps and Qs. Or, as my parents would say, I was *"tishe vody i nizhe travy"*—more quiet than water and lower than the grass. Unnoticeable; off the radar. No running in the apartment. No stomping up the stairs. No loud radio playing. No bugging them about watching TV in the middle of the day. I stayed outside most of the day and rang the buzzer for entry only when my bladder was about to burst. And then I was quick about my personal business and out of the apartment like a shot. A shot from a gun with a silencer.

The adults, when they were home, walked about with serious faces and stooped shoulders; Papa, hands in his pockets, fingered his switch-blade and jingled coins. He discovered maintenance projects around the house and spent time working in our basement or in the yard behind our house. Last year, he had made a raised garden bed (using metal from the junkyard where we scrounged for parts and where I found a beautiful doll with one eye missing. I also found a doll's eye, but it didn't fit this doll.) where we grew tomatoes and flowers (even though Papa's personal preference was for wildflowers) and he would spend time there every evening, staking and tying up tomato plants or picking flowers for a bouquet to greet Mama when she got home from work.

My radar sensed that something was amiss and, with all the guilt that had been pounded into me over the years, I naturally thought it was all my fault. I'd probably said something or behaved in a way that was *grubo* or *nekul'turno* and they were trying to figure out the punishment. Hard to top exile at five, but I was sure there was an equivalent for seven-year-olds. I hoped to conduct some intelligence gathering while they were out but, oddly enough, I was never left alone in the apartment anymore.

Furthermore, our evening walks had come to an unexplained halt. Instead, every evening after supper, when he wasn't working in the garden or basement, Papa sat on the upper ledge of our front stoop, smoking one unfiltered Camel after another. The ritual was almost an art: the tap-tap-tap of a fresh cigarette on his thumbnail to pack the tobacco and then the twist-twist-twist of the cigarette into his yellowed handmade *mundshtuk*. A flick of the stainless steel Ronson ("world's best lighter") and the orange-red glow of a fresh cigarette being lit followed by a strong inhale and an equally strong stream-of-smoke exhale. Watching. Waiting. Smoking. Watching.

In my childhood innocence and egotism, I thought he was coming out to watch me play and, in retrospect, I may not have been far from the truth. I played stoopball with the others, slamming our communally-owned pink Spalding (that's spawldeeeen to the uninitiated) precisely into the second step that gave it a ricochet bounce. I jumped rope to the various and sundry rhymes that didn't require partners. I raced my Sixty-eighth Street sewer rat friends up and down the block in pickup games of stickball and "freeze tag," testing the limits of my "run faster, jump higher" Keds.

Every so often, I would take a break from all the frenzied activity and come sit with Papa on the ledge. Actually, I sat on the ledge opposite him so that I had a good view of what my urchin friends were up to—lest I miss something good—and could talk to him face-to-face.

"What are you doing up here?'

"What am I doing? I'm smoking. You know Mama doesn't like it when I smoke in the house."

"Yah. She walks around wrinkling her nose, coughing and oooofing. Are you watching for something?"

"Just cars."

"Remember when we lived on Berry Street and we used to watch cars out the window? And we always counted the pink ones?"

"And who did the counting?"

"When I was really little, you did. Then, when I got bigger, we both did. And then I did by myself. Except you wouldn't let me look out the open window by myself."

"You still remember that? Such a good memory—it'll help you in school." The gray eyes shifted to a black Oldsmobile making its way toward Fourth Avenue. A family of five: three kids playing punchbug in the back, the parents arguing in the front seat. I could tell because they had all their windows rolled down in the blistering New York summer heat. and I distinctly heard evidence that not all was bliss inside the vehicle:

"Shaddap!"

"YOU shaddap!"

". . . OWWWWW! Idiot!"

"Jerk!"

And, above it all, the adult voices:

"I don't weah Sugah Pink frosted lipstick, ya baaastahd. Whose is it?!"

"Shaddap ya nag!"

And then, the final pronouncement from the front,

"Knock it off and shaddap back there or I'll give ya sumthin' ta whine about."

After which the car plunged into silence and came to a stop at the red light a few hundred yards from where we sat.

The light turned green and the black car was followed closely by a metallic blue Rambler, which Papa proceeded to ignore.

As I sat there and watched him, I noticed that it wasn't every car that drew his attention, only the dark ones. For a moment, my brain raised the remote possibility that we'd be buying a car and that I'd be driven to school rather than having to walk like the rest of the neighborhood kids. I imagined myself in the back seat of a long black Cadillac pulling up to the front entrance of PS 170 while the strains of the school song wafted gently on the breeze: "Hail Lexington! To you all praise is due. Dear Lexington, we'll loyal be to you."[36] As the limo rolled to a soft stop, and the liveried chauffeur came around to open the door for me, I pictured myself walking gracefully up the front steps in lace-trimmed ankle socks and black patent Mary Janes. No lining up at the side entrance with the rest of the Bay Ridge rabble for *me* anymore! I'd have poufy dresses to wear to school, and Someone Else would have to iron my handkerchief and pin it to my waist *just so* in the morning . . . I could have an elastic band to hold my books together like the cool kids, instead of that stupid blue and brown plaid book bag that immediately labeled me as Unhip and Different.

My reverie was interrupted by the siren song of the Ice Cream Truck making its evening rounds. That Mister Softee tune that was irresistible to anyone under the age of twelve: Dum-da-da-da-da-DUM-da-DUM-da-DUM-da-DUM-da-DUM-dum. Dum-da-da-da-da- DUM-da-DUM-da-DUM-da-DUM-da-DUM-dum. My friends scattered to their apartments after the first Dum-da-da-da-da-DUM to beg for ice cream money; I slipped off the ledge, cocked my head to one side (in a way that I thought particularly appealing and effective), sidled up to Papa and asked, as politely as I could: "Papa, may I please have some money for an ice cream?"

"Ah? An ice cream? Didn't you have one earlier today?"

"No, because we didn't walk past the Dairy Queen, remember?'

"Oh, right, we didn't. Well, how much do you need? A nickel? A dime?"

---

[36] The first strains of our school song, aptly named "Dear Lexington" and sung to the tune of the Canadian National Anthem. The remainder, if memory serves, went something like this: "As we backward gaze on our student days, your teachings we'll admire. All our work and skill, we hope always will reflect your lofty desire! Sing to our school, Dear Lexington: symbol of all our hopes and work well done. Cherished through all the years be Lex-ing-ton!" Pretty heady stuff for an elementary school.

And just like that, without further interrogation or ado, a shiny quarter was produced and slipped into my hand. I was about to launch myself off the three steps of the stoop when the baritone stopped me:

"*A ty kuda?*"[37]

"To the ice cream man, he's just down the street!"

"Why don't you stay here and wait for him to come up the street?"

"But Papa! He's already stopped! See, everybody's there!! I'm going to miss him! He won't stop again!!" I could feel the panic rising from my stomach to my throat, taking my voice higher up the scale with it.

"He'll stop. If I have to, I'll go out and stop him."

"But . . ."

"No 'but.' Just wait here. *Ya skazal.*"

There it was, that final phrase against which there was no arguing. *Ya skazal.* I said so.

I parked my keister on the lower ledge of the stoop, hung my head, and pouted. I rolled the shiny quarter around in my grimy little palm, sure that I'd have to return it to its original owner unused. And pouted some more, trying unsuccessfully to produce a tear or two. I heard the music getting louder as that mint green truck with the lit up neon soft serve ice cream cone on its roof came closer and closer. I heard—rather than saw—my father's summer shoes slip past me down the steps. The next thing I knew, the music was quite loud; I looked up and saw the mint green truck with the Ice Cream Man at the window, waiting for me to place my order. I ran across the sidewalk and between two parked cars, quickly surveyed the daily offerings, and opted for the creamsicle. Orange ice outside, creamy vanilla inside. Popsicles were forbidden to me because my parents (Mama mostly, who seemed to have acquired quite a bit of nutritional knowledge since her enforced Diet) believed they had no nutritional value. I could have ice cream. The creamsicle provided a happy medium between the two. I got change back from my quarter, which I promptly returned to Papa, who told me to keep

---

[37] Rough equivalent of "Where do you think you're going?"

it and drop it into my piggy bank—the one with TRIP TO EUROPE emblazoned across the top. The change had a one-way trip: there were no withdrawals from this bank, deposits only. In my world, all seemed well, at least for the moment.

And so it went, every single night after supper unless inclement weather forced us inside. On such occasions, I was allowed to play alone in the play space Papa had built for me in the basement. The flip side of every blessing, it appears, is a curse: I was totally unsupervised. Untethered. Free to do as I pleased. I could play school with my dolls or I could try to build, say, a chair with my little tool set and the scraps of wood we always had lying around from one of Papa's many home maintenance projects. Yes, that's right, Papa and I clearly were ahead of our time: I—a *girl*—had my very own tool set. Real tools, too, only on a smaller scale than Papa's.

On the other hand, I was terrified to be by myself in the basement of our apartment building. Papa had installed a door with locks into our private basement space to keep the curious and malevolent out, but it was never the humans who scared me. It was all those things that are Unseen, the ones that brush past you when no one else is around, the ones that make odd noises and waft their fragrances under your nose, the ones that dwelled in all the dark nooks and crannies of the basement, waiting for me to let down my guard . . . and then . . . *then* . . . It was too terrifying to ponder. But ponder I did, unfortunately for me.

My outstanding and overworked imagination usually led to my scaring myself witless, tearing out of our space, slamming the door shut, and speeding up the four flights of stairs like my hair was on fire to our apartment. Frenzied banging and a frantic *"Papa, eto ya, pusti!!"*[38] were all I could manage before *it* got me. He always seemed to open the door just as I felt the icy tentacles on the back of my neck, ready to snatch me away into the *unknown*. I trusted him completely and knew he'd fight it off and keep me safe, if push came to shove. But, just in

---

[38] Papa, it's me, lemme in!!!!

case, I made sure to throw all three locks into the *closed* position once I was safely inside 2R.

While it may appear to some that I spent all my time racing around with my buddies, in point of fact, the truth was quite the opposite. I was a bookish child by birth, and my strong preference was to stay inside and read a book, any book: I was, and still am, a book omnivore. OK, with the exception of books on hard sciences or *math*. I could spend hours in the non-Papa chair by the window in the living room. The lighting was good, as was the view, since I could turn around and look out through our fire escape onto our back yard and its flowers and tomatoes. I also could keep track of who, in the buildings across the way on shady Sixty-seventh Street, had done their laundry and what kind of underwear they had by whatever was flapping in the Brooklyn breeze on any given day. My reverie inevitably was cut short by Mama's insistence that I go "play in the fresh air." It must have been a recommendation from the *Mother and Child* book she kept hidden in her nightstand—the one I found during one of my snooping escapades when both my parents were out. The interruption predictably came at the most suspenseful or interesting part of the story I was reading. Just as there was no arguing with Papa's *"ya skazal,"* it was pointless to raise any objections to Mama's trying to get me out of the house. Sometimes I simply capitulated and took my book downstairs to the front stoop, where I could claim to be breathing fresh air while reading. Fresh Brooklyn air, scented by Pre-EPA emissions from all the cars and trucks going by or idling at the red light a half-block away.

It is only on the downhill slope of my life that I can begin to understand what must have been going through Papa's mind.

The mother and sister he tried to save by putting them on an eastbound train as the Germans were retreating, the ones he never saw again, his promise to find them broken.

Almost being shot point-blank in the NKVD basement interrogation room.

The *chernyye marusi* that showed up at night, the men who dragged you out in your bedclothes and threw you bodily into the black cars that then drove off into the night. And you were never seen again.

Remembering my mother's father, who was imprisoned on trumped up charges—how many millions shared that fate?—and died of asphyxiation in a prison cell intended to house three, but into which over forty men were sardined. Mitrofan was on the short side and was simply squished to death by the others. The wrinkle in his forehead looked as though it had been made by the four tines of a fork. And when the Komosomol at Mama's college found out about it, they tried to have her expelled. The only thing that saved her was her "*otlichnitsa*" status and a professor who risked her own job to stand up in Mama's defense.

Everyone and everything Papa had both loved and hated and left behind for the safety, security, and liberty of life in the United States. That new life was now under threat, and all because of one stupid letter—a concept no American raised in the land of the free because of the brave could ever understand.

And, of course, with the 20/20 hindsight some of us develop during our so-called golden years, I now understand why Mama didn't allow me to join the girl scouts. To her, they were all too reminiscent of the Komsomol and the type of people who joined the Communist Party.[39]

Suffice it to say that the *chernaya marusya* never came for Papa, Mama, or even me and, after several months of watching and waiting, Papa decided to go back to our old way of life. Just like that, one evening after supper and clean-up, he said,

"*Nu chtozh? Khoroshaya pogoda! Poydyom proydyomsya?*"

Good weather and a walk? You betcha. Hand in hand, straight down Sixty-eighth street to Fifth Avenue, cross the street and head down Fifth, stopping to window shop and turning into the Dairy

---

[39] Pavlik Morozov, the subject of many poems, an opera, biographies. Idolized by the Soviet authorities for ratting out his father. Search the internet if you're interested in learning more about this little Judas. Not devoting any more space or thought to the Fink.

Queen. One sugar cone, vanilla ice cream dipped in hot fudge. No sprinkles. Extra napkins. I can still taste the cold vanilla ice cream melting and commingling with the crunch of chocolate, both flavors melting and merging into each other in an intricate chocolate-vanilla swirl of deliciousness. Oh, yum. It tasted even better than I remembered. Not only that, but I got one on the way home, too. Without even asking. It was, for me, a truly banner day (I wouldn't dare, even now, to call it a "red letter day" for fear of a long distance smack from the Other Side of the Veil).

I wish I could remember what we talked about on that first day of our deliverance from the *chernaya marusya* phantom threat, but I can't. I can reconstruct only a few of our conversations in toto, those from moments seared into my reserve of remembrances. All I can resurrect from that day is the memory of Papa smiling again and letting me skip beside him as we made our way down Fifth Avenue. And the ice cream. I definitely remember the ice cream. And our race back up Sixty-eighth street on the way home. Which Papa won, again.

20

The Russian people, despite their conversion from pagans to Christians in 988, retain a near-infinite number of superstitions and beliefs dating back to their origins. One of these involves whistling: *never in the house!* It'll bring bad luck and you'll never have any money (which is pretty bad luck in anyone's book, I guess). My parents were well-versed in all manner of "don'ts," including the ban on whistling *inside*. If you must whistle, do it *outside*.

One thing I never learned from Papa was how to whistle, and it bothers me to this day that I still can't. He had a terrific assortment of whistles that he used to summon me from wherever I was playing with my little ragamuffin friends. First, there was the gentle "whoop?" Then, if I didn't hear (or pretended not to), there'd be a second, louder version of the first. If I still didn't get the message, there'd be the ear-drum-shattering "fyoooop!" charging through several notes and, if I didn't respond, there'd be the sound of his running footsteps to corral me. It usually went something like this:

Sound of thundering running footsteps.

"Aha. So *here* you are. What, didn't you hear me whistle?"

"Uh.uh.uh.uhmmmmmm." (That blasted pathological truth-teller gene would be the source of my unhappiness in life and eventual demise, I was sure.)

"I said, didn't you hear me whistle?"

"Uhm. Uhm. Maybe . . ."

"*A nu-ka,* the truth."

"Uhm. Uhm. Uhmmmmmmmm."

"*Nu, vsyo.* Now you're coming with me. Say good-bye to your friends."

And I would be summarily perp walked back to the nearest park bench he'd been sharing with one of my friends' fathers, plopped onto the bench next to him, and Papa would pick up where he'd left off in the conversation. Just like that. I was doomed to sit out the evening in exile, listening to two men shoot the breeze, my little friends cavorting in our imaginary fort down the hill. No smack, no yelling, only the barely endurable sitting still, my feet not touching the ground. And no swinging of the feet either, lest I be accused of rocking Satan on my feet. Absolute stillness and silence.

I can remember only one instance of Papa hitting me. Back then, fathers meted out punishment with hands, belts, or pretty much anything close to hand to wax our errant behinds, and no one said "boo" about it. It was just the way things were: "Wait 'til your father gets home" was enough to terrorize any kid back then. Except me, because Mama was a Hot Stove Method Enforcer. If she caught me doing something "wrong," the punishment was immediate and memorable. Funny, all these years later, I remember the punishment(s), but not the crimes. With one notable exception, and that would be the transgression that got me Exiled.

I guess we *Grechenkovy* come from a line of Maternal Enforcers. Take Papa, for instance. That his mother spared no Enforcer Efforts in raising Papa in no way diminished Papa's love for her. He named his only child after his mother, after all. But there was one story he told about his mama that stuck in my brain for keeps and still resides there to this very day.

After Papa's father, Fedor, died, things started to go bad for his family. Starting from the priest's extortionist fee[40] to having to sell off their horses (but one) and cattle (but one cow), the Fedor Grechenkovs were reduced to one pair of boots—left from Fedor—for the entire family when winter came. Russian winter with its merciless freezing temperatures and waist-deep snows.

Think on this: it's 1917. Pre-revolutionary Russia. Countryside. No electricity, no plumbing, none of the creature comforts we all enjoy and take for granted. The surviving Grechenkovs have used up their supply of water. Maria turns to her ten-year-old man of the house and says,

"Kolya, we need water. Go down to the river and bring back a bucketful. Put on your father's boots and be sure to come right back. The wind is picking up and you'll freeze to death."

Which is exactly what Kolya did. Except the last part. I guess he sort of forgot—still being a kid and all—when he saw all his buddies playing on the frozen river. Some already had built forts on opposite sides of the river and were hurling snowballs at each other, cheering when they hit the enemy fortress. Others had strapped skates to their boots and were skating between the two forts, delivering enemy secrets in exchange for not getting pelted with iceballs. Kolya set down the bucket and ran down the slope to the river. He didn't have skates but found that he could slide pretty well if he followed the ruts someone else had made. The boys in the near fort spotted him and called him to come play on their side—Kolya had inherited his father's legendary strength and had a throw that could break through enemy defenses. No one even felt the cold, they were so wrapped up in the fun and laughter.

---

[40] When Fedor died, Maria went to the village priest, Father Aleksiy, to ask him to conduct the funeral mass and burial. The priest said his fee for that was 13 rubles. Maria, in shock, asked, "But Father, where am I going to get 13 rubles? I have two children!" Father Aleksiy's response? "13 rubles or he can lie there like a dog." Maria went house to house in their village, begging a few kopeks here and a few kopeks there until she got the 13 rubles. And her son—my Papa—in disgust, lost his faith and instantly gained an aversion to all things related to priests and religion.

Back home, Maria waited and waited for Kolya to come home. Waited and waited and waited. And, when the sky started changing colors at the end of the short winter day, she realized that her fears probably had come true: he'd fallen through the ice and drowned. Maria bundled herself up as well as she could, but Kolya was wearing the only pair of boots they owned, so she had nothing to protect her feet. Still, she had to know if her boy was alive or dead, so Maria set out barefoot in the middle of Russian winter through hip-deep snows to search for her son.

Imagine her surprise as she approached the river and heard laughter. On hearing children's voices, she broke into a run, listening for Kolya's voice and, not hearing it, searching among the boys for his jacket and hat. She had trouble focusing because of the panic and the wind that was picking up snow and flinging it brutally into her eyes, which started to tear up in response, blinding her even more. She ran all the way down the bank and onto the river, where she found her presumed drowned Kolya slipping and sliding all over the ice.

He never saw her coming.

The next thing Kolya knew—as he told it—his Mama had knocked him on his keister with one blow (she was, in addition to being beautiful, tall and strong). Pinning him down with one knee, she used both hands to drag Fedor's boots off Kolya's feet, one at a time. Both boots were encrusted with snow and ice around the heels. Maria picked up both boots, swung them as far back as her arm would allow and brought them down full force on the back of Kolya's head. Again. And again. And again. He said he saw stars every time she hit him. She was crying and screaming at him the whole time about how she thought he was dead, how she told him not to dally, how she told him to come straight home.

Finally, exhausted by her physical and emotional exertions, Maria got up from her knees and helped Kolya up. There was no blood anywhere, but she asked him if his head hurt. Kolya said that yes, it did hurt.

"Good," replied his mother, "maybe it'll cure you of your stupidity" and, wrapping her arm around his shoulders, walked them both back home. Barefoot. And neither one of them got sick. At least, not then.

After this particularly close encounter, Papa suffered at first from headaches and then, later, migraines his entire life. There was nothing to ease the pain, no matter where he went or whom he asked, until . . . Until he and Mama were in the flood of refugees walking through Europe and asked a farmer if they could sleep in his barn overnight. With his permission, they heaped straw into a makeshift bed in the corner away from the cows and were preparing to sleep when one of Papa's migraines hit. Mama ran to the farmhouse and knocked on the door; when a little old man opened the door, she poured out the whole story to him and asked if he had anything that might help. The old man (whose name I never learned) went back into the house and came out with a bottle filled with some sort of liquid with grasses and seeds, which he carried out to the barn to Papa. The old man said to him: drink this entire bottle, one finger's worth at a time, until you finish the bottle, maybe two weeks or so. This will help stop the headaches for now. But, when you're done with this tincture, come back. I will give you another bottle, and that will cure your headaches for the rest of your life.

As Fate and the Vagaries of War would have it, however, in the course of the next two weeks, the place where they were staying came to be in the crossfire between the retreating Germans and the advancing Allied forces, and Mama and Papa had to grab their paltry possessions and find transport farther West. By the time Papa had finished the first bottle, they were nowhere near the old man's farm. His headaches had cleared up and stayed gone for years, until they came back with a vengeance.

And when the really bad one hit him, Papa was alone in the house with his ten-year-old daughter.

That was me.

21

I was supposed to cook spaghetti. To go with the meatballs Mama had prepared in the big stainless steel frying pan with the matching lid.

Mama's meatballs looked nothing like Across-the-Hall-Mary's, who knew from meatballs, being Italian and all. Mary's "gravy" took all day to cook and included the dropping in of a couple of anchovies. Mama's "sauce" took about forty-five minutes—or as long as it took to cook the "meatballs" through—and included opening a can of tomato sauce and throwing in a bay leaf. Mary served her meatballs and gravy over spaghetti. Mama served ours over mashed potatoes. In other words, the two second-floor apartments' concepts of meatballs were quite different.

Mary's meatballs had freshly grated cheese in the mix. I know this because she sent Mark to the cheese store a couple of blocks over from our house one day to buy some kind of Italian-sounding cheese, and I decided to tag along. Until that day, I'd only known cheese to come in slices. Imagine my surprise when I saw not only huge wheels of cheese, but small balls of it floating in liquid or waxed and suspended from the ceiling. I didn't much care for the aroma of the place—it reminded me too much of the "fresh from the cow" milk I'd been forced to drink at my parents' friends' house in Canada. Not only had I watched Auntie

Varya milk the cow—who *knew* that's where milk came from?!?!?—I had to submit to a glass of it. While it was still warm and foamy. My entire life, I'd gone along thinking that the nice milkman made it in the back of his truck and poured it carefully into glass bottles before delivering it to our doorstep. No wonder I'm lactose intolerant in the downhill slope years of my life—it's all about the childhood trauma. But I've digressed.

With the wedge of cheese wrapped in white butcher paper, Mark and I trudged back to his apartment where I watched Mary mix and make the small round meatballs. She added all kinds of tiny dried green things into the mix, along with an egg and some cheese that she had just grated. She also threw in some onion and garlic, both of which she had chopped into tiny pieces. After all this was mixed up to look like meat loaf, she took tiny scoops of it and rolled it into little orbs smaller than the golf balls we'd occasionally find in the sewer down the block. She lined them up in circles in her big frying pan—like Mark did when he played defense with his little green plastic soldiers—giving them a quick fry, moving the pan all the time so they wouldn't stick and become flat. When the meatballs were done, they'd receive their final baptism in the huge pot of gravy on the stove.

OK, so I didn't know that the little green things that came in bottles were dried herbs and made the meatballs taste better. How would I know what those things were if I'd never in my life seen them? Mary even had a three-story wooden rack where she kept the bottles with mysterious ingredients lined up in alphabetical order. Small clear glass bottles with sage green tops and labels announcing the contents: curry powder, charcoal seasoning, oregano, cayenne and so on. I wondered what would happen if you mixed everything together . . . would you have the most amazing and delicious flavor in the world? What would happen if you mixed say, oregano, cayenne, and cinnamon? Or nutmeg, bell pepper flakes, and a mysterious white powder labeled "MSG?" The possibilities were endless.

We had nothing in our apartment like this tiered tower of tastes.

Mama hated to cook—it was Papa who taught her how—and never bothered to explore flavors that weren't onion or garlic (on rare occasions and only for certain foods) or, for baking, vanilla, orange zest, or lemon zest. She bore her cooking burden with stoicism, but had no interest in perfecting the art or expanding her repertoire.

That said, I was not a total ignoramus about seasoning. For instance, I knew about using onion and garlic from watching Papa in the sausage-making ritual every year a few days before Easter. Mama would buy all the ingredients—veal, pork, casings, onion, garlic—and Papa's job was to cut all these things into tiny bits and mix them together (except the casings, of course) with salt and pepper. When supper was finished and the dishes were done, Papa would get down to work by first, sharpening the Big Knife and second, by cutting us a piece of bread to share. Then he'd cut a garlic clove in half, rub the cut sides all over the piece of bread and, for the final coup de grâce, sprinkle salt liberally across the top before cutting the piece in two. As soon as we bit in, both of us would make I'm-in-Heaven faces and voice our approval through closed masticating mouths: Mm. Mmm Mmmmm. Fueled with gluten and garlic, we would move on to the task at hand: mincing for Papa, watching for me. To this day, I have no idea why they didn't use the meat grinder Mama used to make filling for *pirozhki*. I guess the making of sausage was a "guy thing," sort of like grilling *shashlyk*.

The next day, I'd watch Mama unearth the aluminum funnel from somewhere in the depths of a kitchen cabinet, wash it with hot soapy water, and then string the casings onto the narrow business end to make the sausages, having first checked the casings for holes by running cold water through them. I found the process interesting even though the schlurp-squish-schlurp sounds of the meat being forced into the casings was less than appealing. I tried not to think about the animals that had been sacrificed so we could make sausage for Easter. However, I'd hear an occasional unsolicited oink or babymoo in my right ear, and my rubber toy cow seemed to have particularly sad eyes on those days.

My job during this process was to stay clear of the work area lest some random malevolent loose hair from my head jump straight into the meat mixture and wind up in a guest's mouth. Mama had a persistent irrational fear of unknown origin of hair falling into food and always bound her hair tightly with a kerchief before cooking or baking. Since I refused to wear head gear inside (that stupid blue spangly hat was bad enough outside in winter), I was not allowed to bring my flyaway mouse brown locks anywhere near the work area of the day. But back to the meatballs.

Mama's meatballs were roughly the size of a baseball and differed from her meat loaf only by shape. There was enough meat for four of these babies—two for Papa, one apiece for Mama and me—each of which was flattened slightly before being nestled into the tomato sauce-water-bay leaf bath simmering on the stove. My job was to make sure they cooked through and to make the side dish to go with it. Even though I knew Papa preferred mashed potatoes (what Slav doesn't, I ask you?), I opted for spaghetti because it required less effort and I liked it better. All I had to do was boil the water, salt it, break the spaghettis in half to make them fit the pot, and then pour the whole mess into the strainer at the end. Of course, there was the obligatory pat (read: two tablespoons) of butter on the pasta before I served it up with the main dish. But, apart from that, it was smooth sailing. Virtually effortless. Which is why I decided to wait until Papa got home and got cleaned up before heating the water on the stove. Maybe, if I'd done things the way I'd always done them, all of what follows could have been avoided. Maybe there's a reason for ritual. Maybe, maybe not.

For some reason, I wasn't outside to greet Papa in the usual manner that day. Normally, I'd be horsing around outside with one of my urchin buddies, pretending to play stoopball while keeping an eye on the Fifth Avenue end of our block. In the winter, I waited for the black clad figure walking quickly, taking the bend onto our street under the Drug Store sign and past the barber shop. The walk was unmistakable, the posture something a West Point graduate could envy. Lunch box in his left hand, *ushanka* on his head. Once I was sure it wasn't some random doppelganger, I'd shout "Papa!!" at the top of my lungs and launch myself headlong at him. Top speed, arms pumping, all the way down the block. The absolute best part was when I was closing in and he'd drop to a crouch to catch me, the sound and feel of my cheek hitting the cold leather of his jacket with a distinct smak! and Papa hoisting me up with an "Op-PAH!" After I pecked him on his cold stubbly cheek, he'd let me down and we'd walk home together, hand in hand, my left in his right.

If memory serves—and it doesn't always—I believe the reason I was inside on this particular day was that I was having trouble with the homework assignment—an unprecedented event in my head-of-the-class life. In a moment of confusion and mental blockage, I'd made the mistake of dropping my guard and asking Mama for help, so confounded was I about the assignment. It didn't go well.

Me: "Mama, can you please help me with my homework?"

Mama: "Help you with your homework? Why? What don't you understand?" (Mama prided herself on her flawless memory and academic record: the highest grade possible *always*, in *every* subject. Upon occasion, she would trot out definitive proof and recite complex mathematical formulas she'd memorized in college. Really. So you can see that the bar was set quite high for me . . . one could say it was virtually unreachable. And mobile, always upwardly mobile.)

Me: "Uhm. It's this thing about abbreviations . . ."

Mama: "Abbreviations are simple. What is there to understand? You just memorize them."

Me: "Uhm."

Mama: "Stop saying "uhm," people will think you're stupid or have a speech impediment. Now, what is it?"

Me: "I don't understand how you can get CA from California."

Mama: "Did the teacher explain this?"

Oh no. Here it comes. Wait for it . . .

Me: "Yes."

Mama: "Were you at school today?"

Me: "Yes."

Mama: "Was your head with you?"

Me: "Yes."

Mama: "Then there's no excuse. Figure it out yourself."

Yes, OK, my head had been on top of my shoulders and I'd been physically present in Miss Fitzgerald's 5-1 class. But the fact of the matter was that I'd been unabashedly wool-gathering—while pretending to pay attention with a few well-placed head nods—during Miss Fitzgerald's explanation and demonstration of state abbreviations. The truth was that I'd been sucked up through a time tunnel to this past New Year's Eve, when we'd gotten all dressed up and gone out to a Party at the Ukrainian Hall, where I'd tripped the light fantastic with my friends and with Papa well into the New Year. True, it wasn't Guy Lombardo and the Royal Canadians and we weren't at the Waldorf Astoria, but as New Year celebrations go, this was the absolute best I'd ever had. I'd been in the middle of a crowd for the final countdown to 1968 and sang along to "Auld Lang Syne" because I'd memorized all the words for the occasion. We certainly rang in 1968 with style!

With memories of that evening—and my special store-bought light blue dress with silver thread trim sewn into it—twirling through my brain (again), I left my homework on the kitchen table and slinked into my room for a consultation with *Zaychik*. Between the two of us, we came up with the idea of asking Papa for help when he got home. Papa's English wasn't very good, so he usually wasn't too much help, but he enthusiastically provided encouragement and support. Yes, that was it: I'd ask Papa. And we'd figure it all out together.

My reverie was interrupted by the buzzer ringing in the kitchen. I jumped up from my bed—where I wasn't supposed to sit—and ran to ring Papa in. It was easier to buzz him in than for him to look through his pockets for the keys. This way, I could be at the top of the stairs when he came galloping up, two steps at a time. I pulled my sweater more closely around me.

"And what are you doing out here? It's cold, come inside, you'll get sick standing out here." Papa quickly spit three times over his shoulder. Americans knock on wood, Russians spit over their left shoulders three times: tfu-tfu-tfu. A slight cultural difference.

He pulled frosty outside air in with him as he walked into the kitchen and I followed in his wake. First, he took off his hat and set it on the shelf in the standalone closet. Then, he took off his warm leather jacket and hung it up in the same closet. By this time, Mama had emerged from their room, where she was getting ready to go to work.

"Are you OK?" was the first thing she wanted to know from Papa. "Why?"

"You don't look well. Something's different about you."

Mama had been born with the "gift" of second sight—it's a blessing or a curse, depending on your perspective—a strange attribute passed down for millennia from one female to the next on the maternal side. She could sometimes see things before they happened. Sometimes, simply by looking at you, she could tell what was wrong. Thanks to this, I was perpetually working on my poker face, on the ability to tell a fib with a straight face, and other shadow aspects of my personality that would—ironically enough—eventually serve me in good stead in my career. This time, though, her focus was on Papa.

"No, I'm OK. I feel alright."

"Are you sure? You don't look right."

"Well, maybe I'll look better after I clean up and shave, eh?" Papa winked at me. I smiled my special "it's just us" smile for him.

"Well, OK. I guess I have to go now. I made some meatballs here in the pan, and Masha will fix something to go with it. Why don't you sit down and rest?"

"There's plenty of time for sitting. First, I'll get cleaned up, then I'll help Masha with dinner, and after dinner we can sit and rest."

"*Nu, khorosho.* But you don't need to help Masha—she's supposed to know how to cook." And, with that, Mama gave me her perfunctory peck on the top of the head the way she always did before going to work. She gave Papa another once-over before planting a kiss on him, pulled on her coat, hat and gloves, and let herself out of the apartment. I shot all three bolts behind her and listened to her steps receding down the stairs.

"Papa?"

"*Da.*"

"Papochka?"

"*Da.*"

"I need help with my homework. Can you help me?"

"I'll try, but you know I don't speak English well."

"That's OK, maybe we can figure it out together."

"*Ok. Nu, davay, chto tam u tebya?*"

And it was that simple. No "was your head with you at school today," no harangue, no guilting or shaming. He walked over to where I'd seated myself at the kitchen table and bent to look at my homework paper.

"So what are you supposed to do?"

"Uhm. Well, you see these are the whole names of states. And I'm supposed to write down their abbreviations."

"*Nu?* What's the problem?"

"I can't remember how to do it."

"Well, I don't know about American abbreviations . . ."

"But how would YOU do it?"

"Well, let's see: ALABAMA. I would just do A—MA; CALIFORNIA, I would say CA—IA."

"Oh." It didn't sound right.

"Maybe I'm wrong. Maybe the Americans do it differently."

"No, no, you're right! I just forgot! Thank you!!" and I proceeded down the list while he was watching me. I knew the answers were wrong, I knew that they were two-letter abbreviations, I knew I couldn't remember and that I'd get a bad grade on my homework the next day, but I plowed ahead with one wrong answer after the next. Because I couldn't let Papa think that he was wrong or dumb. I'd rather get in trouble at school than let him think he couldn't help me. Even though I was three grades ahead of him in formal schooling.

"*Nu, khorosho.* Then I'm going to go ahead and shave before dinner."

"OK. Is it OK if I finish my homework before I start the macaronis?"

"Of course. School always comes first. Finish your homework."

I labored away in pencil, thinking that I'd erase everything when I finally figured out the right answers, but only out of Papa's sight. I turned on the burner under the meatballs and set it on low. I thought about walking over to the bathroom to sit on the edge of the bathtub and watch Papa shave, because it was one of my favorite things to do. I loved the entire ritual: the way he'd squeeze the shaving cream out of the tube into a little bowl, the way he'd work up a lather with his shaving brush, and the way he'd brush the foam onto his face. I'd watch and mimic as he puffed out first one cheek, then the other. He usually managed to cut himself while shaving his chin and had to reach for the styptic pencil in the mirrored medicine cabinet. When he was all done, he'd pour about a nickel-sized puddle of blue aftershave in his left hand, rub his hands together, and then pat them all over his face, making ouch noises, huffing and puffing and laughing. If I close my eyes and think back to those times, I can almost detect the aroma floating gently around me and under my nose.

This time, however, I took the practical road and decided to finish my homework—errors and all. I had worked my way diligently down the list to about MONTANA when Papa came rushing out of the bathroom with shaving cream on half his face.

"What's that smell?"

"What smell?"

"*That* smell? Can't you smell it?"

I went straight to TERROR mode and my hands started shaking, because I'd never seen Papa like this. His eyes were wide open, his face was flushed to almost purple, and he was running from the bathroom to the kitchen, looking for the source of this smell.

I smelled nothing. I watched, terrified, as he ran the water in the kitchen sink, cupping his hand to catch it and smell it. He rushed back to the bathroom and I ran to my pink room, grabbed *Zaychik*, and retreated to the corner of my bed that met the wall. I was clutching *Zaychik* when Papa rushed into my room,

"*Tttty---ty g-g-g-gde?*"

He was stuttering, stammering, trying to produce words that re-fused to come.

"I'm here," was all I managed to squeak out. "Should I call the doctor?"

"*N-n-n-n-n-nu-nu-nu da!*"

As he rushed back to the kitchen sink, I jumped off my bed and headed for the black phone on the kitchen wall. I took the receiver off the hook and heard the dial tone, turned back toward the sink where Papa was still trying to sniff the water and . . .

And I saw him stand straight up.

And his arms suddenly went arrow-straight, but his hands still grasped the sink.

And then he half-turned as if to look at me and toppled over onto his back like a tree that had been felled.

And I watched as the dark blue-red pool of liquid started to spread over our light-colored linoleum in front of the stove.

I heard banging on the door. I heard Mary's voice calling to me. I opened the three locks to let her in.

I remember how she looked when she glanced down at Papa on the floor, the growing dark blue-red puddle under his head.

I remember that she crossed herself the Catholic way, which is the reverse of the Orthodox way.

I remember her telling me to get a pen or pencil to put between Papa's teeth.

I remember her sending me across the hall to their apartment to call Mama at work and to call a family friend. I opted to call Peter's Tato, Uncle Peter, since they lived a block away and owned a car. Mark tried to help me dial because I couldn't do it—my hands were shaking so much, but I could only remember their phone number in Russian, a language Mark didn't understand. Through a ten-year-old's version of a Herculean effort, I managed to still my hands enough to dial Peter's phone number. Funny, but I still remember that number. To this very day. But I only remember it in Russian.

In those pre-911 days, I remember dialing "O" for Operator over and over and over to get an ambulance to come to our house and being told that it would be a long wait.

I don't remember what happened then. I suppose the ambulance came and took Papa away.

I suppose Uncle Peter met Mama at the hospital and drove her home.

I stayed in Mary's apartment until Mama came home. Mary and Mark told me that they heard me scream twice, and Mark added that the "second one was a real doozy!" But I don't remember screaming.

I don't remember Mama coming home that night, but I'm sure she did.

I don't remember going to bed.

I don't remember getting up the next morning, or having breakfast, or dressing for school.

All I remember from that day—the Day After—was me stopping in front of Miss Fitzgerald as my classmates were filing into the classroom and taking their seats. I remember telling Miss Fitzgerald that I didn't do my homework last night because Papa had to go to the hospital.

And she asked me what happened.

And I got to say out loud the words that had been stuck in my throat since I saw the dark bluish-red puddle.

And then I cried.

And Miss Fitzgerald hugged me tight.

And she told me not to worry about the homework. And she asked the two Greek girls, Despina and Johanna—the numbers two and three in class—to watch out for me. (Despina's dark hair had been cut pixie-style and she had tiny gold studs in her ears. Johanna had waves of shoulder-length hair that refused to be contained by a single ponytail holder and hazel eyes that changed color depending on what she wore. The three of us had maintained our one-two-three class standing ever since we were lumped together in second grade.)

I loved Miss Fitzgerald all the more for her kindness.

And for hearing the anguished words from my mouth and the unspoken petrified ones in my terrified heart.

I still have trouble with State abbreviations and the sight of blood.

22

I had a memory blip the other day. A visual. I'm ten years old, it's dark and cold outside, and I'm standing under a lamppost across the street from a very large building somewhere in New York. I think Mama's on my right side, but I can't be sure it's her—memory's a funny thing—maybe it's one of our family friends, like Uncle Peter. I just can't pull the image into the forefront of my brain. But here's what I do remember: all the windows are lit up.

Papa is inside somewhere.

Someone, I can't remember who, told me to stand here because Papa would come to the window and I could see him. I wasn't allowed to go upstairs because I wasn't yet fourteen. I'd managed to pass for twelve, which allowed me to stay in the waiting area unaccompanied, but Mama didn't notice the other sign—the one that said you had to be fourteen to go upstairs because certain floors were restricted. I was too scared to point it out to her when she lied to the *dezhurnaya* about me being twelve. Mama was told that I was too young to go upstairs and she, in turn, told me that I was to sit down with my book and *not go anywhere*. Don't talk to anyone. Don't go anywhere. Sit *po-chelovecheski*.

I lowered myself into the closest armchair near a lamp and sat as *po-chelovecheski* as I could. The lighting was dim, there were other people—I didn't notice individuals, I noticed forms—and the chair was too big for me and uncomfortable. That's all I remember. And I remember sitting. And that I was really hot in my black and red plaid wool buttoned-up coat. I didn't know if I was allowed to unbutton it, so I just sat *po-chelovecheski,* turning red in the face and sweating into the two plaits I'd braided that morning. The steady hum of wheels turning, voices echoing, elevators pinging their arrival and departure, was interrupted by occasional staccato PA announcements paging one doctor or another and announcing "code blue" and other things I couldn't fathom. It was as though I'd been catapulted into a foreign country where everyone spoke a language I didn't understand. Sorta like our family speaking Russian in the US of A.

Outside the sitting area the lights were so bright it hurt my eyes. I didn't know if I was supposed to look there or not, so I periodically stole glances at the long corridor with the elevator banks to the right. I remember seeing people shuffling along in slippers, pajamas, and those funny hospital gowns that left their legs exposed so they looked like the cranes in Russian songs and stories. I also noticed that most of them were wheeling some sort of contraption with a bottle suspended from it and were accompanied by a nurse or beefy guy in a white uniform. I wondered if the men were nurses, too. They weren't wearing caps the way all the nurses were, though, so I guessed they were there to help the sick people in case they fell. In my world, only ladies were nurses; men were doctors, but these guys definitely didn't fit the doctor type. They looked more like Sal the pizza place owner or Dom, the owner of the butcher shop a couple of blocks down from our house.

I wondered if Papa was attached to some sort of contraption he had to wheel around "upstairs."

I wondered if Papa was well enough to walk around.

I wondered why you had to be fourteen to go to the upper floors.

It must have been Mama who came to get me, because it couldn't have been anyone else. Or could it? I don't remember. All I remember clearly is being walked outside the hospital into the cold night and how good the blast of cold air felt on my face. I was walked across the street and stopped under the lamppost. It was one of the old-fashioned iron kind of lampposts you no longer see, with lines and curves molded and hammered when the metal was still hot. I was told to look up to the fourth (or was it the fifth?) floor and count six windows over from the right. I did. And there he was.

Papa!

He was in one of his summer T-shirts, waving at me, and I'm pretty sure I saw him smiling. I yelled up at him, but his window was closed and there was some kind of fancy metal grate in front of it, so I'm pretty sure he didn't hear me. But I know he saw me because not only did he wave, he also showed me his arm muscle—he used to bend his arm at the elbow and flex his biceps to show me how strong he was. It was one of our private jokes with maybe just a hint of a threat to me. I laughed and waved frantically. I jumped up and down. He laughed and flexed his arm again to show me how strong he was, that he was invincible, that he'd be home soon. And I believed him because he'd always told me the truth.

And then they made me go inside.

The plaid wool coat scratched my neck where I'd bent it back to look upstairs. And I'd gotten away without wearing the stupid blue hat outside.

Indeed, based on those two facts, it had been a banner evening all the way 'round. For the first time since That Night, I felt the butterfly wings of hope flutter ever so gently in my heart. Maybe everything would be all right, maybe all this would disappear like a bad dream in the morning light when the sun shines, reassuring and bright, in your eyes, bringing you back to the safety of your own room and warm blankets from a dark and threatening place. Maybe, just maybe, we'd be able, some future day, to look back on this episode in our lives and smile at God's reminder of how very fragile our lives can be, having come close to the edge of the precipice, but not tumbled in.

From the safety of our happy Life, when no medication-taking schedules interfered with dinner or walks or repair projects.

A day when I would no longer be afraid of Papa losing his ability to speak or crashing to the floor, leaving a growing pool of dark red liquid under his head.

A number of years later I was pretending to watch a Knicks game on TV in my godmother's den in Farmingdale, New Jersey. (By then, I was a rabid Knicks fan and my heart belonged to Dave DeBusschere —unless I was watching the Celtics and eyeballing John Havlicek.) I was quietly eavesdropping on a conversation between Mama and my godmother, waiting for a scoop of some sort. My radar went off immediately when one of them mentioned Papa. And that's when I learned that the secrets you hear while eavesdropping may not always be juicy. And that words, once heard, could never be unheard.

The upper floors of the hospital were restricted to the "mental" cases.

Papa had tried to throw himself out that window and it took three orderlies to restrain him.

Of course.

He was very strong.

23

I had been left to my own devices again. My being left alone was something that had become the norm in our Family Minus One. Papa was recovering in the hospital and Mama was away visiting him or working, cleaning the twenty-fourth floor of an office building in Manhattan at night. I had pretty much gotten used to having the apartment to myself with only our across-the-hall neighbor, Mary, to "listen for" me.

Most of the time I busied myself with homework, reading or playing school—developing lesson plans, homework, and tests for my imaginary pupils. Sometimes I'd listen to the radio, moving the station dial around until I found music in keeping with my developing tastes. I was, however, meticulous about returning the dial to its original position, because I knew that if Mama caught me secretly listening to the Beatles, the Exile episode from five years ago would look like a walk in the park . . . so to speak. I was too afraid to turn on the new Admiral color TV without permission—I'd have to ask permission to change the channel back then—and the telltale warmth emanating from the set would doubtless give me away, resulting in who knew what kind of disciplinary measure. And there was no one here to defend or intercede for me.

On this particular afternoon, Uncle Peter was driving Mama to the hospital to pick up Papa, who was being discharged and sent home. As usual, I spent this unsupervised time snooping through the closets and my parents' nightstands. I was never quite sure *what* I was looking for (adoption papers, maybe?), but I was sure that some kind of secret something had been hidden away from me and was waiting to be discovered. And, before you ask: Yes, as a matter of fact, I *did* read the Nancy Drew books. I also read the Hardy Boys. And anything else I could get my hands on at the big library.[41]

I had snooped through Papa's nightstand and found a big fat nothing other than an old copy of the Hobo News (we Russian kids not-so-affectionately referred to the *émigré* New York Russian paper by that name because of its Cyrillic banner: *НОВОЕ РУССКОЕ СЛОВО*) and a few books on Russian history. This led me to conclude that anything of a secret or dubious nature would be found somewhere in Mama's possession (of course). Since this wasn't my first foray into the fine art of snoopàge, I knew that whatever of import she had in her possession would be hidden well.

I'd found their paperwork and references from the DP camp in Germany underneath a bunch of old greeting cards and yellowed newspaper clippings of recipes (never made) in the top drawer of Mama's nightstand. They'd lived and worked at the camp in Germany with

---

[41] As an aside, there's a reason for the use of the phrase "big library." I'd voraciously and indiscriminately read my way through the kids' selections at the library closest to our house, so was allowed to walk to the BIG LIBRARY blocks and blocks away. That's right, by myself, you "stranger danger" hysterics. In NYC. Across streets and avenues. *Alone.*

As I think back on those days, I remember that one of the best days of my little life was the day I graduated to the "adult" section and was allowed to go *upstairs* to select books. My heart beat so fast I thought it would come out of my rib cage at the very thought of those stacks and stacks and stacks of books I'd never even seen before. The first sight of the upstairs didn't disappoint: I was so overwhelmed by the sheer number of books and the rows and rows of stacks that I might have even stopped breathing for a few seconds. It was that impressive. Even the Librarian seemed nicer. Bliss.

thousands of other refugees after The War, all of them waiting and hoping that someone from a Western Democracy would sponsor them for
entry into a country that was not the USSR. (These refugees were the
lucky ones: they were not repatriated like the Cossacks in Lienz. Most of
the latter opted for suicide over returning to Stalin's USSR, where their
fates were predetermined and the trains to Siberia with armed escorts
and fierce, barking *ovcharki* on chains awaited them. Mothers simply
grasped their children to their chests and stepped off the mountains into
the rushing Drau River below rather than be subjected to the inevitable
in the USSR.) With previous successful discovery in mind, I opened
the door to her nightstand, being careful not to leave any fingerprints
on the glossy exterior panel.

Mmmmhhmmm. A large pink heart-shaped box, ribbon bow still
intact, faint scent of chocolates from a long ago Valentine's Day. On
top of that, a smaller cardboard box with a gold lid held memories of
Schrafft's fine chocolates. I shook each one gently, then held my breath
and softly lifted each lid in turn.

Nerts.

Black and white photos of family friends.

A photo album with pictures from my baptism and other (apparently) festive occasions in our apartment, some with and some without
me.

A book of some sort was gathering dust on the bottom shelf, so I
gingerly pulled it forward. AHA! This must be it!! It had a romanticized
picture of a woman and her baby on the cover. It was a Russian book.
The title was *Mother and Child*. This, then, *must* be it! This must be the
repository of everything having to do with my adoption. I peered at
the picture and noticed that the woman looked nothing like Mama and
the baby looked nothing like me in my baby photos. Artistic license?
Perhaps.

The only way to find out was to open it.

I steeled myself for impending doom, closed my eyes, took a deep
breath, and oh-so-gently lifted the cover. I opened my right eye first

and saw . . . a printed page with a black and white version of the cover picture. Hmmm. I opened my left eye, no longer fearing what I might find, and discovered . . .

A book. A book on how to raise a child.

I scanned a few pages (finally! Russian school had paid off!) from different parts of the book and realized that Mama either hadn't read this book or didn't agree with the author, because I couldn't remember a single instance of her following their suggestions . . . especially on discipline. Which only strengthened my conviction that Mama wasn't my real mother. A tad disappointed, sadder, and feeling quite sorry for myself, I replaced everything exactly as I'd found it, closed the nightstand door, and used the hem of my shirt to wipe off the few fingerprints I'd accidentally left behind. No one would be the wiser. Except me.

For once, my timing was impeccable: the buzzer rang just as I finished polishing the nightstand. I scooted to the kitchen and buzzed to unlock the foyer door. Then, I opened our apartment door and yelled, "Who is it?"—our version of IFF.[42] And I heard Mama's voice, telling me it was OK and that they were home.

Wow!! Papa's home!! Yay!! Now we could go back to our regular life! Papa and I could resume our walks past the Dairy Queen in the evenings! He was usually good for two ice cream treats: one—going, one—coming back, with the admonition not to tell Mama because it was our secret. I always had the same thing: a sugar cone with vanilla ice cream dipped in chocolate, the kind of chocolate that hardens when it comes in contact with ice cream. No nuts, jimmies, or other fripperies; I was a vanilla-meets-chocolate in a sugar cone purist. He'd hand me a quarter and I'd bring him the change, which he always told me to deposit it into my piggy bank *svinke v spinku*." The ceramic one with thistles, shamrocks, and "TRIP TO EUROPE" painted in bold black letters along the slit in its back. It was a strange kind of bank, because I was allowed to make deposits only, no withdrawals.

---

[42] Identify: Friend or Foe. For those of you with no military background.

We'd walk down the street and across Fifth Avenue to the hardware store, where he'd continue to teach me about tools, gadgets, nuts, and bolts, and why you used which ones where. I was pretty sure he'd (again) tell me the story of how he and a friend played a trick on a fellow DPer named Fedot who was selling stolen watches on the black market. One night, when Fedot stepped out for a little fresh air and left a disassembled watch on the table, its myriad pieces glinting under the suspended light bulb, Papa and a friend "nationalized" one of the little screws that went inside. No matter how hard Fedot tried, he couldn't get the watch to work and would walk around the compound, staring down at the ground, repeating *"винтики, болтики, винтики, болтики"*[43] in search of the one piece that was missing. They took mercy on Fedot after about three days and returned the little screw and everyone had a good laugh at his expense, including old Fedot himself. And then Papa and I would start chanting, repeating *"винтики, болтики, винтики, болтики"* louder and louder until we'd both erupt in wave after wave of unrestrained laughter. I still chuckle at this stunt nearly seventy years after the incident. Maybe not the stunt so much as Papa's retelling of the affair.

We could go to the Times Square Store, inspect all their fishing equipment and think about which reel to buy, discuss whether I could now fish without a bobber, or weigh the plusses and minuses of various sinkers. I'd intentionally walk past the bikes, slowing to a near-stop, lured by the siren song of the violet Schwinn twenty-six-inch girls' bike I'd been eyeballing for months. I would always ask for Papa's opinion on this particular violet beauty, and he'd always remind me that I already had a bike: the twenty-inch pink two-wheeler I'd learned to ride in our basement (owner's side only).

So much to do in our little world, now that he was home.

I stood at the top of the stairs, shivering a bit in my lavender sweater—they'd let all the frigid February air in when I buzzed the

---

[43] "vintiki,boltiki, vintiki, boltiki" = little screws, little bolts, little screws, little bolts

foyer door open. I was waiting to hear Papa's rapid step and then to see him taking the steps two at a time, the way he always did. But I didn't.

Instead, I heard the hushed tones of adults whispering things to each other the way they did when they didn't want children to hear.

Then I heard them start up the steps. Slowly.

I thought that maybe they were playing a game with me to see how long I'd wait before running down the steps to meet them. I bounced up and down on the landing in front of 2R, hugging my sweater to myself, nearly jumping out of my slippers in joyful anticipation.

And then I saw him.

Uncle Peter was holding Papa under his left arm while Papa gripped the banister and s-l-o-w-l-y moved one leg up to the next step. Again. And again. They stopped for a rest at the landing where the stairs turned toward our apartment. Mama, who had made curtains for the landing window and kept an assortment of plants on the sill, pretended to check them for moisture. No one looked up to see me because they were more concerned with not letting Papa miss a step or have a fall.

After what seemed like hours, they started up the final flight of stairs, Uncle Peter supporting Papa under his left arm and Mama bringing up the rear with the carpet bag that held Papa's clothes from the hospital. I knew those six steps like the back of my hand—I was responsible for washing all the floors in the building every Friday after school—and I knew how fast Papa used to come up them. Until today. Today, rather than sprinting up them two at a time, he was having trouble simply getting from one step to the next.

My hands had turned blue and started shaking, probably from the cold.

I think I forgot to breathe while I viciously chewed my lower lip to keep it from quivering.

And then, right before he got to our landing, Papa looked up and saw me. He gave me a feeble half-smile and said,

"Don't be afraid, I won't fall down again."

I should have laughed. I should have made some sort of half-funny, half-brave comment about what had happened That Night. And I really, really wanted to believe him, but my arch-nemesis—always present in the shadows, always waiting for an opportunity—*fear* wouldn't let me. I was starting to breathe faster and faster at the thought of being alone with Papa and having a repeat of The Night That Everything Changed. So, I did my best. I tried to made a brave face, but I couldn't get any words to come out of my mouth. And I couldn't even smile. For the first time in my life with Papa, I was struck dumb. And I was struck dumb in front of the person who most needed to hear me say something. Something off-hand and encouraging. Or even to tell a bold-faced lie and say it takes a lot more to scare me than that; after all, I was of the Grechenkov breed. *Grechenkovskoy porody.*

Instead, as I moved to the side to let the whole procession in, I caught sight of the bandage over the stitches on his head. And what was left of my heart squeezed so hard that I actually shuddered. I remembered, in a flash, what had happened The Night When Everything Changed, especially the sight of Papa on the floor with his head in a growing dark blue-red puddle. And in that instant, I knew that, despite my hopes and prayers to God and the Saints and anyone "up there" who would listen, things would never be the same again. The Papa I had known all my life had disappeared The Night That Everything Changed and had been replaced by a man who was feeble, much older, and Not The Same.

No one had warned me about this.

Not a single soul—and certainly not Mama—had told me what to expect when Papa came home.

Shivering nonstop, I pulled the sweater as tightly as I could around me and followed the trio into the apartment.

If in writing

"Hope is the thing with feathers
That perches in the soul
And sings the tune without the words
And never stops at all"

Emily Dickinson was right, then perhaps I still had some. Because in the place where my heart used to be there was a tiny hummingbird flapping its wings.

I closed the door behind me and shot the bolts on the three locks.

And walked into the brightly lit kitchen.

And, just like that, I'd gone from kid to caretaker. But I was a very responsible ten-year-old.

24

To say that our lives went back to my definition of normal would be to stretch the truth. Quite a bit. In fact, in the spirit of full disclosure, I have to say that my life never went back to its carefree days. I always had a niggling fear gnawing at either my stomach or my throat, and it manifested itself in a couple of different ways. For instance, I barfed every Friday, right before the weekly afternoon spelling test. It wasn't intentional because I was a champion speller and had even had my name published in the newspaper for my spelling achievements, but somehow it happened every Friday at lunch.

The girls' bathroom off the gym-cum-lunchroom where I'd perfected my upward throw of soaked toilet paper wads that stuck them to the ceiling like so many papier-mâché snowballs now was reduced to echoing the sound of me retching my guts out. Whether I'd eaten the school lunch, my own from home, or nothing at all, the result was the same. I'd then be sent to the office and Mama would be called to come get me—something she didn't appreciate because it meant putting on her girdle and stockings and walking the six long city blocks to school, her purse over her arm. I think Mama suspected I was faking it just to come home, but I really wasn't.

In the spirit of being brutally honest about growing up in those New York City years I have to admit that Mama's distrust was not unfounded, albeit dated. I tried faking illness for two days in kinder-garten, shortly after I'd started school. Two days in a row, since I didn't know any better (yet). [Brief aside: if you didn't speak the language and didn't understand what anyone was saying to you, wouldn't *you* be a tad reluctant to keep immersing yourself in this environment? Hmmmm?] Besides, I'd spent the first five years of my life listening to our elderly neighbor Yelizaveta Rudol'fovna's stories of how she got out of going to school by faking illness. As I reflect on those tales, I have to give Yelizaveta Rudol'fovna quite a bit of credit for creativity in this school-avoiding regard. I never did get the opportunity to practice some of her better dodges, but that was mostly because they involved a nanny—a gilding of the lily that my parents' status as DPs-turned-hard working immigrants did not allow.

Since I had morning kindergarten, my symptoms magically eased throughout the morning, and I felt well enough to go play in the park by the afternoon. It seemed like a pretty good arrangement to me until I repeated the "my tummy hurts" complaint on the third day. At which point, Mama flung me over her lap and administered some "discipline" with her open palm to my bunnypajamma'd rear, repeating mantras that I came to know like the back of my hand: "I'll teach *you* how to lie!" and "how *dare* you lie to your Mama?"

After Mama felt that her lesson had been properly administered—there were beads of sweat on her forehead—she spun me around toward the kitchen sink, where I dutifully brushed my teeth and washed my face. I was fed breakfast, stuffed into my school clothes, and marched off to school, being lectured all the way on the pitfalls of lying, my sniffles and occasional hiccups notwithstanding. In light of this episode (and maybe a few others), I really couldn't blame Mama for being a tad suspicious of my weekly stomach upset.

I also got sore throats a lot more often—probably as a result of NOT saying things or of swallowing tears as they started to form a Spalding ball in my throat—but never got to stay home from school. [I suspect Mama's training as a Soviet teacher and, later, school principal, played a role in this. Maybe the fact that their town had been overrun and occupied by the Germans during WWII also had an impact on her inclination to have *Alles in Ordnung*. But I've digressed. Again.]

Instead, Mama would hand me several coins and tell me to stop at the drugstore on the way to school and buy throat lozenges. She specified Sucrets—for some reason she thought they were more "medicinal" than the other brands, maybe because they came in a metal box and were individually wrapped. But, since she wasn't there to supervise the purchase, I always got the Pine Brothers cherry kind. They were soft and really stuck to your teeth if you chomped down on them. You could spend quite a bit of time focused on getting your teeth to slide back and forth to dislodge the "medicine," time during which you could block out the sound of Kevin Ronald trying to read out loud with that naaaasal voice of his tripping over unfamiliar words. (For all you lit majors who think you know better, Kevin Ronald will reappear in this narrative. I choose not to describe him here; however, suffice it to say that he very clearly had been misplaced in our "smart" 5-1 class.) Besides, cough drops were the only "candy" we were allowed to have and eat in school, so I figured I might as well get something I liked and that would amuse me throughout the day. I'd let loose a pretend cough in class and then quietly raise my wooden desk top, extract a cough drop, and pop it into my mouth. I usually had the last one on the walk home from school and would ditch the box along the way, thereby getting rid of any evidence of non-compliance with Maternal Rules and Regulations.

I had been told that Papa's doctor told him to stay home for a while to make sure he was all better. To that end, the doctor had sent him home with a cavalcade of capsules and tablets that Papa had to take at specific times, some with food, some on an empty stomach. And, since That Night had affected Papa's ability to remember when to take which medicines—among other things—I was put in charge of administering the evening doses after I got home from school.

So, the world kept turning despite this earth-shattering event in our lives. I still went to school at the same time. Mama still went to work after I got home from school. I still had to take the trash down to the scary part of the basement from where Papa had rescued *Zaychik* all those years ago. And I was still responsible for washing the hall and staircase floors every Friday. On the face of it, everything looked kinda normal, sorta like it used to Before.

Sorta.

But it wasn't at all the same.

Papa wasn't allowed to eat many of the foods we used to eat, like the fried *pirozhki* or *kotlety*. No butter, only margarine. And the only baked goody he could have was angel food cake because it didn't have any egg yolks or butter in it. Neither Mama nor I had ever heard of such a cake, much less did Mama know how to make it. She did find it at the A & P during her weekly shopping, and from that point on, we always had some on hand in case Papa got a hankering for something sweet and not *verboten*. I was told that Papa had something called *skleroz* and the special brain doctor said that dietary changes could improve Papa's condition. For Papa's sake, I pretended to like angel food cake. But the fact is, I really detested it. The texture was weird—it was like eating compressed cotton candy or a lighter, much sweeter version of WonderBread—and it was suspiciously *white*. [Sidebar: Twelve years later, I married a man whose favorite cake was *angel food*. I learned to bake it, but I never learned to like it. Evidently, Karma has a sense of humor.]

Time went by in our adjusted Universe, sometimes quickly, sometimes slowly. There was only a handful of memorable moments, but each one is indelibly etched into the tablets of my memory.

I remember one evening in particular. I'd finished my (pretend long) homework assignment and had heated up Mama's soup for our dinner. I'd carefully cut and set out the bread for Papa and the bowls for our dessert: canned fruit salad, one of my favorites, and the only canned food we ever had. I always hoarded the one or two cherries in the can because I loved them most of all and always ate them last, after the pears (ick) and pineapple wedges (not so ick). I folded the napkins into triangles, set them to the right of our plates, and set the silverware on top of them. Just a big spoon for soup and a small one for the dessert. I made sure the salt shaker was full and on the table—Papa and I both loved our salt. Besides, if you don't have a salt shaker on the table, any Russian who sits at your table will tell you it's crooked. *Stol krivoy.* I had ensured that our table was straight. All systems go.

I checked under the lid of the soup pot and saw the soup boiling madly, so I quickly turned off the burner and ladled a full bowl for Papa and a smaller serving for myself. Convinced that everything was OK and that I hadn't accidentally cooked Mama's homemade hand rolled and cut noodles into oblivion, I called Papa to the table. I heard the TV go off and watched him walk slowly into the kitchen. We both stood in our usual places, Papa slightly behind and to the left of me, facing the icon of the Virgin Mary holding the Christ Child in the north corner of the kitchen. Papa started reciting the Lord's prayer:

"Otche nash, izhe yesi . . ."

I knew the *Otche Nash* as well as anyone, but it never occurred to me to recite it along with Papa. It seemed good and right and reassuring to let him be the Head of Family, responsible for the safekeeping of my body and soul. So, I continued to cross myself in the right places of the prayer and to add my child's request, *"Bozhen'ka, blagoslovi!"* at the end with a genuflection (sincere). I was pretty sure God understood and couldn't be mad at me for this minor transgression, seeing as how I was doing such a good job administering Papa's medicines.

Papa sat down at his place and I slid into mine, next to the old brown radio I listened to every morning before school.

I don't remember much of our conversation. I only remember this part:

Papa was looking at me while I pretended not to notice. Finally, I couldn't stand it anymore and looked up and into those grayish-blue eyes of his. They seemed a tad damp. And he said,

"So, you see, *detochka*, your Papa is now old and feeble. Look at how my hand shakes when I eat the soup."

The Poker Face kicked in, the Lying Man on my left shoulder let loose, and I said,

"What do you mean? You're not old, you're just a little bit unwell. But you're getting better all the time. And look, MY hand shakes, too, when I eat soup." And I intentionally faked a rather authentic-looking Parkinson's shake, sending drops cascading from my soup spoon into the bowl.

We stared into each other's eyes. I kept trying to maintain Poker Face and the shaking. Actually, the fake shaking wasn't all that fake. I was terrified that Papa was going to tell me something horrid, something from which there'd be no retreat or recovery, something that couldn't be unheard.

But he didn't.

He took a deep breath and let it out with a "*da*" that sounded like a croak, picked up a piece of bread and the salt shaker, sprinkling some white crystals on the soup and on the uneven slice of seedless rye I'd cut from the loaf. When we were done with the soup and moved on to dessert, he spooned up the cherry half that I'd intentionally placed in the middle of his bowl, reached across the table, and plunked it into my dessert bowl, causing a series of ripples to splash across the bowl. It reminded me of Papa showing me how to skip stones at the lake on vacation.

"*Ty zhe lyubish eti vishni?*" he asked, as if he didn't know.

"Uh-huh."

"*Tak vot i moyu skushay,*" and he tried to smile as he encouraged me to eat that one, too.

And I tried to smile, as well.

And we both failed miserably, but in the interests of maintaining some semblance of order in our disordered Universe, we looked into our dessert bowls and pretended that things were just fine. [Sidebar. I learned much later in life, that FINE is an acronym that can be deciphered as follows (children should look away or cover their eyes): F$%#ed Up, Insecure, Neurotic, and Emotional. Clearly, someone of a more poetic or creative nature than mine had had a similar life experience.]

The responsibility for washing the dinner dishes had fallen to me since Papa could no longer use the excuse he'd used all my life to explain his willingness to do the dishes: getting the industrial grease off his hands and out from under his fingernails from his days as the mechanic at the Jaguar Match Company. And, while I didn't mind the additional chore too much, I got the willies every night from standing in the place Papa fell from that January night. I almost expected the same thing to happen to me and surreptitiously sniffed the air around me while at the big white sink to detect any foul odor that might overwhelm me and cause me to repeat Papa's actions. In a way, I almost wished it would, since then Papa and I would be on a level playing field again. But it never did, and I continued to wash the dishes and scrub the pots, putting a bit more elbow grease than usual into the routine.

Life also wasn't the same because Papa moved much slower. He had gone from the seventy-eight rpm I always associated with him to a sixteen rpm.[44] He once told me that sometimes he got dizzy for no good reason, so he didn't venture too far from home. As a result, I didn't insist on outings to look at fishing reels or even on walks to the Dairy Queen a couple of blocks away. Instead, I pretended to busy myself with increasingly long homework assignments that kept me at the kitchen table while Papa watched TV or read the HOBO news in his chair in the living room, square glass ashtray on the right armrest. This way, I could pretend to be doing my homework while watching the clock to administer the right medication at the right time, as well as fix the side

---

[44] If you don't know what rpm means, you're clearly too young to appreciate this metaphor. As a former teacher, I hereby give you the following advice: if you don't know, look it up. I, myself, was a member of the "We Never Guess, We Look It Up" club at school. You, however, have Dr. Google to ask and don't have to run to the neighborhood library or your encyclopedia set. And I'm not sure this is a better way to go about learning things.

dishes that went with whatever main course Mama had semi-prepared. These days, I usually went with rice or some version of potatoes and the frozen *vegeTAHblz* Mama bought at the A & P.

I never again fixed any form of noodles or pasta for us. I didn't want to risk a repeat of That Night. Ya never know how one small move might affect the fate of nations. Not to mention the fate of one small Brooklyn family. I had become more superstitious than ever, risk averse, and pastaphobic.

As time went on, Papa grew restless in his seemingly endless "recovering" state—how many times could you re-read the Hobo News, after all—and started casting about for a project that wouldn't require long periods of standing. He finally decided that the maple tree that had taken over one corner of our small back yard had to go. I tried to plead on its behalf—I'd been nursing a secret urge to make my own maple syrup ever since reading a book about sugaring in Vermont—but Papa told me that this tree had deep roots that could spread and damage the sewer or pipes. In other words, it could cause more damage than it was worth. In retrospect, I like to imagine that the little tree fought back with all its might, because it took Papa weeks to cut it down, grind down the stump, and finally remove the last of the roots. Like any other true craftsman, he was proud of his work and gave me a piece of the sawed-down trunk as a memento of the Great Maple Battle. For years, I kept it in the glassed-in shelf of the bookcase in my room. Next to the studio portrait taken of us when I was about five and still had blonde bangs. Just the three of us, all dressed up in our finest outfits, me in the middle, hands folded demurely showing the dimples on my knuckles.

There's so much I don't remember. I wish I could reconstruct more of our conversations. I wish I could remember some of the things he taught me like how to weave a flower wreath, how to make furniture out of wild grasses and weeds, and whether bubbles in puddles mean it's going to rain all day or be over quickly. I do remember him telling me that if there's dew on the grass and plants in the morning, there won't be any rain that day, even if it's overcast.

I wish I could remember how to fix a faucet or tell if a car is malfunctioning and why, but those are things that Papa told me and I didn't pay attention back then, figuring I could always ask him in some faraway later. I hung around him while he was repairing things, pretending to pay attention, but mostly I just enjoyed being around him. He always had a funny or cautionary tale from his childhood to tell me, and I simply soaked up his words and cadences and laughter, catching the random whiffs of his aftershave mixed with the sweat of an honest working man.

One time Papa pulled off a huge surprise on me. And, since it was so memorable, I'm going to share it with you. But first, a little background (Lit majors, pay attention):

I had spent the first ten years of my life mostly as a tomboy. I played with boys because their games were more interesting than the girls'. Let's face it, playing house or beauty parlor gets old in about five minutes. You can wonder about how to do your hair or what to serve for dinner that evening only for so long before you want to run away screaming, tearing out your pretend freshly-coiffed locks.

Boys' games were full of action, plots, ambushes, making forts, and other really fun stuff. It was especially fun to run through the girls' perfect little "houses" with their perfect little dolls and perfectly arranged hair, causing havoc and disruption wherever we went. I must've been pretty good at these games—especially the ambush plotting—because I always was treated as one of the guys. Don't get me wrong, I also played with girls, but I didn't enjoy their company as much. If a guy had an issue with you, you'd settle it fair and square with a punch or two and then shake hands and fuhgeddaboutit. Girls were different: they made up stuff about you and said nasty untrue things about you to other girls and to their parents, all of which had the potential of creating a living hell for me at PS 170. And I couldn't even pop them one in the mouth—despite my training with Papa—for fear that I'd get punished at home for hitting a girl. Go figure.

Which brings me to another memorable moment in my collection of Papamoments.

I suddenly found myself in a very strange predicament in fifth grade. Nasty Kevin Ronald's family had moved into the PS 170 district from who-knows-what-planet in the middle of the school year, and he was placed into my "smart" class. Clearly by mistake, but we'll come back to that.

I don't know what set him off: the fact that I was the undisputed "number one" in class (maybe he'd been a big fish in a small pond in Moosebreathburg?); or, the fact that I was an astonishing base runner during recess games of punchball with the boys; or, that I simply ignored him because he wasn't much to look at those days. Short, squat, albino with a piggy snout for a nose, both a lisp and a stammer, topped off with an incredible nasal drone for a voice. But, for some reason unbeknownst to me, Kevin started paying attention to me in annoying and embarrassing ways. For instance, sneaking up on me from behind and yanking my braid so hard I could hear my neck snap. Making fun of my (unpronounceable) last name. Calling me a Commie. Stupid ten-year-old catcalls, all of which contained some version of "ugly," "stupid," or worse in combination with my name. Trying to trip me at gym or recess. You get my drift. But his favorite place of attack was from the base of the light post I had to pass on my way home from school. He'd hang on with one arm and make gestures I didn't understand with the free arm, catcalling and harassing me until I was out of sight. He always kept out of my reach . . . no doubt because he'd heard about my right jab. And, though I hated to admit it at the time, he was a faster runner than I was, especially when he had a head start. Perhaps because he was lower to the ground than I was and had a different center of gravity, his bowlegged little legs pumped faster than mine, though my stride was much better.

I had tolerated this incessant persecution in silence. I told neither Miss Fitzgerald nor my parents, maybe because I was afraid to get the Ronald kid in trouble (and then the persecution would worsen) or because I was ashamed I'd let it go on for so long. In any event, toward the end of the school year, in the spring, the dam burst and I told Papa everything, including how ashamed I was.

Papa responded in true Papa form: 1) he calmed me down and let me finish crying while sitting in his lap; 2) he asked me what I wanted to do about it, and 3) said he'd talk to Mama after she came home from work and they'd decide what to do. I had been shouldering this burden all this time, much like the Atlas at Rockefeller Center—where I skated during the winter months—but I felt the world had been lifted from my shoulders that evening and was able to fall asleep as soon as my head hit the pillow.

I guess Mama and Papa had discussed my dilemma and come to some sort of conclusion, but they didn't tell me what it was. Mama actually offered to walk me to school (Oh. My. God. *What* was she thinking? I was ten years old, for cripes sake! I could take the subway by myself into Manhattan and she was offering to walk me to school?), an offer I quickly declined, thank you very much, and scooted out the door. I descended the steps two at a time, raced along the black runner on the first floor, threw open the inside door, was through the foyer in two steps, and lunged out the building's front door and down the stoop before anyone even realized I was gone. I had a little change in my pocket left from last week's allowance and stopped at the corner drugstore to load up on cough drops. Not only was this an ideal location to catch my breath, it also allowed me a critical vantage point from which to see if Mama was following me. Assured that she wasn't, I proceeded via one of my routes—they varied day by day—at a more leisurely pace to Dear Lexington, where I fell in line behind Cassie (Cassandra) Alexandropoulos in the school yard. Cassie and I shared the burden of unpronounceable last names: misery loves company.

At the end of another routine day of fifth-gradeness with its reading, spelling, math, recess, and music (yay!), we packed up our homework, books, and notebooks by 2:50 pm and sat quietly at our desks with our hands folded. Waiting for the clock to tick over to the 3:00 pm dismissal bell. I wondered what torment Kevin Ronald had in store for me that day and desperately searched my nervous brain for another route home or for a particularly withering retort. By the time the bell rang, I had come up with nothing and had resigned myself to another episode of haranguing by my irksome lisping foe.

We walked silently, two by two, out the classroom door, a few steps along the hall to the stairs, and down three flights to the ground level. A teacher was posted at each landing to ensure we a) didn't talk and b) didn't shove each other out of the way and over the railing in the desperate lunge for the freedom and sunshine that came with pouring out onto the sidewalk like so many uncaged rats. I can still hear Mrs. Spencer, the vice principal with a nearly-bass voice and old-timey high class New York pronunciation that's been lost to the ages (and influence of the Bronx, no doubt), commanding "Wohhhk thehyah! Wohhhk thehyah!", encouraging us to proceed in as orderly a fashion as was possible for a multi-score multitude of urchins down the stairs and out through the heavy side doors to Seventy-first Street and freedom.

After I'd cleared the doors and stood near the iron fence surrounding the school pretending to re-balance my books, I kept an eye out for the Ronald kid. True to established practice, he'd made it to his favorite lamppost and was scrambling up to his perch. I took a deep breath, determined to ignore him this time (like I had every other day since his matriculation into my educational institution), squared my shoulders, and proceeded to walk at a quick-march pace toward Sixth Avenue. And, like every preceding day since his arrival, Kevin was warming up to his verbal assault as I drew closer. I could hear the nasal singsongy harangue in his preferred poetic style: iambic tetrameter.

There goes that stupid Russian bitch
She makes my ass go fart and itch

He'd pause to make farting noises and scratch his rear with exaggerated hand gestures and total lack of aplomb or restraint, much to the amusement and delight of his sycophantic Neanderthal crew. How they kept their knuckles from dragging along the sidewalks was a mystery to me.

Kevin must have spent precious homework time each night coming up with the following day's rhyming diatribe. That his grades continued their downhill slalom was a surprise to no one, as was the accompanying increasingly bad classroom behavior. In fact, I'd silently cheered each time Miss Fitzgerald had beaned him straight between the eyes with the reprimanding "TO ERR IS TO MAKE A MISTAKE" eraser from her desk. I silently wished he'd sprout a horn in that spot on his forehead that would serve as a warning to all who saw it: I am the Devil's Spawn, stand back.

I hugged my books closer to my body and picked up the pace. No matter, the torment and laughter at my expense grew louder and seemed to follow me. I could feel my ears burning and my eyes starting to fill with tears of frustration and humiliation as I walked more and more quickly up the street. And then I looked up.

There he was.

Leaning casually against a streetlight, lit cigarette in the *mundshtuk* between his fingers, hat tilted rakishly on his head. I couldn't believe my eyes. The man who never walked far from our home anymore had walked six long city blocks to meet me after school. I broke into a blisteringly fast run and rammed straight into him, dropping my books, throwing my arms around his waist, and hugging him so close I could barely breathe.

"*A nu-ka,* which one is he? Show him to me."

I turned around in time to see the Ronald kid climbing off the lamppost, laughing out loud with his cronies and starting off for his walk home. Toward where we were standing.

"*Nu,* which one?"

"The one with the striped shirt."

"The white-haired one? That short one?"

"Uh huh."

"*Kak zovut?*"

"Kevin Ronald."

"OK."

Papa took a long drag on his cigarette, blew out the smoke, waited a few seconds for my tormentor to get closer, and then stepped gently into his path. Kevin tried to go around him, but Papa just moved back into his path. Kevin tried to duck down, sidestep and break into a run . . . unsuccessfully because Papa had caught him by his shirt collar. A full two feet (plus) taller, strong from years of physical labor, Papa swung the albino around so fast I could almost hear his neck snapping.

I really didn't hear what Papa said to him, but I did see him pointing at me with the cigarette hand and using the same hand to emphasize certain points in his lecture to Kevin. When Papa finally let the little weasel go, Ronald scurried off toward home like the rat he was leaving a sinking ship. Kevin's cronies had abandoned the ship as soon as they saw Papa and had beat feet to their homes before Papa's avenging strongarm could get to them. No matter, the Ronald kid was the unelected top dog in their pack and took the punishment for the team.

And, just to show you that—even at the age of ten—I was far above those louses, I didn't even gloat. I believed so firmly in Papa's strength, power, and authority that I was convinced the Ronald gang would leave me in peace from that moment forward.

Papa, being considerably older and wiser than I was, came to school to meet me every day for a week. Just to make sure that his lesson stuck.

25

Over the sound of the KitchenAid whipping up yet another cake experiment (more process, less thought . . . get me out of my head, Lord, it's a "no fly" zone), I heard the television anchor asking, "What's the best advice your father ever gave you?" and in a nanosecond I was whiplashed back to that June day in 1968.

We were standing in our kitchen, the three of us: Mama somewhere behind me—I could feel her presence and saw her only in my peripheral vision, Papa in his trademark starched white shirt (thank you, Wu's Chinese laundry and the brown paper packages tied up with strings I picked up on my way home from school) and dark slacks. I had had to call Mama at work last night to tell her to come home because Papa had another seizure—again, on my watch—and had started vomiting up his dinner and everything else in the world, it seemed. Mama told me to call Papa's special doctor and tell him what was happening, and she would be home as soon as she could. I pulled Doctor Mihalko's card out from behind the phone on the kitchen wall and, willing my fingers to stop shaking and dial the number, I eventually managed to get his answering service and leave a message. Frankly, I did not believe that he would call me back: I'd had to call for an ambulance at least three times when Papa had his first seizure, being told by the Operator during the last call that it would be more than an hour before they could get to us. Suffice it to say that, in my view, the New York City health establishment left much to be desired.

Much to my surprise, Dr. Mihalko did call back, and fairly quickly. I explained to him what was happening with Papa and told him, in response to his question on where Mama was, that she was at work but was on her way home. I asked him if she should call him when she got home and he said she should. The long wait for Mama's return began.

For the first time in what seemed like a very long time, I was actually relieved to hear Mama's key in the door locks. She immediately went to Papa, who was stretched out on the living room sofa, just as he sat up and started to throw up. She cupped her hands under his chin and yelled at me to get something to catch the vomit. Even more panicked than before, my brain went into momentary paralysis and I couldn't imagine what would work, so Mama yelled at me to get a pot from the closet. I got it there just in time.

After the waves of nausea and vomiting subsided, Mama helped Papa into their room, changed him out of his street clothes, and tucked him into bed, turning off the lights as she left. Then, she was able to call the doctor and find out that he had a bed waiting at the hospital for Papa and that they should come directly there the next morning.

Mama spent the rest of the evening quietly packing a hospital bag for Papa with his pajamas, toothbrush and toothpaste, shaving cream and razor, and slippers. Mama also found an old wallet of hers and filled the change portion with all the change she had so that Papa could call home from the public phone in the hospital. She called my friend Peter's father, Uncle Peter, and asked him to drive them to the hospital in the morning. She spoke Ukrainian, but I understood everything she said. Funny, but when you grow up around Other Slavic kids, you naturally come to understand their languages—Polish, Ukrainian, whatever. Mama spoke those languages, but Papa refused to, on principle, he said, because he was Russian. Invariably, he would add a final phrase, like a period at the end of a sentence: *"oni i tak menya poymut"* . . . and they really **did** understand him anyway.

So, there we were, we three, in our kitchen. As the icon of the Virgin Mary and Jesus hovered protectively over us in the light blue corner under the ceiling, over Papa's right shoulder, I remembered a phrase from Mass: "the Trinity one in essence and undivided." He was dressed for the hospital, having survived the night, and we were waiting for Uncle Peter to come to drive Papa to the hospital. No subway today. Only a prayer to the Virgin and Her Son for protection and mercy. And, from me, a fervent silent prayer that everything in our trio would go back to the way it was Before: before the seizure, before the blood, before the medicines, before all the vomiting the night before. Before: getting dunked in the Serdyuks' water barrel after a rain shower; fishing in the lake; jumping into the really deep end off the huge tree; racing home up the length of Sixty-eighth Street; running down Sixty-eighth Street at full tilt and jumping up to Papa's "OP-PAH!" and kiss on the cheek. Before.

But no. The scales fell from my eyes as I studied Papa and saw that he was suddenly older, feebler, and unsteady on his feet. In my heart of hearts, I somehow knew that jumping off the big tree into the deep end of the lake was a thing of the past not to be repeated, but I desperately believed—or wanted to believe—that the hospital would restore Papa to us almost exactly the way he was Before. I was willing to give up the racing, the deep part of the lake, and even dancing in the Pavilion if we could only have a healthy Papa back. I tried some deal-making with God, promising to do anything He ordered me to do if I could have my Papa back. I'd take care of his medicines and dinners, I'd get books for him from the library, I'd bring the Hobo News to him when I picked it up on the way home from Russian School at that one kiosk by the subway station in Manhattan. Anything. Tell me to do anything and I'll do it. Just bring him home safe, as healthy as possible, and we'll make do. We'll adjust to anything but pleasepleaseplease bring my Papa home.

Papa crossed himself and bowed from the waist as his prayers came to an end. We followed suit, Mama softly whispering "amen," and me crossing my toes where no one could see. I thought God probably wouldn't mind my adding a little non-religious, non-Orthodox turbo boost to my prayers, just in case. As I looked up, I saw Papa turn toward me and take a step closer so he could reach me. I can still feel his hands on my bony shoulders and can hear the gentle voice instructing—almost imploring—me: "Go to school, *detka*, study." Perhaps because he'd had to leave school after second grade to go to work to provide for his widowed mother and sister, he prized education above many, many other things.

Papa's gray eyes glistened where the tears had popped out at the corners, and I could see the focus wrinkle in his forehead between his eyebrows as he tried to find the right words for me. In retrospect, I suppose it was either because he thought I was too young to understand adult concepts or because he knew something that he would not—or could not—admit to anyone but himself. I don't know whether he did this without prompting, but in the interest of staying true to the story, I have to admit that he did tell me to help Mama around the house and in the garden. I treated those tidbits as the white noise I assumed them to be and focused instead on his voice, the feel of his hands on my shoulders, and the different colors playing in Papa's eyes. I so wanted to remember it all while he was away at the hospital, so that I wouldn't feel as alone as I had during his first hospital stay, when I sat in his chair while Mama was at work or otherwise not at home. Keeping it warm for his return.

An autodidact, Papa had read everything he could lay his hands on over the years and could engage anyone in discussions on topics ranging from The Bolshevik Revolution (he was, after all, an eyewitness and survivor), to gardening, to auto repair. In fact, Papa was the only person I've ever known who could diagnose a car's problems by listening to it run. Still, I think he felt the lack of *formal* schooling acutely and, in the same way that a thirsty person appreciates a drink of water, knew the value of this thing he had missed. I suspect he might have been quite a great man had he had the opportunities other, non-fatherless, children his age did. On the other hand, in my eyes he always was a great man and maybe that was his purpose after all.

The door buzzer interrupted our little tête à tête loudly and rudely, jolting Mama and me out of our silence and into action to buzz back. Sure enough, it was Uncle Peter, who came upstairs ostensibly to help with the bags, but in reality to help Papa down the stairs. Hat in hand, he stepped over the threshold into our apartment and, in the gentlest voice I'd ever heard him use, asked if *Mikolaychiko* was ready to go. (*Mikolaychiko* was the pet name their family had given Papa after he helped take care of Auntie Tonya when she had rheumatic heart fever. Papa was the only one who was strong enough to carry Auntie Tonya to the bathroom and back. He even stayed home from work to take care of her so that Uncle Peter could continue to work and draw a paycheck.)

In keeping with tradition, we sat down for a moment of silence in the kitchen—the way we all did before a trip, before escaping from the German advance, before leaving for college, before vacation, before . . . well, I guess, before a trip to the hospital. I was keeping my toes crossed all this time, believing their clinging together would make God know that my prayer and promises were really sincere and incline Him to respond in my favor. And, after what seemed like an eternity, Papa said,

"*Nu chtozh? Poyekhali?*" and everyone shoved their chairs back from the table and stood up, making final pre-departure checks. I ran into my room to get my shoes, but was stopped at the threshold by Papa's voice,

"*A ty kuda?*"

Stunned, I turned around and explained that I had to get my shoes on so I could go with him to the hospital. All the grownups were stuck in a freeze-frame, as if this had come out of the blue and they were totally unprepared to deal with the issue of my tagging along. Finally, Mama broke the silence gently and said that children weren't allowed on Papa's floor and that there would be so much paperwork to fill out that I would be bored.

"It's OK, I'll bring a book and wait in the waiting area like before.

I won't be bored," I pressed. But I knew the window of opportunity had closed when Papa said,

"Why don't you stay here and read. Or, if you like, turn on the television and watch one of your programs. There's no need for you to go all the way to the hospital—hospitals are for sick people, and I don't want you to get sick."

I swallowed the growing lump in my throat and felt it squeezing tears into my eyes, but I refused to cry. Instead, I said, looking at Papa,

"Well, OK, if you say so."

"*Nu vot i molodets!*" Papa attempted a smile.

And I attempted a smile back, promising to draw a picture for him of me in my ballet tutu, en pointe.

My face felt like it was going to crack, so fake was my smile as I stared into Papa's eyes. And I realized he was doing the same thing: making a brave face so that no one will know your fear.

Mama unlocked the door and the three of them moved into the hallway and ever so slowly down the stairs, Uncle Peter holding the carpetbag in one hand and supporting Papa under the elbow with the other. Mama checked her purse for keys and wallet, clicked it shut, and started down the stairs. I trailed after them in my house slippers, leaving a doorstop at the foyer door so I wouldn't lock myself out.

Uncle Peter had been double-parked all this time, yet he hadn't said a word about it or tried to rush us out of the house. He'd left enough room for cars to get by on the driver's side, but if either of the two cars he'd blocked on the right had wanted to get out, it was tough noogies. I stood on the top landing from where I had a view of all Sixty-eighth Street; oddly enough, there seemed to be no activity on our block other than ours.

Uncle Peter helped Papa down the stoop steps, then helped him into the back seat of the car. Mama slid in next to Papa on the burgundy leatherette bench seat and slammed the car door shut. In one final un-controlled impulse, I launched myself down the stoop, across the side-walk, between two parked cars, and into the street next to Uncle Peter's car. There was no imminent danger to me—life or limb—since there wasn't a car in sight. I gestured to Papa to roll down the window and, as he did, I leaned in and gave him a big kiss on the cheek. And, before Mama could yell at me about cars and leaving the front door open, I ran back up the stoop in time to watch Uncle Peter's left blinker come on and the car slide gently off toward the light on Fourth Avenue. I waved wildly in their direction as the car turned right and disappeared into the general flow of traffic.

I turned slowly toward the heavy front door and pushed it open.

I crossed the foyer, pulled the doorstop out, and let the foyer door slam shut.

I walked down the hall and up the stairs to our landing.

I opened the door to 2R, stepped through, and closed it behind me, throwing all three locks.

I could still smell Papa's aftershave and see the depressions in the kitchen chairs where we'd all sat.

I wondered how long Papa would be gone this time, and looked up at the icon to see if, maybe somehow, it would miraculously start talking and give me the answers I so desperately wanted to hear.

But both Jesus and His Mother remained silent.

I walked into the living room, turned on the TV, and sat *po-chelovecheski* in Papa's chair. He'd left a half-smoked Camel in the ashtray on the right arm rest—a first. Papa smoked all his cigarettes down to the nub, so this was quite a surprise. I took it as tacit permission to finish it and scurried into the kitchen in search of matches. Search complete, I moseyed into the living room, put the cigarette between my lips, and lit a match. I touched the flaming tip to the end of the cigarette, inhaled the way I'd seen Papa do all my life, and took a long deep breath. And . . . aaaaaaaakhakhakhakha! I coughed so hard I started retching, my eyes were tearing over, and snot was running out of my nose. I dropped the offending article into the ashtray and ran to the bathroom to splash cold water on my face. As I turned the C faucet on full blast and tried to bend down to it, my eyes noticed the tile pattern on the floor and the room started spinning all around me, including the ceiling. I slammed my behind onto the toilet seat and waited for this to end or death to come—I wasn't sure which I preferred.

But this little unexpected turn of events did come to an end eventually, and I regained my equilibrium. I washed my face and even combed my hair. And then I realized that Mama doubtless would be on her way home.

OH NO! If Mama found out that I'd been smoking, she'd kill me. I had no doubt about it whatsoever. What to do, what to do? Aha! First, under the auspices of helping around the house, I emptied Papa's ashtray, washed it with soap, dried it, and put it in its rightful place. I also did a bit of dusting and fluffing of pillows to further add credence to my cover story. The cherry on my cover story cake was my brushing my teeth so hard that my gums bled and my tongue lost most of its epithelial cells. I was pretty sure there was no evidence of smoking on my breath, but just in case, I ate a few Pine Brothers cherry cough lozenges I had stashed in my desk.

By the time Mama came home, I had already fixed dinner, set the table for two, and was sitting in the living room, in my appointed place on the couch, watching TV. Mama gave me a brief synopsis of what happened in the hospital and said that Papa was all settled in and had enough change to call us in the evenings or afternoons, before Mama went to work and after I came home from school. She tried to make everything seem normal when our world had been turned upside down and shaken.

I did not ask if Papa would get better.

I did not ask when Papa would come home.

I did not mention my attempted deal with God.

I did not say to Mama all the things that were roiling inside me like, please tell me we'll all be ok, please tell me Papa will come home, I'm sosososo scared, can I please sit on your lap so you can hug me?

And, in return, Mama never told me whether she was scared or sad or anything.

We went on as if nothing had changed in our lives, except that Mama would go visit Papa several times a week, taking him fresh pajamas and the most recent issue of the Hobo News.

Papa did call in the evenings and I did get to talk to him, but it wasn't the same. I was afraid to tell him about my problems because I was afraid the worry would keep him from getting better. I told him funny things, some of which I made up on the fly, just to hear his robust laugh rolling through the telephone wires to my ear.

One of the days Mama was going to visit Papa, I was struck by a lightning bolt of inspiration and decided to make a treat for him, since I was convinced he missed our real food, subjected as he was to hospital food all this time. I walked across the hall and knocked on Mary's door because she was such a great cook and told her my plan. She was almost as excited as I was about it, and even sent Mark down to the neighborhood deli to buy a few key ingredients. Mostly, Mary supervised as I made and rolled dough into circles, counted a few blueberries and a bit of sugar into the middle, and then sealed them the way Mama had taught me. I brought a huge pot of lightly salted water to boil and dumped my dumplings—*vareniki*—into the water and watched them float to the top when they were done. I used a slotted spoon to fish them out and then wrapped them in aluminum foil. Twice, to be on the safe side.

I walked into Mama and Papa's room, where the packed carpetbag stood ready, unzipped it, and removed the top two layers. I gently placed the wrapped *vareniki* on top of Papa's pajamas and covered them up with his underwear and socks. We all congratulated each other on a job well done, made quick work of mopping up in the kitchen, and were all in our appropriate places when Mama rang the buzzer to come up.

I buzzed her in, shouting down the stairs, "Who is it?" to make sure it wasn't some evildoer trying to gain entry into our splintered world. Relieved to hear Mama's "*eto ya*," I stood on the landing, waiting for her to come up, checking my clothes for telltale signs of flour. Not a whit, not a jot. Success!

Mama told me later that night, when she came home from visiting Papa, that they had both been stunned to find my little surprise in the bag. But the best part (for me) was when Mama told me that Papa actually teared up when he realized that I had done this for him. So touched was he by this one single gesture of mine that he kissed every single *varenik* before eating it.

I didn't ask if they had turned out OK, because I knew that my message had been received: I love you, I miss you, please come home, I'll make you more. I love you, I miss you, please come home. Just come home.

Come home.

Please.

26

Уходят люди . . . Их не возвратить.
Их тайные миры не возродить.
И каждый раз мне хочется опять
от этой невозвратности кричать.[45]

F ast forward fifty years. Half a century later, on the anniversary
of his death, I'm still the ten-year-old girl with a black ribbon
braided into her hair, forced to wear an iceberg-lettuce-green
dress to her father's funeral. I have loathed and avoided that color all my
life, largely due to its insult to my broken child's heart. Told by my mad-
with-grief black-enrobed mother that "children do not wear black" and

---

[45] *1961*

Евгений Евтушенко. Стихотворения.
Серия `Самые мои стихи`.
Москва: Слово, 1999.
People leave . . . You cannot bring them back.
You can't revive their secret worlds.
And every time I want to scream
From this not-bring-them-backingness.
[My translation]

powerless to do anything about this affront to—and dismissal of—my overwhelming grief, I buried my resentment deep inside a crack in my heart, convinced all the more that She was my *stepmother*. My fevered little brain kept up a steady drumbeat: *my REAL mother would let me wear black. My REAL mother would let me wear black. My REAL mother would let me wear black.* But, crushed by her own sudden and unbearable loss, my mother had no room or time for me.

Friends and neighbors saw to my basic survival needs, but I had lost the only person who had seen into, understood, and loved my child's heart and soul. I realized in those early days that I would forevermore be one of those sad children from the fairy tales I read that made me cry: an orphan. Orphan. *Siротà*.

It all began one morning with the phone ringing while I was getting ready for school. For some reason, I didn't rush to pick it up per my normal practice. Maybe Mama beat me to it because she was closer, I don't know; rather, I don't remember. I do remember, however, Mama calling our family friends down the street who owned a car and screaming single words over the phone in Russian: *"Vsyo! Konets!"*[46] It's odd, but I don't remember either finishing dressing, getting my school things together, or walking to school that day. I don't remember if I ate breakfast and I don't remember if I ate lunch at school that day. I must have, right?

What I do remember quite distinctly was that, as the school bell rang for dismissal, my teacher—Miss Fitzgerald, whom I worshipped for a host of reasons—offered to give me a ride home. I fell in love with Miss Fitzgerald on the first day of fifth grade for her unerring precision in hurling the mauve, six-inch "To Err Is To Make A Mistake" eraser from the center of her desk to the center of either Gustavson's or Eriksen's forehead.

[A brief digression, but a somewhat important one: because they were tall for their age, both Robert Gustavson and Steven Eriksen sat

---

[46] "It's all over! It's the end!"

at the back of the room where they raised Cain like the two normal fifth grade boys they were. I leave it to you to figure out which one was Swedish and which one Norwegian; we could tell by the patterns on their sweaters. Miss Fitzgerald didn't care. She was an equal opportunity Themis. The most important school lessons we learned that year, we learned on the first day of school.

Specifically, when Miss Fitzgerald's face turned red and she yelled, "Jesus, Mary and Joseph! God give me patience with you people!!!", that was the first heads up or, rather, heads down warning. Because immediately after that she would reach for the eraser, and the best position for the innocent was heads down, hands clasped over hair on top of our iron maiden desks. We learned that from the unfortunate incident with Jimmy O'Rourke—known on the playground for his slow reaction time—who went home with an undeserved knot on his noggin on the first day of school simply because he was slow on the uptake and missed the tell. On top of it all, poor O'Rourke got it at home, too. Back in those days, the parents **always** sided with the teacher, no matter what.]

Back to the story of that sunny June day. On this particular day, for a reason at that time unbeknownst to me, Miss Fitzgerald offered to give me a ride home. *In her car.* The numbers two and three in class—the Greek girls Despina and Johanna—overheard and started whining the *Miss Fitzgerald gimme a ride too pleeeeeeeeeeeeeeeeeeeze* refrain. Even though they lived next door to each other *right across the street* from the school. My nose was distinctly out of joint as we all trooped behind Miss Fitzgerald out of the school and to her car on Seventy-second Street. I admired the black-roofed gold Cutlass SS as the interlopers piled into the back seat. I was slightly mollified by the thought that at least I got to ride up front with Miss Fitzgerald. This was one of the *best* days of my little life so far and I couldn't wait to get home to tell Mama all about it. Maybe I'd even send a note to Papa in the hospital so he could share this glorious event with me. WOW!! Not only my favorite teacher in the whole world, but a ride in her car. Just the two of us! I can't remember a word of what she said, I was so in love with her and the car and this whole life-changing experience that I even forgot to become nauseated. It was, indeed, sublime. My entire memory of the experience has a golden glow to it.

Alas, before I knew it, we were in front of my house. I remember Miss Fitzgerald asking me if I knew how to open the car door (I did, miraculously enough) and whether I was going to be OK. I thought it a tad odd, but dismissed the thought because of all the unexpected, unadulterated joy and privilege I felt at being given a ride home by my very favoritest teacher in the whole wide world. I still remember the faint scent of her perfume and the music the gold bangles on her right arm made every time she moved. She had beautiful dark curls tipped with sunshine, freckles, and her green eyes danced when she was happy.

I bounded up the steps of the stoop, swung open the front door into the foyer, and pressed the button for 2R so Mama would let me in. The buzzer sounded, I pushed open the curtained door into the hall, ran along the black rubber runner as fast as I could, and took the steps up-stairs two at a time. I hung a sharp left into our apartment door, threw it open, shouting "Mama! Mama! Guess what! Miss Fitzgerald . . ." and stopped. Our neighbor, the very Italian Mary-with-a-beautiful-soprano-voice, was standing in our kitchen with Mama. Strange, I thought, as I pulled up next to them to complete the circle.

A peculiar stillness hung in the room. Mama's face was darker than I remembered it being that morning and she looked like she'd been crying. Mary stood opposite her and the space between them was very small. I remember Mama getting a small white pill out of a drug store bottle, giving it to me, and telling me to take it. She handed me a glass of boiled water. (My parents never drank water straight out of the tap. Old habits die hard, even in the days of chlorination.) I think a silent pause followed, but I am not too sure about that part.

I remember her placing her hands on my shoulders.

I remember her looking me in the eyes.

I remember her starting to cry as she said, "Masha . . ." and swallowed a sob, *"Papa umer."*[47] And then she cried.

And I don't remember anything else.

Except one thing: when I woke up the next morning, I couldn't move.

The days afterward are caught in a blur of freeze-frames for me: Not being able to move when I woke up in the morning. Mary somehow getting me into a cab to take me to Dr. Schaumberg's office, who diagnosed me with "hysterical paralysis." I didn't see how I could be hysterical, since I hadn't uttered a word or cried a tear since I'd heard the news. All I knew was that I couldn't move by myself and I had trouble holding my head up.

In fact, I was something akin to the Tin Man in *The Wizard of Oz*, only I wasn't standing up. I was in my small pink room with the bed facing out to the sky and all the stars, wondering which one he might be, but I did not cry. Since hearing the news, I had been Gobi Desert dry. Mama seemed to produce gallons of tears in an endless stream, dripping clear blobs onto the black fabric of mourning dresses she was rapidly stitching together on her old Singer sewing machine. And I could not cry. Simply couldn't do it.

I couldn't cry, couldn't move, and could only observe the world around me with a detached neutrality. I suspect that my physical inability to move simply reflected my inner detachedness from the world. Perhaps my little body was simply refusing to take part in a life that no longer included Papa. It was the harshest blow I'd ever been dealt and, as such, I was something akin to "punch drunk." Nothing made sense anymore.

Time out.

To Sleep, Perchance to Dream?

Those of you who believe only in the things you can see, smell, touch, and taste should skip the next few pages.

---

[47] Papa died.

If, however, you believe that the Unseen is vaster and greater than the Seen . . .

If you believe in a Power Greater than Yourself and in the angelic realms . . .

If you believe that our loved ones never truly leave us . . .

Then go ahead and keep reading.

This is 100 percent true; it really happened. If you don't care or don't believe me, skip to the next chapter or call me a liar and toss this book. Your choice.

My job is to tell the story. Because it gave my ten-year-old shattered heart some measure of healing and a ray of hope. And sometimes that little tiny ray of light is all you need to keep putting one foot in front of the other and showing up for life. It's the one gossamer thread that links your tiny spark to its Divine Origin.

The night of the day that Papa died, I was tucked into bed in Mama and Papa's big bed, not my own in my own pink room. Probably because I wasn't moving or talking and Mama could keep an eye on me better, but I don't know. It's one of the many things I don't know about those days—or don't remember. They say that our brains block the memory of traumatic events, which probably explains my inability to recall all of what happened then. It probably also explains why I can't recall the route of my husband's funeral procession at Arlington Cemetery. (Coincidentally or synchronistically, both men died at seven in the morning. On dates that were numerologically identical.)

Enough of the prologue. Here's what happened while I slept:

Uncle Peter and Uncle Stosh come to collect me and take me to the funeral home.

They lift me under the arms and somehow manage to get me down the stairs and into Uncle Peter's car. The car is black with a fake leather burgundy interior. I surprise myself by not barfing in the car or even feeling nauseated.

Uncle Peter pulls up in front of Makeyev's Funeral Home and both he and Uncle Stosh help me out of the car and "walk" me into the funeral parlor; the room is packed with people.

I am lowered onto the prayer bench in front of the coffin for a few minutes, then lifted onto a chair next to Mama.

I am sitting in the front row at Makeyev's, staring at what used to be Papa in the coffin. He's wearing one of his light summer suits and his hands are crossed as for communion. I'm watching him breathe because I know this can't be real.

And I'm right.

A transparent part of Papa sits up, leaving the heavy "real" part behind, looks at me, smiles, and says, "Would you like to see where I'm going to live now?" And I nod "yes" because I still can't speak.

PapaSpirit moves out of the light wood coffin, I stand up, he takes my hand, and we walk out of the funeral parlor together, leaving all the people behind. It's a bright sunny day when we walk outside; but, instead of staying on the sidewalk, Papa leads me out into the black paved street where, oddly enough, there is no traffic. Don't get me wrong: sure, there are parked cars, but there are no moving cars. In Manhattan.

We walk up the street, which starts to climb higher and higher until the street runs out and we're walking on a rainbow. I don't remember what we talked about, but I do remember the walk being easy, peaceful, and light. The rainbow leads us to poofy white clouds that we actually walk on as we climb higher and higher still.

Papa asks me if I'd like to see his room, since this is where he'll be living now. And I say "yes," because I've magically regained the ability to both walk and talk freely.

The "room" is a room in name only, because what I see is a limitless space of such indescribable luminosity, such a wondrous combination of his two favorite colors—blue and green—that to this day, I have not been able to find an earthly color that even approaches it. Maybe amazonite, but it still pales by comparison. There was a very nicely made up bed with crisp clean white sheets on it for Papa to sleep on in his new home. I didn't ask to sit down on it, because I'm not allowed to sit on beds. Beds are for sleeping only. It looked very welcoming.

Then Papa asked me if I wanted to meet his new family. I remember looking up at him, wondering if it meant that I was no longer "his family" and how bleak and even black the future looked with that possibility.

And that's how I met his Mama, a very beautiful, kind, and gently smiling young woman in her long white robes and wide light blue belt. She seemed very gentle and loving and had a kind of glow around her; in fact, she looked nothing like the pictures of her I'd grown up seeing. She stretched her hand out to me and tenderly caressed the right side of my face as if to say that everything is as it should be, that everything would be all right, and maybe even that she loved me, too. At least it felt like that.

In the distance, I saw an old man in white robes with long white hair and a long white beard. His eyes twinkled so much when he looked at me that it appeared as though stars were dancing in his eyes. I thought that he made a wonderful new father for mine, because I could feel how much he loved Papa and how happy he was to see him back home. He even seemed to make up for the father Papa had lost when he was ten.

Out of the wispy clouds came a young man with dark, shoulder-length wavy hair, a beard, and soft, dark-brown eyes. Papa introduced him to me as his brother, but I'd seen pictures of this young man before in church and knew immediately who he was. He smiled at me, too. And I smiled back, because that was the only way I could react to someone who so obviously loved me and Papa, who would take care of Papa when I wasn't around. I thought they'd probably set off for a great fishing spot to start things off right. I wished I could come along.

But, no.

Papa smiled down at me and said these exact words (well, not exact since they were in Russian, but you'll get the drift) to me:

I have to take you back now, but now you know where I'll be. And remember: whenever in your life you have troubles, or life is difficult for you, all you have to do is call me and I'll come back to you to help. You can always, always count on me because I will always, always be here for you.

And then it was time to go. I waved good-bye to Papa's new mother and brother, took one last look at his new home, put my small right hand in his coarse, large left one and we walked out. Down through the clouds.

Down the rainbow.

Down the paved part of East Seventh Street.

We turned left into the funeral home and then right, into the parlor where all the people were sitting.

He led me to my seat in the front row, smoothed my hair gently, then PapaSpirit slid through the wood into the coffin and laid back down into his "real" self.

That is exactly what I saw the night of 12 June, over fifty years ago. As real today as it was then.

I remember the days after in camera-like format. I can practically hear the clicking sounds of the shutter and the hiss of film advancing.

Advance.

Stop. Click. Mama at her sewing machine, stitching together yards and yards of black fabric into dresses for herself, dripping enormous tear blobs onto the fabric, where they were absorbed into the darkness, leaving even darker traces of themselves.

Advance.

Stop. Click. Womenfolk taking turns to bring food to us. I guess Mama had stopped cooking, but I didn't notice since I wasn't moving, talking, or eating. They were all very kind. They all sat and watched us eat, probably to make sure we did. Then they would wash our dishes and go home to their own families, dishes, and lives.

Advance.

Stop. Click. Uncle Stosh and Uncle Peter holding me under my arms to get me from our apartment, down the stairs and the steps of the stoop to Uncle Peter's car. I remember that I didn't get sick in the car, probably for the second time in my life, but I don't remember the rest of the trip. The car was black with a dark red fake leather interior.

Advance.

Stop. Click. Uncle Stosh and Uncle Peter walking me into the Makeyev funeral home, holding me under the arms. (Makeyev's was the funeral home of choice for all Russian, Ukrainian, Polish, and other name-your-Slav immigrants. The elder Mr. Peter, founder of the establishment, spoke all the languages. He spoke them badly, mixing and matching languages to the best of his ability into something resembling Proto-Slavic, I suspect. But at least he could communicate both his sympathy and funeral costs effectively. Flower car and limousine extra.) I remember the room being full of people and flowers. I remember my godmother screaming, *"Akh, ty moye zolotse! Bednoye ty detya! Sirotka ty moya zhalkaya!"*[48] and clutching me to her, weeping, but I did not cry. I could not cry. I was suffocating from the overwhelming stench of carnations.

[I have to insert a brief cultural note here, and it has to do with weeping. There is a particular way of crying (in the Russian culture)—perhaps "keening" would be a better or more understandable word—that has its own style, phraseology, and cadences. The word for it is *golosit'* from the masculine noun *golos,* "voice." I find it odd that a masculine noun was used as the basis for a word that applies to a traditionally female activity, but that's just me.

Russian women my mother's age were really good at it, having had lots of opportunities to practice the art during WWII and the Soviet horrors that both preceded and followed it. It was—for lack of a dictionary description—a combination of howling and plaintive cries to God and the deceased asking "Why?" and other related questions such as begging the deceased not to go, and so forth.

Except for her screaming, "Kolya!! Kolya!!!" at Papa's grave side and

---

[48] "Oh, my little golden thing! You poor child! My sad woeful little orphan!"

attempting to throw herself into the grave after his coffin was lowered, Mama did not keen. Therefore, I never learned how to *golosit'* properly—even though my godmother was particularly good at it—and to behave *à la Russe* at funerals.

In fact, come to think of it, I believe it was then that I lost my Voice. Not in a laryngitis way, but in the way Ariel voluntarily gave her voice to Ursula in *The Little Mermaid*. I suspect it was somehow tucked into Papa's coffin along with a handful of earth from Russia, symbolically returning him to the dust from which he'd come. Some fifty years later, I'm still searching for it and wondering if I'll ever find it again. Maybe that'll be Papa's "welcome home" gift to me the next time I see him. That, and my old fishing pole.]

Advance.

Stop. Click. I remember Mama rising to look at me from the front row while Uncle Stosh and Uncle Peter lift me by the arms again to carry me to the front. I remember her all in black, with a black lace mantilla; her olive complexion had darkened even more. She gasped and started to heave great sobs. Her white handkerchief, looking much the worse for wear, stood out amongst all that black. I caught a whiff of *Krasnaya Moskva* mixed with sweat.

Advance.

Stop. Click. I remember the first time I looked at Papa in the polished wood coffin and realized it wasn't him. For instance, this man's nose was pointy and Papa's wasn't. He was wearing one of Papa's suits and a tie, but he didn't look like him at all. Instead of wearing his gold cross, he had an Orthodox cross pinned to his lapel; his wedding band was gone. The longer I studied this man, with his arms crossed like for communion, the more it seemed to me that he was breathing. I could see his chest going up and down. I remember observing for what seemed to be a long time. I could hear noses being blown and women crying gently. I was lowered to my knees in front of the coffin—to pray, I suppose, as if I knew what prayers to say—and stayed there awhile, watching Papa breathe. A couple of women started to keen softly behind me in that uniquely Russian way.

Clearly, this had been a colossal mistake or someone's idea of a great joke to pull on me. I immediately suspected my detested god-sister, Iudochka, and decided that I would definitely pound her into the ground—parents' orders notwithstanding—once this was all over. Everyone would have a good laugh at my expense and then come back to our house for a meal, some vodka toasts, some dessert with whipped cream and a maraschino cherry on it (my favorite!), followed by singing and dancing. We would move the fake mahogany cocktail table out of the way, roll up the rug, and play the Russian dance music record we'd bought at the ROVA market last summer on the hi-fi at 33 1/3 rpm.

At one point, I realized that I was the only one who could bring this charade to a close, so I pulled gently on Mama's sleeve and whispered, "Papa's breathing!" She assured me that he was not. But the longer I scrutinized him, the more truly I could see he was breathing. I let some minutes pass before I made another attempt, this time by pointing at Papa's chest and proclaiming, in a slightly louder whisper, "But Papa's breathing." Someone behind me blew his nose very loudly, but I couldn't tell who it was. I looked up at Mama and watched the white edge of her handkerchief ride along her face, mopping up clear beads. She laid a soft warm hand on my head and explained, patiently, very patiently, that Papa wasn't breathing now and wouldn't breathe again. And then she helped me sit down on a chair in the front row.

I remember her telling me that Miss Fitzgerald had come and had brought flowers. I looked at the arrangement and thought it very pretty, probably because it didn't have any carnations in it.

And then my brain started to whirr.

I realized, with growing horror, that this was all my fault. It was all because last summer, when we saw Papa off at the bus stop for the return to New York City, I didn't cry. Every single time prior to that, I had wept when he left. Great heaving sobs. This time, however, he had talked me into not crying, convincing me that I was a big girl. For him, I kept it together. The tears rolled into a colossal throbbing ball in my throat, but I didn't let them move up into my eyes. I couldn't talk, but I didn't cry. And if only I had, he'd be alive right now.

There were toasts, of course, but they happened after we had buried Papa. In keeping with Russian Orthodox tradition, we buried Papa three days after he died. In the place where he told Mama to "bury me with the Russian people," within walking distance—if you cut through the woods—of where we'd spent the last several summer vacations. I remember isolated fragments of that day, but not the whole day. (Many years later, I'd have the same memory blips about my husband's funeral, so maybe this was preparation for an event nearly forty years in the future.)

Advance.

Stop. Click. The funeral mass in the church we'd gone to ever since I could remember. I'd probably been baptized there, but no one told me if that was the case and, in fairness, I never asked. It was dark inside Holy Trinity. I remember the lights in the chandeliers and all the candles lit and the way the shiny wood floors reflected the candlelight. I remember that someone pushed me to the front of the church where we'd never stood—we were middle-to-the-back kind of people. I remember standing near the coffin, holding a candle that dripped wax on my hand, and Mama telling me to hold the candle straighter so I wouldn't drip wax on the floor. The wax was warm on my hand.

Advance.

Stop. Click. I remember the clouds and clouds of incense that threatened to suffocate me billowing from the priest's censer every time he swung it either around Papa or us. I remember the warm glow of the candlelight on Papa's oak coffin. My friend, Olya, was standing next to me and crying buckets. So was Mama. So was just about everyone there. Except me. Because I could not.

Advance.

Stop. Click. I remember the priest sprinkling soil into the coffin at Papa's head and feet, telling us that it was from Russia—returning

Papa to the earth whence he'd come. I wondered who had brought it with them when they left Russia and why in the world you'd drag a bag of dirt with you through war-torn Europe. And Papa *hated* the Soviet Union.

Advance.

Stop. Click. I rode in a large black car with seats in the back that faced each other; it was gray inside. My godfather, his wife, and Iudochka rode with us. And the only thing I remember is that I did not get sick riding in the car, probably for the third time in my life.

Advance.

Stop. Click. It's sunny and warm outside when we step out of the car. I smell fresh dirt and it reminds me of all the times we'd dig for worms to go fishing. For some reason, I remember the rusty old can we used for them: it was steel and blue and had a lid to keep the worms from escaping.

The gravel was the color of beach pebbles and crunched beneath my feet as we walked along the path toward a tall mound of fresh red dirt next to a large hole in the ground.

Advance.

Stop. Click. A group of people dressed in black is gathered around the hole in the ground. Family friends. People whose houses I'd been to and who had been to ours, for as long as I could remember. The New Jersey group—Baba Khristya and Deda Mitya, my godmother and her husband (Krestnaya and Kolya Koom), Uncle Shura and Auntie Liza (my godmother's brother and his wife)—some of whom had not been able to visit Papa at Makeyev's to say their farewells to him nattering at the funeral director to open the coffin. He kept refusing, saying it was against the law. He didn't realize what he was up against, though, with these survivors of war horrors who wouldn't back down until he did what they asked. So he complied with their wishes and opened the coffin.

Advance.

Stop. Click. I get shoved out of the way and toward the back of the crowd. I wanted to see Papa again, but they wouldn't let me near. I remember Baba Khristya in her black lace mantilla leaning over to kiss Papa good-bye. I remember the sound of my godmother's keening.

Advance.

Stop. Roll film. The priest is waving his bronze censer and it sends gold flashes into my eyes every time the sun hits it on the upswing. The relentless sun ceaselessly beating down on my head, the clouds of incense seemingly intent on suffocating me, the sounds of women's lamentations in Russian over the choir intoning Old Church Slavonic hymns, and the hornking of men blowing their noses all combine to create an image of hell in my mind.

I am shoved to the back of the crowd while everyone finishes their last good-byes with Papa. After about a thousand repetitions of the "*Upokoy Gospodi usopshego raba tvoyego Nikolaya*" prayer asking God to give rest to His departed servant Nikolai . . . I hear the funeral hymn I know begin, "*So svyatymi upokoy, Khristye* . . ." asking Jesus to rest the soul of my father with the saints. Over the human voices, I hear a strange mechanical squeaking and wonder what it might be. I figure it out pretty quickly because Mama, screaming, "Kolya! Kolya!!" tries to throw herself in after the coffin as it's lowered into the cement-lined hole. Several hefty men hold her back by the arms. It was the first and only time in my life that I heard my mother scream. To this day, I can hear the anguish and panic in her soul-wrenching cries of that one word.

I stand by myself at the edge of the crowd until someone in black remembers I'm there. Someone else hands me a long-stemmed pink rose with no thorns and pushes me toward the hole in the ground. I hear the *thunk* of the coffin hitting the bottom and smell the bonechillingscent of raw earth; Someone tells me to drop the rose onto the lid in the hole in the ground. I drop the rose and am shoved aside as the crowd moves forward to drop their flowers onto Papa's coffin and say "farewell." But some say "good-bye."[49] Which is what I did.

Cut.

Advance.

Stop. Click. I am standing at the edge of the crowd, careful not to step on the neighbors' graves. Iudochka pops out of the crowd like she was fired out of a cannon and runs to me, practically exploding with news: Papa turned all black as soon as they opened the coffin.

And I do not pop her one because I think it's probably a sin to punch someone at a cemetery, especially when the priest is swinging his censer and everyone is intoning the excruciating soul-searing funeral hymn,

Veechnaaayaa paaamyaaaaat'

Veeeechnaaayaaaa paaaaamyaaaaat'

Veeeeeeeechnaaaaayaaaaaa paaaaaaaaaaamyaaaaat'

Eternal memory. Indeed.

Advance.

Stop. Click. We pile into the waiting cars for the short drive to the restaurant at ROVA. It's the second time in my life that I go to a restaurant, so I'm not sure about how to act. (The first time was when Papa took us out to lunch at a place with booths and red leather seats after church one Sunday and I had rice pudding for dessert.) We're in a separate room that's long and narrow, with sheer white curtains on its many windows. Someone plants me in a chair at a table with grownups who ignore me as the food arrives and vodka is poured.

I'm not hungry.

Menfolk make toasts.

Everyone eats.

Except for one little old man whom I had never met, but who sat in

---

[49] Just as you have two parting expressions in English—"farewell" and "good-bye"—we have something similar in Russian. The word for "farewell" carries with it a shade of "please forgive me" and permanence. "Good-bye," on the other hand, is like the French au revoir, "until we see each other again" and implies only a temporary parting.

a chair near me and cried and cried and cried. Mama in her black dress and mantilla tried to get him to eat, but he refused. He had one shot of vodka along with the others at the first toast "for the remembrance of the soul of the departed." Maybe he was one of those angels who Papa told me roam the earth, giving people an opportunity to be good or bad, to receive them or not. I think we did what we were supposed to do because, at some point, he disappeared.

I'm too young to drink like the rest and no one thinks to make me the kid drink we all got during parties: a whisper of whatever hooch the grownups were drinking mixed into a glass of ginger ale. The over-worked waitress brings me a grape soda and pats me on the shoulder. I hate grape soda.

I can't eat and the smell of food is making me nauseated.

And I still can't walk by myself, but if I lean a bit to the left in my seat, I can see the cypresses where Papa hid the fishing poles he'd made out of tree branches for us so we wouldn't have to carry them all the way back up the hill to the Serdyuks'. That was the year we somehow forgot our regular fishing poles at home. But such intrepid fishermen were we that the minor setback was only that, and we managed to catch our fair share of assorted lake fish all the same.

I sit. And remember the departed.

Advance.

Stop. Click.

We somehow return to apartment 2R in Brooklyn. I somehow go back to school on Monday, even though it takes me three times as long to walk the six city blocks to get there and every step is wracked with pain. I lumber, Frankenstein-like, into the 5-1 line right before the bell rings.

I straggle behind the others, getting shoved into the railing and buffeted by successive waves of kids as I struggle up the stairs to my fifth-grade classroom. Miss Fitzgerald is waiting outside the door in the hallway, as always. My classmates scramble to their desks, elbowing each other out of the way. As I finally drag myself to our classroom door,

Miss Fitzgerald folds me into so tight a hug that I can barely breathe. But I can cry. Out loud. Buckets. Class starts late. No one looks at me.

Advance.

Stop. Click.

The Sunday after we bury Papa is Father's Day. Mr. Babuk stops by with Olya and her brother for a brief visit. We kids peel off from the grownups and head for my tiny pink room. I show them the Father's Day card I made for Papa: on the front, I drew a picture of me in a pink tutu en pointe. In a fit of bravado and trying not to cry, I say, "Well, guess I won't be needing this anymore," tear the card into little pieces, and throw it into the trash basket under my desk. Levko doesn't know what to say or where to look. Olya cries. I do not cry. I do not make eye contact with either of them. I stare into the trash basket and see a piece of crayoned pink tutu on paper.

Advance.

Stop. Click.

School ends in two weeks and I flunk all my fifth grade finals.

Miss Fitzgerald lets me retake all of them with help from Despina and Johanna. Probably because Miss Fitzgerald knew I knew the material (as the perpetual number one in class).

I like to think that she may have loved me a little bit, too.

Advance.

Stop. Roll film.

End of a gym day at the end of the school year. We tie our sneakers together and sling them over our shoulders on the way out of school. Kevin Ronald, the bane of my existence, has climbed up onto the base of the lamppost I have to pass on my way to the crosswalk and is preparing for another assault. He stopped picking on me after Papa had a brief chat with him about a month ago, but now all bets are off. (I'm not sure whether it was Papa's size, his fedora, the cigarette smoke, or the way he delivered the message that made Kevin shrink to an even smaller size and run home as fast as his beat up brown school shoes could carry him.) He's swinging his sneakers around like some sort of medieval mace.

As I near the lamppost, Kevin lets his sneakers fly, shouting "Sh-sh-she got to take her tethts over jutht cuz her *thtupid father died.*" The rubber sole smacks me on the right side of the face, but it's the words that hurt more than the humiliating clout. I hear laughter.

I look up, hoping to see Papa waiting on the corner where he schooled Kevin on how *not* to treat me. But he's not there.

Fade to black.

*To this day, I cannot bear the scent of carnations. They are a funeral flower. (Note to self: leave instructions in will stipulating **no carnations**. Violators will be disinherited and haunted. Ya skazal. I said so.)*

Months later, as the weather grew colder and the winds started to howl up and down Sixty-eighth Street, I went snooping into one of our stand-alone closets in search of something. I don't remember—there's much I don't remember about that time—what the target of my snooping was, but I was rifling through the old coats and jackets. Having slid open to the left the right-hand door, I stepped up onto the lower ledge to reach the upper compartment. I swept my right arm back and forth while my left hand hung onto the little door for balance.

And then I hit something.

It was cool and smooth in one part and seemed to have some kind of fur attached to it.

I pulled it out to examine it further.

I jumped off the closet ledge and looked at it. And then my breathing really stopped.

It was Papa's *ushanka*. I clutched it to my heart and then, very slowly, I lifted the inside to my nose. I inhaled deeply. And there he was. Exactly the way Papa had smelled my whole life—masculine, hard working, a hint of sweat and a touch of aftershave. The one that was a very light blue in its glass bottle. I kept smelling it and smelling it, thinking that if I did this long enough, surely he'd materialize in the kitchen for me.

But he didn't. No matter how much, how long, or how hard I tried to inhale his fading scent from the well-worn hat. No matter how many times I envisioned running down Sixty-eighth Street toward Fifth Avenue as he rounded the corner, head down into the wind. Cheeks red from the cold. Ear flaps lowered. The slap of his leather coat's cold lapel against my cheek as he lifted me up with an "OP-PAH!" and the feel of his stubbly rosy cold cheek against mine. I could feel the emery-board-like scratchiness of his face where yesterday's shave had been forgotten. He always shaved at night because he got up so early in the morning. I almost had it, for a moment. He was almost here. And then I opened my eyes.

The light was bright in the kitchen and I was alone. With the hat. I put it back where I'd found it before it could lose its magic.

Later, when Mama came home from the doctor's office, I almost knocked her over as she came through the door. I remember stammering and speaking very, very quickly, trying to get the news of this great discovery out before I messed it up with the wrong words. I remember opening the upper compartment of the closet and grabbing the hat. I remember inhaling Papascent from the inside and waving it at Mama, shouting in a fit of pure joy, "Look!! It smells like Papa! It smells like Papa! Here, try it, look!! Sniff it!! Smell it, here, look!!!"

And I remember how she looked at me and what she said. She said only one word, "*Da,*" and turned away.

I can't remember if she made dinner for me or not, but before I knew it, she had changed into different clothes and headed out the door to her job cleaning offices in Manhattan at night, after all the business people had gone home for the evening. I was left alone, with only our neighbor Mary to "listen for me" in case anything went wrong.

I was crushed that my fantastic discovery had been ignored. But at least I could continue to pull the hat down from its hiding place and bring Papa back into my life simply by getting a whiff of Papascent from his *ushanka*.

And then, one day, it was gone. Just like that.

I had come home from school and Mama had gone to work. I pulled up a kitchen chair to the closet, slid open the upper part, and saw hats. Women's hats. My hats (most of which I detested). But all of Papa's hats—the *ushanka*, the fedoras, the summer straw skimmers—were gone.

My heart sank into my heels. Because I knew where they'd gone.

They'd gone where she'd thrown *Zaychik* a few years ago. And now there was no one to rescue them: the trash had been collected that day.

I slid the closet door shut, pushed the kitchen chair back where it belonged, and went to sit in Papa's chair in the living room. Mama had changed the slipcovers to the "summer" lavender ones. I watched the light outside dim until the lines of the furniture started to blur.

A big girl now, I did not cry.

27

I guess Mama wanted to make me feel better, but everything turned out wrong—typical of our relationship throughout the years. One of us would try to do something nice for the other, and, invariably, it would get messed up and have the opposite effect of what was intended. Mama had made me bring my fishing pole along when Uncle Peter drove us to New Jersey for vacation. I hadn't wanted to bring it because it was nestled so nicely next to Papa's blue one that they seemed to be having a heart-to-heart talk. But there was another reason: I had never, ever cast a line in my life.

When Papa and I went fishing, he always baited my hook (even though I was a major player in bait acquisition or production), always cast the line for me (having spit on the bait three times for good luck), while simultaneously showing me when to release the button on the reel. I'd never done it myself before. My line still had the float on it from last year, so I'd know if a fish were to bite, but I was pretty sure I wouldn't be able to get a fish off the hook because, quite simply, I'd never done it. My job, when fishing with Papa, was to wait until the float started to bob, to let the line go while the fish was making up its mind, and then to pull up really fast and hard when the float went all the way under water. At that point, all I had to do was reel in the fish without falling into the water (not always a given) and wait for Papa to remove it from the hook and then string it on our improvised fish holder: two popsicle sticks and some line. This way, we could keep the fish in the water (and alive) until we were ready to leave. I did not know how to take a fish off the hook or how to make the improvised fish holder, so I worried about what I would do with a fish if I were to catch one. I knew how to skin and filet one, but I didn't know how to get it to that point. And I didn't have Papa's big switchblade to knock the fish out by conking it on the head before decapitating and eviscerating it.

So, one bright July day, dressed in our bathing suits and cover-ups, Mama and I marched ourselves from the Serdyuks' property to the lake, my flip flops sticking to the tar and occasionally popping off my feet. I glanced over to the woods where Papa taught me how to build a fire, roast bacon on a stick, being careful to catch the drippings on a piece of bread, and then how to put a fire out and make sure it stayed out.

Papa was careful about fire ever since he almost burned down his family's barn when he was seven. It wasn't intentional, it's just that he'd been sneaking a smoke (yes, at seven, you Snowflakes. Quick, call family services!) and suddenly saw his father approaching. To Papa's astonishment, the episode ended without a swat, yelling, or his premature demise. No muss, no fuss. And how many of us have had moments like that: the moment when you know—beyond a shadow of a doubt—that life as you know it will cease to exist because a parent is going to *kill* you, and then he doesn't? He laughs. Maybe even cuffs you gently on the head. And you're bonded for life over a shared secret, one you'll never tell your mother. Just the menfolk, the *muzhiki*. Yeah.

But I've digressed.

Back to the fishing story.

Mama and I crossed the parking lot in front of the building used as a cinema for Russian films on week-ends, heading toward the fishing spot right outside Dunya's Diner. I stopped between the two skyscraping cypresses that crowded the entrance to check whether Papa's homemade fishing pole had survived the winter. On our last day of vacation, he'd hide the fishing pole in the right cypress; on our first day of vacation, he'd check to see if it was there, and it was! Every year! Today it was gone. Maybe Papa took it with him when he moved into his new home.

We passed the outdoor dance floor where a stout fellow with half his left foot missing played his accordion on Friday evenings. Women, still free from their menfolk who'd arrive from the city on Saturday morning, danced with each other and sang along to war songs and romances. *"Zachem, zachem, so mnoy ty povstrechalsya? Zachem narushil moy pokoy?"*[50] they'd croon, eyes directed into the night, filling with tears, remembering their youth and the boys they'd loved who never came back. Until someone—usually Grisha's mother—would pipe up with a raspy *"Enough* of this already! Give us a lively one!" And Frol would, keeping time with his right foot, women in colorful summer dresses swirling on the dance floor, some of their children joining them on the hardwood, their heels keeping time with the music. When Frol took a break, we'd walk over to the weekly bonfire and throw sticks, leaves, and anything else we could find into the blaze, faces illuminated, listening to the snaps and crackles and watching filaments of fire rise into the sky.

As we passed the rowboats, I noticed two men and a blond boy with a crew cut, about my age, maybe younger, milling around the fishing spot. They all turned to look as two females approached what was clearly a place claimed by and for men. For the first time in my life I felt out of place in a male environment.

Mama exchanged greetings with them, asking if it would be OK if I fished there (from the tone of her voice, "no" was not an anticipated response). They skedaddled to the left, closer to the boats, clutching their sweating beer cans in their fists, having deep discussions about whose planes were the deadliest strafers in the War. Like every other grownup I knew, they'd had personal experiences on which to base their opinions.

My stomach was starting the *gonna barf* waltz.

---

[50] Why oh why did you meet me? Why did you disturb my peace?

My hands were starting to shake.

I carefully unwrapped the bait I'd made earlier that morning, trying not to crinkle the wax paper too loudly and attract attention to myself.

My hands shook harder, as Mama urged me to "Go on, show me how you can fish. You spent all that time with Papa fishing, I'm sure you know how."

I couldn't tell her that I was a Fisherman Fraud, that I only held the pole, that I didn't know how to do anything else, that Papa had done everything for me.

I slowly unhooked the line.

I baited the hook with our secret family recipe.

I pretended to spit on it three times. I say pretended because my mouth had gone completely dry.

I pulled up my black-red-white striped pole with its metallic red reel, slung it behind me as far as I could, closed my eyes, pressed the black button on the reel, and flung it forward. I heard a "clunk," an "owwwwwwwwwwwwww" and male voices yelling at me. Evidently, I'd hit the release button on the reel at the wrong time and had beaned the blond kid with my bobber and hook. The men were yelling something about me not knowing what I was doing and how I could have blinded the boy, Mama was barking at me to reel in my line and apologize to the boy, and people everywhere had stopped to stare. Even Dunya came over to the window to check out the latest *skandal*.

I was crushed and mortified.

I dutifully and slowly reeled in my line.

I apologized to the crew cut boy and his uncles.

I set the hook just so on one of the guides on the fishing pole and tightened it up the way I'd been taught.

I broke up the bait and threw it in little pieces to the fish hiding among the water lilies.

The expression *"smatyvat' udochki"*[51] had developed a new and sad meaning for me.

I wrapped up my fishing pole and walked all the way back uphill to the Serdyuks' compound.

I walked across the grass, ignoring old Man Serdyuk in his chair on the tiny porch from where he used to yell at all of us kids.

I walked past the picnic table under the cherry tree that never had cherries to our room.

I opened the screen door, turned the key in the lock, walked in, and stashed the fishing pole in the corner by the big bed where Papa used to sleep.

Feeling much older but not necessarily wiser, I locked the door on my way out without looking back into the corner and let the screen door slam shut, knowing full well that Old Man Serdyuk would yell at me for it. I simply did not care.

I walked to the lake, key in hand, flip flops sticking to the tar.

I did not look at the woods as I walked past them.

I did not look for Papa's fishing pole when I walked between the two cypresses.

I sat down on the lower right corner of the beach blanket and handed Mama the room key.

To her offer to buy me an ice cream I breathed a quiet, "No, thank you. I'm not hungry" and stared at the light playing on the lake. I forgot to take off my cover up and got sunburned in funny places.

My childhood was over.

---

[51] The expression, translated literally, says "to wrap up your fishing poles." It means to get ready to go, but in this instance it's a Russian pun, since what I did was exactly that.

28

That first Papaless summer, we returned to the Serdyuks' place—the scene of so many happy memories, now all in the past tense and non-reproducible. We packed light because Mama had to carry the suitcase by herself, and it was probably close to a mile, maybe more, from the Cassville bus stop to the Serdyuks' property, and at least a part of that was uphill. I remember the smell of the melting tar under our feet, Mama's heels sinking into the roadtop, her constant switching of the suitcase from one hand to the other. Walk, walk, walk, pause, put suitcase down, shift purse to other hand, pick suitcase up with free hand. About every fifteen to twenty paces the drill would be repeated. I don't remember if we said anything to each other during that walk, but I do remember that not once did Mama ask me to help her. I guess she was as determined to do that by herself as she was to get me out of the city in the summer.

I remember coming down the slight slope past the woods where we went mushroom hunting. Down a bit farther and then right onto the light gravel driveway where grass had sprung up in the middle between tire tracks. I remember hearing the gravel crunch under my summer sandals and seeing the Old Man with his cane, sitting in his usual perch attached to the main house.

Serdyuk was always there, surveying his domain and scaring off any interlopers. In years past, I'd wondered if he even slept there, because the only times he wasn't there, Serdyuk was either eating his meal (and looking out the window), going to the bathroom, walking his property (to check for anything we might have done to damage something), or doing his weekly chauffeur routine by driving his renters to the big grocery store miles away.

I rode next to him once on one of these excursions.

Once.

It was a true "once and done" because it was a hot day, the car was packed with nattering Aunties in the back, and I was wedged between Serdyuk and his wife in the front seat. The Old Man Smell combined with the Missus' Old Lady Smell combined with the Aunties' dime store perfumes to make me range from nauseated to nearly unconscious from the hypoxia that resulted from me holding my breath. The fake leather seats had been heated to "broil," which is what happened to the back of my legs when I sat down and immediately was glued in place. And, although my experience riding in cars was limited, it seemed to me that we were proceeding at an agonizingly tortoise-like pace. I took a deep breath and leaned toward Old Man Serdyuk on the next turn to peek over at the speedometer. Yeah, buddy, we were doing a break-neck twenty miles per hour. All the road signs I'd seen had announced boldly: forty-five. No wonder the cars around us were laying on their horns in a cacophony of C minors, F sharps, and foghorns. Some people were leaning out their car windows, shouting "Sunday driver!" and other things I didn't understand—even though the words were English—and making funny shapes with the fingers on their hands. It seemed like years passed before we finally arrived at the Food-A-Rama and air-conditioned bliss.

But, getting back to the Old Man Serdyuk theme, we always knew where he was when he was mowing the lawn: the telltale sound of his riding mower let us know whether we were at DEFCON 4 (increased watchfulness and strengthened security measures such as plausible excuses for being in a *no go zone*) or getting close to DEFCON 1 (i.e., nuclear war [Serdyuk's wrath, emphasized by the waving of the cane] is imminent). Oddly enough, the Old Man's wife, Varvara Sergeyevna, was an incredibly nice and gentle woman and appeared to us to be proof positive of the saying that opposites attract.

But as I think back to the feel and sound of the driveway gravel crunching under my feet, I remember looking at the grass on the front meadow. It was summer green and freshly mowed and that first whiff of fresh cut grass wrenched me back to last summer, when we ranged free all over the property and tried to sneak into the Old Man's garden just to see if we could undetected. In all the times we managed to penetrate the chicken wire perimeter we never actually picked anything, not even once. It was the getting in and out under the radar that was the challenge and made it fun.

Like in the movie theater when the film slipped off its spool, flashes of scenes from summers past took over the present moment: the different clubs I created and devised initiations into, our espionage efforts against Iuda's aunt and mother, the grape arbor where Grisha and I had hidden a time capsule on our last day there that we'd pinky sworn to open the next summer when we reconnected in the same place. Next summer was here, but it seemed as though I wasn't. At least not all of me and certainly not the me I was when we got the capsule together and hid it under one of the posts supporting the grape vines, next to the place Papa and I used to dig for worms.

There was a nice bench with a back and arms, like in the New York City parks of my early childhood, in the shade underneath the enormous walnut tree in the front meadow. The walnut tree dropped walnuts at random, so you never knew if you were going to get beaned by one of the green golf-ball-sized orbs when the wind kicked in. It was to your own benefit and well-being to keep your eyes peeled and moving from treetop to meadow—you could easily slip or trip over one of the dropped green balls and end a budding career in stickball. The walnut was close to the cherry tree off the branches of which we'd picked and chewed hardened sap last summer. I remembered how sweet it was and how quickly it was gone, and how we'd scouted out all the other trees in a vain search for more.

Grisha's mother had been sitting on the bench, bickering with Old Serdyuk—aggravating the Old Man was one of her favorite forms of entertainment—when we came into her field of vision. I remember how she cried out Mama's name and rushed toward her. I remember how Mama dropped the black and red tartan plaid suitcase and threw her arms around Auntie Zoya. I remember the sounds of their voices as they hugged and cried and cried and cried, and I just stood there with my head down, looking at the pale pieces of gravel on the driveway.

Eventually, they both came up for air and handkerchiefs and that's when Auntie Zoya noticed me. With an "*oy, bednen'kaya Mashen'ka*" she jumped over to me, hugged me really tight, and cried all over me, cementing the "poor little Mashen'ka" concept even more. And, while I stood there like some sort of department store dummy, hugging her, my eyes were completely dry. But my heart hurt and I couldn't breathe and I felt like I was shouldering the entire weight of the walnut tree on my ten-year-old frame. I would be eleven later that summer, but it was the first birthday about which I cared not one whit. I was having trouble just keeping my head above water, so to speak, on a day-to-day basis.

By this time, Varvara Sergeyevna had heard the commotion and came swooping out of the big house with a light shawl over her shoulders and straight toward Mama, and they both cried all over each other. Auntie Zoya tried to break up the pity party by picking up our suitcase, but that only redirected Varvara Sergeyevna's attention to me, alas. Sweet and kind though she was, she had that funny old lady smell women seem to get late in life, and that made me hold my breath until everything went fuzzy and my legs started to feel rubbery. Fortunately, Auntie Zoya decided we'd had enough crying on the driveway, picked up our suitcase (again), and, taking Mama under the arm, led her to our usual room. Varvara Sergeyevna asked me if I remembered the way to our cabin and, receiving an affirmative response from me, ran to her kitchen to finish pickling cucumbers, promising to bring our key along later.

Yes, we were back in the same room, with the same worn and yellowed lace curtains. The same two beds—one double, one twin; the same dressing table and mirror that kept losing reflection space to mirror rot; the same yellow flypaper dangling from the ceiling near the bare light bulb. Actually, judging by the body count, it looked like the Serdyuks had splurged on a new strip this summer. Same hook and eye closure on the screen door, same two steps down to the kitchen from the other door in our room. Because it was all so very familiar, it made me feel The Absence even more.

Everywhere I turned my gaze, *he* wasn't, and I felt my aloneness stabbing me in the heart with every place I looked. He'd never come striding past the (non-bearing) cherry trees on a Saturday morning with just his week-end bag, freshly shaved and smiling. He'd never dunk Grisha and me in the rusty old water barrel after a downpour. Our fish cleaning stump was where we'd left it, but Papa wasn't. Everywhere I turned, he used to be and wasn't anymore. And wouldn't be ever again because what remained of him was up the other road a ways, perpetually resting. Despite the sun and fresh air, despite the long bus ride and the walk to the Serdyuks', I simply wasn't hungry when Auntie Zoya called me into the kitchen. I didn't see how I could be expected to eat anything when Papa's chair at the table was empty. While everything was right where it should be, it was all wrong.

Grisha found me later that day when I was sitting at the picnic table under the cherry tree in front of our cabin, pretending to read. It was a fake cherry tree, actually, because it never had any cherries, but it did produce that sap we liked to eat. After we exchanged an initial "hey", there was a long, long pause. We'd been good summer buddies for years and even wrote to each other during the year, but at that particular moment, neither of us knew what to say. Grisha was the first to break the silence with "I'm sorry about your dad." And all I could say in return was "yeah" because it felt like I had a tennis ball stuck in my throat. That, and my eyes were welling up. But I knew I'd never cry in front of a boy—it could damage my reputation as "one of the guys," so I whirled around on the bench to extricate my legs, daring the splinters to find me, and said, "ya wanna do something?" And that's where we left The Topic.

The only time we would revisit the issue would be over forty years later, during a brief reunion that ended catastrophically. A totally different story that doesn't belong in this one.

I have to give Mama credit for trying to provide me with some sort of vacation time out of the City that year. For the most part, I was left to my own devices, except when we went to the lake. Going to the lake meant changing into my bathing suit, putting on a cover-up, shouldering the bag with Coppertone lotion, towels, and a snack of some sort and then walking all the way back—past the woods, past Pushkin Park, past the priest's house, past St. Vladimir's cathedral, to a hair past the Cassville bus stop. Instead of crossing the street for the bus stop, we'd turn right into the Russian émigré compound with its movie theater, Russian book and trinket store, and the restaurant where we had the reception after we buried Papa. We'd bear left through the two tall cypresses, walk a bit farther, and turn into the fenced off "beach" area of the lake, where we'd pick a nice spot to set up camp.

The first time we walked this familiar route that summer, I made a beeline for the cypresses where Papa hid our makeshift fishing poles the year we forgot our fishing gear at home. But such inveterate fishermen were we that a minor oversight such as this was not a deterrent to keep us from our beloved activity. Papa had cut a couple of branches off one of the trees in the woods behind our cabin, had strung them with fishing line and weights obtained I knew not where, and even attached a float to mine. On the last day of our vacation, he took the float off my rod, stored it in his pocket and, having wrapped the line around the rods and set the hooks, stored them very carefully in the left cypress. They, like he, were gone.

After we set our beach blanket down on a relatively flat grassy surface and Mama pulled the Coppertone bottle out of the bag to start basting me with its contents, I surveyed the lake, the people on their beach blankets, kids in the water, boats at the boat ramp, and Dunya's Diner. The old witch was still there—I could hear her yelling at kids to "make up yooor mahynd! I no have all day!" just like all the summers past. Boys were still jumping off the big tree into the deep end and younger kids were splashing around in the shallows near the perpetually unmanned life guard stand. The people around us looked familiar, and I saw a few women look at us and then start whispering. That's right, I thought, look at the new zoo animals: widow and orphan. I plopped myself onto the blanket to let the Coppertone fade and gossiping stop. Maybe if I plastered myself to the ground and pretended to sleep or read, I'd move myself out of their radar's range and they'd go back to chewing over the latest *skandal.* I could feel their eyes on me and caught random phrases off the breeze floating over me, *"bednen'kaya,"*[52] *"bez ottsa,"*[53] *"vdova, a yeshchyo molodaya"*[54] and so on. I hated their pity and I hated them for hammering more nails into my heart with their pretend sympathy. Mama either didn't hear them or was ignoring them. She was pretty good at letting things run off her back, like water off a duck, or at least she was making a pretty good show of it. I flopped onto my stomach and buried my face in my arms, pretending to sleep.

It was like that pretty much everywhere we went, from the Serdyuks', to Abdul's mini mart (where, last summer, Iuda's aunt shamelessly and consistently flirted with Abdul to get lower prices and occasional freebies when we shopped there) to Ochagov's Russian store with its books, papers, magazines, and other Russian realia, to St Mary's church at the cemetery. Everyone would take a long look at us and then turn away and start whispering. Maybe it was the fact that Papa had made friends everywhere by chatting people up and now he was AWOL, or maybe

---

[52] Poor little thing

[53] Without the father

[54] A widow, but still so young

it was Mama in her black dress with large dark circles under her eyes. Whatever it was, the reaction was the same everywhere and it nearly killed me to straighten my spine and hold my head up—reminding myself that I was *Grechenkovskoy porody*—when all I wanted to do was curl into a ball and let the world and all its *living* people leave me alone. Don't touch me, don't talk to me, leave me alone to die.

But leave me alone they didn't and I learned to function through my grief—a skill that would come in very handy later in my life. So, in retrospect, maybe this first gut punch from the Fates was in preparation for what would come later. Whatever it was, it hurt like the dickens, and I couldn't imagine how or when it would ever go away. And I couldn't imagine laughing again; hell, I was having trouble breathing. It seemed as though every time I started to catch a breath, something would happen that would hit me like a two-by-four between the eyes and remind me of my changed status.

For instance.

That summer, inflatable rafts were the de rigeur item among the kids on the lake. And not only those cheapo plastic ones, but the kind that were fabric coated and meant to last for years. After watching "everyone else" playing and floating on their rafts, I brought my raftless status to Mama's attention by asking if I could have one. It was the first time that I heard Mama say, *"Ne mogu,"*—"I can't." As in, she couldn't spare the money.

I had no idea that we were that poor . . . I mean, we still had the six-apartment building in Brooklyn, it's not like we were out on the street. However, our diet had changed somewhat and included more liver and a stew Mama made out of chicken gizzards and tomato sauce that, for some reason, I really liked. Up until that moment, I'd thought that, since Mama was only cooking for the two of us, there was no reason for anything more complicated like we used to eat when Papa was alive. It only now hit me that we were eating the cheapest cuts of meat, and I could feel heat rushing to my cheeks from the shame of our status. Which was right behind the shame I felt for my unreasonable request for a raft. I resolved to do better by wanting less and asking for nothing and imagined that Papa, wherever he was in his new home, would be proud of me for my resolve: a genetic feature of the Grechenkovs (although the uninformed may have referred to it as stubbornness or obstinacy).

Svet ne bez dobrykh lyudey.[55] Every time someone did something nice for us or was kind to us above and beyond the call of Christian Duty, Mama would repeat the above phrase with an element of mild surprise in her voice. It came to mind when I remembered how it felt to be the *only one* without a raft to float on that summer. And the reason I know that the phrase is true is that, out of the blue, on a hot summer day, an old friend of Mama and Papa's from back in the Regensburg DP Camp days showed up lakeside with her new husband—the fourth, thus far, to the best of Mama's knowledge.

After they finished crying all over each other and Motya finished examining me and branding me with the "she's a copy of Nikolay" stamp of approval, Auntie Motya's (a rhyming "Tyotya Motya" in Russian) wide candy-apple-red lipsticked smile grew wider and wider as she looked at me, sitting on the blanket with a book, and asked,

"Why are you just sitting here? Why aren't you out in the water with the other kids?"

I really didn't want to own up to our lowly indigent state to someone I'd only met once, so I turned on the mask and said,

"Oh, I don't feel like it. I'm reading a book instead." I couldn't make eye contact with anyone because the pathological truth teller was dying to come out and I couldn't let her. Because, if she came out, all the words about Papa would spill out of me and force me to cry. Which I still hadn't done in public (except for that one time at school with Miss Fitzgerald). So, keeping my eyes fixed on the blanket and book, I could continue to respond without inadvertently blurting out the truth.

In retrospect, I have to give Tyotya Motya a great deal of credit for her observation skills. Here's why: after talking and talking and

---

[55] The world is not without good/kind people.

talking with Mama, she asked me where my raft was. Uh oh. Oh no. Fortunately, Mama jumped in with some excuse as to why I didn't have one, something along the lines of it not fitting in our one suitcase.

"Oh, is that all?" Tyotya Motya asked and, turning to Hubby Number Four, said,

"Go bring the car around, we're going to go buy Masha a raft."

Which is exactly what she did. She paid no attention to Mama's protestations; in fact, she overrode Mama almost immediately by grabbing my hand, throwing my cover up over my head, and telling Mama to stay where she was, that we'd be back shortly.

I think Mama started to cry, but I could be wrong. Maybe it was only the sun in my eyes and the funny way she looked at us hustling off the beach.

I was so dumbfounded that I forgot to get nauseated in the car, where I got to sit up front next to Tyotya Motya and smell her perfume and listen to her stories about how she and my parents met.

Considering how things had been going for me this year, it was one of the happier moments in my life. Especially since she let me pick out whichever one I wanted, and I opted for the blue-and-gold one, an homage to Dear Lexington and Miss Fitzgerald. When we returned to the lake and Mama, I threw off my cover-up and flip flops and charged into the lake, raft and all. I paddled it out past the little kids and jumped on top, where I lay on my stomach like a beached beluga and watched all the goings-on from a distance. I can't remember it distinctly, but I suppose I even smiled because I'd reached Nirvana. I knew, somewhere in my broken heart, that Papa had played a part in sending Tyotya Motya my way. And, when I sent a thought bubble up to him in his amazonite room to confirm this hypothesis, a gentle breeze blew across my back and ruffled my hair in response.

Svet ne bez dobrykh lyudey, indeed.

I wonder now whatever happened to Tyotya Motya. Did she stay married to Husband Number Four? Or was there a Five? Six? Did she try to keep up with Elizabeth Taylor or Zsa Zsa Gabor in the husband race? It matters not—not then and not now. All that matters is that by doing this one good and kind thing for an unhappy child, she bought herself some good Karma. And a warm place in the broken heart of that child.

Even though we were back on familiar vacation territory that summer, our daily schedule was quite different from what it used to be in happier times. For instance, instead of heading to the lake or to the woods for mushroom picking in the morning, we'd walk all the way to the cemetery—a pretty long walk, even through the back fence short cut—to visit Papa. Sometimes we'd pick wildflowers along the way to stick into a jar Mama had found somewhere because Papa loved wildflowers. Back then Mama hadn't picked out the headstone yet, so it was easy to identify Papa's resting place by the large white Orthodox cross at his head and the mound of reddish dirt over the rest of him. He had a pretty good spot, actually, not too far from the road or the church, a water spigot close by, and almost no neighbors nearby to speak of so he could really enjoy some peace without worrying about having to engage in civilized conversation with people he didn't know.

Mama was pretty good about the not crying (too much) in public thing, so our walk was usually long and silent. I pretended to look for wildflowers or mushrooms along the way so I could look anywhere but at her. But, once we were through the back gate and in the cemetery, she'd start to breathe faster and faster and, as soon as we were in sight of Papa's white cross, her sobbing would begin. Mine did not. I neither sobbed nor cried, but developed a propensity for passing out. I didn't do it intentionally, but the sun would get really hot and, before I knew it, everything would go black. Whoever was near me usually caught me before I face planted on someone's grave or the gravel path. I almost face planted in the church one day during a family friend's funeral; it must've been all the heat, clouds of incense, sobbing women, and an open casket that combined to turn my lights out. Still, *svet ne bez dobrykh lyudey*, and that's when the nice funeral director caught me as I started

269

to tilt forward and took me outside to sit on the church steps, where he taught me how to pour water on my wrists to cool off.

Anyway, as we approached the white cross, Mama's weeping would become more and more vocal until, as we reached Papa's place, she'd blurt out "well, you see, Kolya, we've come to visit you again." And, through her sobs, she would tell him about what we did the day before, what kind of flowers we had picked for him today, and how much we wished he was with us. What Mama didn't know, of course, (since I hadn't told her about my dream) was that Papa and I were in telepathic communication the whole time. Every once in awhile, I'd hear his voice or his "come here" whistle; I'd catch a whiff of his aftershave and, at night, while I was pretending to be asleep, I knew the breeze that was moving the curtains was Papa coming to say goodnight. Because right after that I'd fall asleep. And sometimes he'd visit me in my dreams. I guess that was his way of letting me know that he was still around, even though, to all intents and purposes, it appeared that he wasn't.

Mama would exhaust herself crying and we'd have to wet down her hankie at the spigot so she could wipe her face and bring herself back to the world of the living. We'd start to walk away, and the last thing Mama would say to Papa was a promise to come back the next day, which we did. As long as we were at the Serdyuks'. It was the new order of things in our broken lives on vacation.

I remember one day in particular, and it stands out for good reason. We had come home from our daily visit to Papa in the cemetery, where Mama had cried the color out of her eyes again. Her eyes seemed to recover some of their color in the evening after a day of not-crying, but her tears bled that color out early in the day, every day, when we visited Papa. I was walking normally by this time, but I still couldn't cry. People might argue "Couldn't? Or wouldn't?" to whom I say something civil along the lines of, if you haven't walked in my size fives, you have no right to judge me.

Anyway, we had returned from the cemetery, and Mama sat down with Auntie Zoya to chew the fat. Grisha was out roaming around solo somewhere, so I was left to my own devices. I figured that this was as good a time as any to go foraging for mushrooms but had to wait until the ladies came up for air before I could interject myself and ask permission to go to the woods. (That's right: ask permission. I had to ask permission for pretty much everything back then.) Auntie Zoya suggested that, perhaps, I should wait for Grisha to come back, but I knew his solo roaming habits—he could be gone the entire day and Auntie Zoya wouldn't notice. So, gently and politely (*po-chelovecheski*), I replied that I wanted to be by myself for awhile and that I wasn't afraid—I knew the woods by heart. Surprisingly enough, Mama supported me on this plan and, before she could change her mind or Auntie Zoya talked her out of it, I grabbed a random basket and flew out the patched screen door in the back, letting it slam behind me. And, of course, both mothers started yelling, but I pretended not to hear and made a beeline for the woods. I made sure to quickly camouflage myself by heading for an area with lots of leafy brush, in case they decided to come look for me. I stopped to let my breathing get back to normal and my heart to slow to the point where it wasn't straining to get out of my ribcage. And then I had an idea.

As I stood there and smelled all the trees and bushes around me, I scanned the woods' floor for evidence of our presence there last year. I looked for, but never found, the circle of rocks Papa had made for our little cooking fire where we'd blissfully roasted pieces of bacon on sticks, letting the grease drip onto our bread slices. The smell of the woods around us, the smoke from our little fire, the sizzle of the bacon, and the flare-ups as it dripped into the flames, made a memory for all my senses. I closed my eyes and could see the fire and Papa's face as the flames illuminated it; I could smell the smoke; I could feel the heat of the fire on my hands as I held the whittled stick over the flickers; I could hear the pops and crackles of the wood being consumed by the little blaze; and, of course, I could still taste the smoky chewiness of the bacon that I'd put on the rough cut piece of white bread. All my senses sprang into action to vividly relive that delicious episode in our vacation story. For a few moments, I was there, and he was so close I could almost reach out and touch his left shoulder through the thin blue summer shirt he'd been wearing. And then I opened my eyes and, just like with Papa's *ushanka*, the bubble burst and I was back in a Papaless summer.

The misery of being whiplashed back into my current state forced me to start moving—move a muscle, change a thought. Alas, there wasn't a single mushroom to be found anywhere. Not even one of the colorful *syroyezhki*, the lowest rung on the mushroom desirability scale. Since it was definitely too soon to go back—and risk being forced to read something in Russian—I decided to throw caution to the winds and *cross the road* to the piney woods without asking permission to do so. I figured that the mothers were busy talking about mother things and would have no way of knowing that I'd broken through the imaginary Maginot Line of the woods' edge. Papa and I had done this a number of times, but back then it was OK, since I was with him. I also figured that, since Papa had promised to help me whenever I needed it, I could always count on him to rescue me if I got into trouble or got lost. So, I walked out of the woods on the opposite side of where I'd gone in, looked left, looked right, looked left again and, seeing no cars, ran across the road. And walked into the piney woods.

There's something special about the piney woods that distinguished them from our "regular woods" stomping ground. The piney woods were more silent, perhaps because the needles the trees shed don't crinkle when you walk on them. The piney woods also were home and host to a special kind of mushroom—*gruzdi*—that was white, shaped like a calla lily, and crunched when you ate it (after it was fried in butter, of course). Very yummy. Of course, you had to slide your foot along the forest floor where you thought there might be a mushroom hiding under a lump of needles to unearth it. On this particular day, the woods seemed especially quiet, quieter than I'd ever heard them being. Truth be told, it was a tad spooky, even for me, but I progressed ever inward, away from the road, following the sun dapples as I went. Once in awhile, I would find a *gruzd'*, remove it gently from its hiding place, and set it in my basket. Flip the needles with my foot, see the telltale white, bend over, pick. Flip the needles with my foot, see the white, bend over, pick. Flip the needles with my foot, see the white, bend over, pick. Flip the needles with my foot, see the white, bend over and whoa. Oh, my. Oh, mymymymymy.

Last summer, during one of the weeks when Mama was back in New York working and we were here vacationing and fending for ourselves, Papa announced that he and I were going foraging for dinner. We had potatoes and onions at the cabin, but if we could find some mushrooms, we'd have a meal fit for a tsar. OK! And off we went.

The pickin's were slim in our little patch of woods, so we crossed the road to the piney woods, where we found a mushroom under almost every tree. Basket full and heads swimming with success and thoughts of that evening's dinner, we ambled out to the road, where Papa stopped to fish his *mundshtuk* and cigarettes out of his shirt pocket. The cigarettes were there, but the *mundshtuk* was gone. We did an about face to search for it where we'd been—I mean, really: Papa had made it himself—but had trouble retracing our steps since we had sort of wandered all over the place. After what felt like an eternity, Papa declared the search over and we went back across the road, through our own patch of woods, and in through the screen door I'd slammed on my way out. And I must say that dinner that night was beyond delicious and I doubted that even the Tsar had eaten so well . . . before the godless communists had murdered him and his family, martyring them in the eyes of the Russian Orthodox Church in Exile.

Anyway, after dinner Papa and I walked up to Abdul's market in search of a new *mundshtuk*. We found a small selection and settled on one that was made out of some kind of dark wood, but it wasn't the same as his old handmade one. Still, beggars can't be choosers at moments like these. And I got an ice cream out of the deal, too. Not that I flirted with Abdul like Iuda's aunt, but I was very polite and spoke Russian with him. Well, I tried to speak Russian with him, but Abdul's Russian was so abysmal and heavily accented that I had trouble figuring out what he was saying. (On the USG 0—5 scale for foreign language proficiency, I'd rate him about a 1+ on a good day). But I guess I made a pretty good listener and polite little girl back then, so he didn't even charge Papa for my ice cream bar. We walked back in triumph, Papa breaking in his new *mundshtuk* and me trying to eat the ice cream before it collapsed under the weight of its chocolate coating. A happy day.

So. There I was, standing still, slightly bent over, ready to pick the next *gruzd'* when I saw it. Plain as day and as light-amber-colored as I remembered it. I set the basket on the ground behind me, bent down, and picked it up. I held it in my hand, examining the details to be sure. Yes, the little gold rim that didn't fit quite right on the wide end. Yes, the tooth marks on the thin end. Inside, it was dark from all the tar that had accumulated in it since Papa hadn't had a chance to really clean it before it disappeared. (I remembered Papa telling me that, if you wanted to kill a snake, all you had to do was take the goop out of the *mundshtuk* and smear it on the grass around your house. Dead snake, guaranteed. Funny how memory works.) I held it up to my nose to see if it still smelled of Camels, but it didn't. I only sneezed from inhaling the dust microbes on it too fast. I held it tightly in my right fist and tried to find an opening to the sky to say "thank you," but couldn't. I quietly slipped it into the right front pocket of my shorts, picked up my basket, and hustled out to the road. I looked up to find him, but all I got was sun in my eyes. I turned my head right to look toward the cemetery— maybe I'd see him hanging out there? But all I saw was a car coming, so I waited for it to pass. Looked left, looked right, looked left again and crossed the road. Crossed through our woods, double checking for other mushrooms, but came up empty. I walked quietly through the patched screen door, holding it behind me so it wouldn't slam, into the common area and found Auntie Zoya and Mama where I'd left them.

The ladies ooh'd and aaah'd over my *gruzdi* and started sorting them in preparation for frying, simultaneously telling me to go wash my hands. I took two steps up to our room to get a towel and the soap, walked out the other door and across the grass to the toilet room with the sink that had only one handle marked C. Having scrubbed my hands into a hospital grade sanitary state, I meandered back to our room, made sure no one had noticed me, and quickly took Papa's *mundshtuk* out of my pocket. I grabbed *Zaychik* and, with sincere apologies, opened a slit along some stitching. I very carefully slid the *mundshtuk* into *Zaychik*'s stuffing and prayed it would not fall out. Later that evening, I would ask Mama for a needle and some thread to "sew on a loose button," which was almost the truth.

I told no one about what I found, especially not Mama: I remembered what had happened to Papa's *ushanka*.

This was one thing he'd left behind for me to find, and I wasn't ever going to give it up. In fact, I still have it. To this very day. Somewhere. But always in my heart.

I so miss him, still.

29

We had returned from our first sans Papa vacation, back to the same apartment and end-of-summer routines. Somewhere along the line, Mama had bought me two parakeets—a yellow and green one and a blue and white one. I can't remember what I named them, but I do remember that the green one was nasty and bit me every time I put my hand on or in the cage. On the other hand, (s)he also danced on her perch in time to any music that was on, so she wasn't a total write-off in my book. The blue one, on the other hand, was much nicer to me but had no sense of rhythm and displayed no interest in anything except food, water, and sharpening her beak on the arrow-shaped white stone we bought in the pet department of the Fifth Avenue Woolworth's and attached to the inside of the cage.

The day before my birthday in August, Mama decided that the birds needed fresh air and set them out on the fire escape outside our windows that faced the back yard. I double checked the cage door to make sure it was closed and locked (ya never know) and watched them jumping about for a bit. I inserted the screen back into the window and, having asked permission to go outside and sit on the stoop, went downstairs in search of a few buddies to bring a little distraction to the day. I meandered up and down the street, but it was completely childfree. I guessed that they either had managed to nag a mother into taking them to the big pool blocks away—out of our normal wandering range, which required the presence of a Mother—or had been dragooned into school shopping. I rang a few doorbells on the off chance that some were hiding out in the relative coolness of an apartment, but came up empty. It appeared that there was no company to be had, and the sun was beating down so hard on our side of the street that I was forced to squint to distinguish objects. Overdone by the sun and boredom, I dragged myself up the stoop steps, into the cool foyer, and rang the bell to our apartment. The buzzer to unlock the door buzzed, and I pushed through just in time to respond to Mama's "Khu eez eet?" with the usual,

"*Eto ya*," and dragged myself up the stairs to 2R.

I washed my hands (without—or possibly before—being prompted to do so) and walked into my room to pick up the book of fairy tales I'd most recently borrowed from the library. Mama was busy in the kitchen making something for our dinner, so I scooted around her and into the living room. Mama had a fan in the kitchen window, and it was creating a breeze throughout the apartment, easing the heat from the dog days of summer to some degree. I plopped myself into Papa's chair and promptly forced a "*Sadis' po-chelovecheski!*" from Mama, reminding me—yet again—to sit like a human being. I blame it on the near-sunstroke condition of my brain that I forgot to ease myself into Papa's chair, rather than allowing myself the full-tilt plop that I practiced when alone.

As I leafed through the pages and stared at the illustrations, something outside caught my eye. I wasn't sure what it was, so I peered out the window to try to refocus my vision on the underwear flapping in the breeze on the clothesline behind the building across from us on Sixty-seventh Street. It didn't help. So I unfolded myself from the chair and walked over to the window over the fire escape. And then I saw it.

Or him.

Him might be more appropriate.

Because, sitting on top of the birdcage on the fire escape, was the most beautiful parakeet I'd ever seen in my entire life. He was almost exactly the same color as Papa's room in his new home and was singing his little avian heart out.

And I knew immediately where he'd come from and who had sent him.

And, on the spot, I named him Nicky.

I took the screen out of the window, reached over to the birdcage, and gently started moving it inside, terrified that Nicky would fly off.

But he didn't. He stayed, clinging to the cage. And, after I had the cage inside, I waited patiently for Mama to come in from the kitchen and marvel at this strange occurrence.

Frankly, there was nothing strange about it at all: it was a birthday gift from a father to his child. Very long distance, through a time-space wormhole, yet so close you could feel his hand crafting this surprise for me, and I sent a mental thank you, hug, and kiss to Papa in his new home.

It was the best birthday gift I'd ever received.

Or ever would receive.

30

For as long as I can remember, three has been my favorite number. True, over the years, I flirted briefly with a few different numbers—five, seven, and even six—but none of them ever felt right. Five couldn't make up its mind between a soft curve and a hard stroke; seven, on the other hand, was too angular. Two strokes—if you wrote it the European way as my parents did—direct, determined, and harsh. I tried six once or twice, but I could never get past the fact that it was two threes and therefore unoriginal. Briefly, I toyed with two because I loved the way it looked in Papa's handwriting—almost like a swan—but it never offered me the comfort of three, which felt natural, normal, and soothing.

I suspect that my affinity for three came, in part, from Church. There were a few places in the seemingly interminable service[56] where

---

[56] A typical Russian Orthodox service lasts close to two hours. And we *stand* for the entire service (except when we have to kneel). There are seats along the walls, but those are for the elderly and/or infirm. But even the sitters have to struggle to stand for certain prayers. Because I found it rather boring to stand and stare at women's backs/hair/shoes, I would migrate between Mama and Papa. I preferred the view from Papa's side, but he'd try to enforce the "men on the right, women on the left" rule from time to time. I'd return to the left, stand impatiently in front of Mama, staring at my shoes, until I could return to the comfort of the

I was prohibited from moving between parents and would do my best to bloom where I was planted and to cross myself diligently and sincerely. Fingers of the right hand folded: ring finger and pinky down into the palm, the remaining three fingertips touching to form a tripod. Forehead, heart, right shoulder, left shoulder, bow. I figured that since I was technically in God's house, it was best to adhere to the rules, written, unwritten, and implied. You never know when He's watching and making note of sins—small and large—to punish you for later, or so I'd been told. Like, if you ate before going to communion or farted in church. (Not kidding. The Russians have an expression for someone who's really cheap: *He'd fart in church for a kopek.* I told you we have an expression for **everything**.)

The Orthodox service is sung in Old Church Slavonic (a made-up language that no one ever spoke but which had a disproportionate influence on the development of the Russian language) and some of the melodies are written on my heart to this day. The Nicene Creed was always preceded with the priest intoning:

Troitsa Edinosushchnaya i Nerazdel'naya!

(The Trinity One in EEEssence aaaaand Undiviiiiiiided)!

Followed immediately by the entire church singing:

"Veeeeeruyuuuuuu vo Edinogo Boga Otsa . . ."

(I believe in One God the Father . . .)

So, not only did I love the melody (still do), but I always thought that the first part applied to Papa, Mama, and me: the three of us, together, in essence one whole, undivided. It made me pretty happy, back in those pre-K years, to think that the entire church was singing about our little family.

Papa, by virtue of having been born *before* the Revolution, knew more prayers by heart than Mama did because he was allowed (forced) to learn them. Mama was born in 1918 and was part of that "new"

---

right side. As I may have mentioned before, I was a tomboy and felt that I fit in with the opposite gender better.

generation of Soviet children: the ones who were taught at school to go home and demolish all the icons in the house.[57] Anyway, I always found it interesting to watch Papa from my perch directly in front of Mama on the women's side of the church as he crossed himself with an almost military precision and mouthed the prayers being sung by the choir. When he bowed, you could tell that he really meant it and wasn't faking it like some of the others I watched with their almost careless flinging of the sign of the cross, the bowing of the head rather than from the waist, the stepping out for a cigarette.

Yes, really.

Since we don't sit for the service, people can walk in and out pretty much as they please, provided they're inside for the "important" prayers like the Nicene Creed and the Lord's Prayer. The only ones who give these transgressors the proverbial Evil Eye are the little old ladies who stand/sit in the back of the church and gossip about everyone. And then cross themselves, muttering, *"Prosti, Gospodi!"* (Forgive me, Lord.) No parish is complete without its share of hypocrites, I suppose.

But here's the thing: Papa was *not* a true believer in his wild and crazy days. In fact, according to censored stories I was told about Papa, he wasn't much of a church goer and didn't display much "church approved" behavior back in the day. He had soured on all priests and the Church following the death of his father and the local priest's extortionist burial fee demands. However, WWII changed him, as it did the millions of others who survived. You'd have to know a bit of *real* Soviet history to understand what it was like on the ground when the war started. For instance, I'll give you Papa's experience:

All able-bodied—and even the not-able-bodied—men were

---

[57] According to the story I heard, Mama actually came home from school one day pumped full of new Soviet thinking and ideals, railing against religion, icons, and the *"perezhitki proshlogo"* (vestiges of the past) in their house. Whereupon *her* Mama—the one who sent her kids out to the woods to pick out a switch for their punishment—said three words to her: "Lift one finger . . ." And that, as they say, was the end of *that* little piece of attempted Sovietization.

rounded up, enlisted, and sent to the Front. Age—too old or too young—was not a disqualifier. Neither was being the sole supporter of your family, as was the case with Papa's family. Uniforms generally did not fit, resulting in some rather comical outfits with sleeves to the knees and pants' hems over the ankles. There were no belts, so the lucky inductees were issued rope instead; the unlucky ones had to supply their own belts or—in the absence thereof—rope. Because there was a dearth of rifles only every third man was issued one. (Thank you, Comrade Stalin, for purging the military of its leaders before the War.) And, of those, only every third one was issued bullets. Yet, each man was to "save the last bullet for himself," according to Comrade Stalin, who declared—among other idiocies—that there were *no* Soviet prisoners of war. Which meant that thousands of Soviet POWS never benefitted from Red Cross packages because, according to their *vozhd'*,[58] they did not exist.

Helmets, apparently, also were "deficit items" and not every soldier was lucky enough to get one. Including Papa. He went through a number of battles with no head protection whatever. He once told me that, when his unit was surrounded by Germans and it seemed pretty certain that they were all going to die, he sent up his first prayer in years and it went something like this:

"OK, Lord. If you get me through this war with no injuries, then I'll believe that You truly exist. And I will believe in and worship You for the rest of my life."

Their unit was overrun, but he and two others managed to escape (AHA! The number three!! And you thought I'd digressed to the point of no return!). They were rounded up by their fellow Soviets, accused of treason, and Papa was nearly shot by an NKVD colonel in the bloody basement of a building. But I already told you that story.

As the war drew to a close and my parents wound up in a Displaced Persons (DP) camp in Germany, Papa realized that he had been spared:

---

[58] Leader

not even a flesh wound. And, from that time forward, he believed. He truly did. And, in his story, I see not only a foxhole prayer; indeed, I see evidence of God's mercy and wondrous works not only in preserving Papa's life, but especially for turning his heart. And so I believe, too. Ever since my little ears heard that story, my heart has beaten in acknowledgement of its own spark of the Divine. Thanks for shining the light on the path, Papa. And for showing me through your example how to truly, irrevocably, undeniably, passionately believe that God is merciful. Because, over the years, I sometimes forgot.

Some years later, after our indivisible family trio had been inexplicably and suddenly reduced to two, my focus on the parts of the Nicene Creed shifted to the very end:

Chayu voskreseniye mertvykh i zhizni budushchago veka . . .

(I await the resurrection of the dead and the life of the age to come . . .)

Secure in the knowledge that this **certainly** applied to our family, I looked forward to the resurrection of our dead and the re-establishment of our family trinity.

Still do.

Amen.

31

If I'm not mistaken, it was William Wordsworth's direction to "fill your paper with the breathings of your heart," something I tried to do while telling you these stories. I wanted someone to hear them while I still remember the details—a storyteller's supplication, perhaps.

In the twilight of my life, I keep a few mementos of those golden happy years of my childhood:

Maria Emil'yevna's amethyst necklace, which I wore to my wedding rehearsal dinner;

Papa's *mundshtuk* and Ronson lighter, even though all the good smells are gone;

Papa's everyday watch, forever stopped on 1306 hours—I wonder about the significance of the numbers;

Black and white photos of an etheric-colored childhood; and,

Color photos of a world turned sepia.

And, every once in a while, but not often enough, I catch a whiff of his aftershave and sense the feel of his stubbly cheek against my soft one on a cold wintry day on Sixty-eighth Street in Brooklyn.

I suspect that's exactly how it'll go the next time I see him.

Do svidaniya, not *proshchay.*

AUTHOR'S NOTE

This book never would have seen the light of day had it not been for Karen Hansen Dobson who connected me with Beth Lottig of Inspire Books. I had been working on this book for years, but had no idea how to turn my manuscript into a true, finished product book. Thank you, Beth, for your professional guidance and advice throughout my maiden voyage to becoming a published author—you've made a lifelong dream come true. Special thanks go out to Sara Davison for her gentle editor's touch and suggestions that helped my voice speak well and truly.

And, to my friends who listened to these stories as oral histories and who read them as I committed them to (digital) paper, a huge thank you for your patience, questions, comments, and support throughout this process. I send you an enormous hug wrapped in gratitude and love across the miles (in alpha order, so don't get your panties in a twist about who read what first. You're all priceless to me.):

Nancy Boughn, Zelda Cook, Christine Davidson, Laura DeBurr, Karen Hansen Dobson, Nathalie Hintz, Meg Hosmer, Susan Lowry, Peggy McCauley, Mark Meeks, Anna Mendelius, and, of course, *Zaychik*, still faithful after all these years.

The author welcomes (positive) comments and questions. You can find her in the following places:

Facebook: Maria N. Grechenko, and/or
email: maria.n.grechenko03@gmail.com

CPSIA information can be obtained
at www.ICGtesting.com
Printed in the USA
BVHW071230290421
606134BV00006B/726

9 781950 685677